References for the Rest of Us

COMPUTER BOOK SERIES FROM IDG

Are you intimidated and confused by computers? Do you find that traditional manuals are overloaded with technical details you'll never use? Do your friends and family always call you to fix simple problems on their PCs? Then the *...For Dummies™* computer book series from IDG is for you.

...For Dummies books are written for those frustrated computer users who know they aren't really dumb but find that PC hardware, software, and indeed the unique vocabulary of computing make them feel helpless. *...For Dummies* books use a lighthearted approach, a down-to-earth style, and even cartoons and humorous icons to diffuse computer novices' fears and build their confidence. Lighthearted but not lightweight, these books are a perfect survival guide to anyone forced to use a computer.

> *"I like my copy so much I told friends; now they bought copies."*
>
> **Irene C., Orwell, Ohio**

> *"Quick, concise, nontechnical, and humorous."*
>
> **Jay A., Elburn, IL**

> *"Thanks, I needed this book. Now I can sleep at night."*
>
> **Robin F., British Columbia, Canada**

Already, hundreds of thousands of satisfied readers agree. They have made *...For Dummies* books the #1 introductory level computer book series and have written asking for more. So if you're looking for the most fun and easy way to learn about computers, look to *...For Dummies* books to give you a helping hand.

IDG BOOKS

MORE

EXCEL 5

FOR WINDOWS

FOR

DUMMIES™

MORE
EXCEL 5
FOR WINDOWS
FOR
DUMMIES™

by Greg Harvey

IDG Books Worldwide, Inc.
An International Data Group Company

San Mateo, California ♦ Indianapolis, Indiana ♦ Boston, Massachusetts

MORE Excel 5 For Windows For Dummies

Published by
IDG Books Worldwide, Inc.
An International Data Group Company
155 Bovet Road, Suite 310
San Mateo, CA 94402

Library of Congress Catalog Card No.: 94-77748

ISBN: 1-56884-207-4

Printed in the United States of America

10 9 8 7 6 5 4 3 2 1

1D/QY/QY/ZU

Distributed in the United States by IDG Books Worldwide, Inc.

Distributed in Canada by Macmillan of Canada, a Division of Canada Publishing Corporation; by Computer and Technical Books in Miami, Florida, for South America and the Caribbean; by Longman Singapore in Singapore, Malaysia, Thailand, and Korea; by Toppan Co. Ltd. in Japan; by Asia Computerworld in Hong Kong; by Woodslane Pty. Ltd. in Australia and New Zealand; and by Transword Publishers Ltd. in the U.K. and Ireland.

For information on IDG Books in the U.S., including information on discounts and premiums, contact IDG Books at 800-434-3422 or 415-312-0650.

For information on where to purchase IDG Books outside the U.S., contact Christina Turner at 415-312-0633.

For information on translations, contact Marc Jeffrey Mikulich, Foreign Rights Manager, at IDG Books Worldwide. Fax number: 415-286-2747.

For sales inquiries and special prices for bulk quantities, write to the address above or call IDG Books Worldwide at 415-312-0650.

For information on using IDG Books in the classroom, or ordering examination copies, contact Jim Kelly at 800-434-2086.

About the Author

Greg Harvey

Greg Harvey is a product of the great American Midwest. Born in the Chicagoland area in 1949 (thus his saying "I'm only as old as China" — Red China, that is) in the dark ages of the Cold War — before the age of McDonald's, MTV, and, certainly, personal computers. On the shores of Lake Michigan, he learned his letters and numbers and showed great promise in the world of academia (quickly achieving Red Bird reading status after being put back as a Yellow Bird, due to an unforeseen bout of chicken pox at the start of the school year). After earning many gold stars along with a few red, he graduated from Roosevelt School (named for Teddy, not FDR) in 1963.

During his stint at Thornridge High School in the perfectly boring Chicago suburb of Dolton, Illinois (named for Tom Dolton, the gunslinger?), he found great solace in Motown music (thanks Phil!) and the drama department (to this day, he can recite every line from the play *Auntie Mame*, verbatim). Bored with what passed for academic studies, he went through high school in three years. Looking back on these formative years, Greg sure was thankful for the great tunes and Auntie's philosophy, "Life's a banquet, kid, and some poor suckers are starving."

In 1966 (ah, the Sixties), he entered the University of Illinois at Urbana, where he was greatly influenced by such deep philosophers as Abbie Hoffman and Mahatma Gandhi. In the summer of 1968, he purchased his first pair of hand-made sandals (from Glen, a hippie sandal maker who'd just returned from the Summer of Love in San Francisco).

During his college years, he became quite political. He holds the distinction of being one of a handful of men and women to attend the "camp-out" protest against women's dorm curfews (back then, not only were dorms not sexually integrated but women were locked up at 11 p.m. on weeknights, 1 a.m. on weekends) and was the last one to leave after all others went back to their dorms. During his subsequent college years, he became a regular at the Red Herring coffee house, the veritable den of SDS activity on campus.

In addition to antiwar protests, Greg attended various and sundry classes in the liberal arts (such as they were in the last half of the 20th century). In the end, he took a major in classical studies (ancient Greek and Latin) and a split minor in American history and French (Greg showed a facility for foreign language, probably stemming from the fact that he's always had a big mouth). In the course of his classical studies, he was introduced to his first computer-based training, learning basic Latin with a CAI program called — what else — PLATO!

At the beginning of 1971 (January 12, in fact), Greg migrated west from Chicago to San Francisco (with flowers in his hair). Deciding it was high time to get a skill so that he could find a real job, he enrolled in the drafting and design program at Laney College in Oakland. After that, he spent nine years working over a hot drafting table, drawing (by hand, mind you) orthographic and perspective plans for various and sundry engineering projects. During his last engineering gig, he worked with a proprietary CAD software package developed by Bechtel engineering that not only generated the drawings but also kept track of the materials actually needed to create the stuff.

In 1981, following his engineering career, Greg went back to school at San Francisco State University, this time to earn his secondary teaching credential. Upon completion of his teacher training, he bought one of the very first IBM personal computers (with 16K and a single 160K floppy disk!) to help with lesson preparation and student bookkeeping. He still vividly remembers poring over the premier issue of *PC World* for every piece of information that could teach him how to make peace with his blankety-blank personal computer.

Instead of landing a teaching job at the high school or community college (since there weren't any at the time), Greg got a job with ITM, a small software outfit, that was creating an on-line database of software information (well ahead of its time). As part of his duties, Greg reviewed new software programs (like Microsoft Word 1.0 and Lotus 1-2-3 Release 1) and wrote articles for business users.

After being laid off from this job right after the Christmas party in 1983 (the first of several layoffs from high-tech start-ups), Greg wrote his first computer book on word processing software for Hayden books (as a result of a proposal he helped to write while still employed full-time at ITM). After that, Greg worked in various software evaluation and training jobs. After a few more high-tech software testing and evaluation jobs in Silicon Valley, Greg turned to software training to get, as he put it, "the perspective of the poor schmo at the end of the terminal." During the next three years, Greg trained business users of all skill levels in a whole plethora of software programs for several major independent software training companies in the San Francisco Bay area.

In the fall of 1986, he hooked up with Sybex, a local computer book publisher, for whom he wrote his second computer training book, *Mastering SuperCalc*. And the rest, as they say, is history. To date, Greg is the author of over 30 books on using computer software, with the titles created under the... *For Dummies* aegis for IDG Books being among his all-time favorites.

In mid-1993, Greg started a new multimedia publishing venture, Media of the Minds. As a multimedia developer, he hopes to enliven his future computer books by making them into true interactive learning experiences that will vastly enrich and improve the training of users of all skill levels.

Dedication

To Gutenberg and all his followers: Thanks for the memories! In the immortal words of Meat Loaf, "Don't worry about the future, sooner or later it'll be the past..."

Welcome to the world of IDG Books Worldwide.

IDG Books Worldwide, Inc., is a subsidiary of International Data Group, the world's largest publisher of business and computer-related information and the leading global provider of information services on information technology. IDG was founded more than 25 years ago and now employs more than 5,700 people worldwide. IDG publishes more than 200 computer publications in 63 countries (see listing below). Forty million people read one or more IDG publications each month.

Launched in 1990, IDG Books is today the fastest-growing publisher of computer and business books in the United States. We are proud to have received 3 awards from the Computer Press Association in recognition of editorial excellence, and our best-selling ...For Dummies series has more than 7 million copies in print with translations in more than 20 languages. IDG Books, through a recent joint venture with IDG's Hi-Tech Beijing, became the first U.S. publisher to publish a computer book in the People's Republic of China. In record time, IDG Books has become the first choice for millions of readers around the world who want to learn how to better manage their businesses.

Our mission is simple: Every IDG book is designed to bring extra value and skill-building instructions to the reader. Our books are written by experts who understand and care about our readers. The knowledge base of our editorial staff comes from years of experience in publishing, education, and journalism — experience which we use to produce books for the '90s. In short, we care about books, so we attract the best people. We devote special attention to details such as audience, interior design, use of icons, and illustrations. And because we use an efficient process of authoring, editing, and desktop publishing our books electronically, we can spend more time ensuring superior content and spend less time on the technicalities of making books.

You can count on our commitment to deliver high-quality books at competitive prices on topics customers want to read about. At IDG, we value quality, and we have been delivering quality for more than 25 years. You'll find no better book on a subject than an IDG book.

John Kilcullen
President and CEO
IDG Books Worldwide, Inc.

Acknowledgments

Let me take this opportunity to thank all the talented and twisted people —
both at IDG Books Worldwide and at Harvey & Associates — whose dedication
and talent combined to make this book a reality.

At IDG Books, I want to thank Janna Custer and Megg Bonar in San Mateo as
well as Corbin Collins (who's always a pleasure to work with), Barb Potter, and
the World's Greatest Production Department in Indianapolis.

At Harvey & Associates, I want to thank Jane Vait and Shane Gearing for their
many contributions to the substance and style of the book. As always, I
couldn't have done it without you!

(The Publisher would like to give special thanks to Patrick J. McGovern,
without whom this book would not have been possible.)

Credits

Publisher
David Solomon

Managing Editor
Mary Bednarek

Acquisitions Editor
Janna Custer

Production Director
Beth Jenkins

Senior Editors
Tracy L. Barr
Sandra Blackthorn
Diane Graves Steele

Production Coordinator
Cindy L. Phipps

Associate Acquisitions Editor
Megg Bonar

Assistant to the Managing Editor
Jodi Thorn

Project Editor
Corbin Collins

Editor
Barbara L. Potter

Technical Reviewer
Ellen Finkelstein

Production Quality Control
Steve Peake

Production Staff
J. Tyler Connor
Kent Gish
Patricia R. Reynolds
Gina Scott

Proofreader
Betty Kish

Indexer
Joan Dickey

Book Design
University graphics

Cover Design
Kavish + Kavish

Contents at a Glance

Cartoons at a Glance

By Rich Tennant

page 277

page 147

page 211

page 99

page 7

page 146

page 98

page 209

page 275

page 303

Table of Contents

Introduction

· ·

*W*elcome to *MORE Excel 5 For Windows For Dummies*, the sequel to that all-time favorite, *Excel For Dummies*. In *More Excel*, you have a chance to deepen your experience with the basic features that you probably already use as well as learn some brand new tricks that you can do with this multifaceted spreadsheet program. In addition to a quick review of the Excel basics covered in *Excel For Dummies*, I've added scads of new information on features that can save you a lot of valuable time and effort when working with the program. For instance, you'll learn how to create custom charts, use automatic subtotals, create templates and new workbooks from templates, find and eliminate errors from you worksheet, perform "what-if" analysis on worksheet data, edit macros that you record to make them more powerful, and how to transfer data to and from Excel when using the program as part of the Microsoft Office package. As though that weren't enough, you also get access to hundreds of my favorite tips and tricks, including shortcuts and tips on what to do when you get into trouble with Excel.

Just keep in mind that when it comes to introducing more advanced features, such as summing data with automatic subtotals or doing data analysis with pivot tables, this book just touches on the easiest ways to use these features to get something done with them. I've made no attempt to present these features in anything approaching a definitive way (this book is, after all, still part of the beloved . . . *For Dummies* series).

About This Book

Like its predecessor, *MORE Excel 5 For Windows For Dummies* is not meant to be read from cover to cover. Although its chapters are loosely organized in a logical order (progressing as you might when learning Excel in an intermediate training class), each topic covered in a chapter is really meant to stand on its own.

Each discussion of a topic briefly addresses the question of what a particular feature is good for before launching into how to use it. In Excel, as with most other sophisticated programs, there is usually more than one way to get a task done. For the sake of your sanity, I have purposely limited the choices by giving you only the most efficient way to do a particular task. Later on, if you're so tempted, you can experiment with alternative ways of doing a task. For now, just concentrate on learning how to perform the task as described.

As much as possible, I've tried to make it unnecessary for you to remember anything covered in one section of the book so that you can get something to work in another section of the book. From time to time, however, you will come across a cross-reference to another section or chapter in the book. For the most part, such cross-references are meant to help you get more complete information on a subject should you have the time and interest. If you have neither, there's no problem; just ignore the cross-references like they never existed.

How to Use This Book

This book is like a reference, where you start out by looking up the topic you need information about (either in the table of contents or the index) and then refer directly to the section of interest. Most topics are explained conversationally (as though you were sitting in the back of a classroom where you can safely nap). Sometimes, however, my control-freak mentality takes over, and I list the steps you need to take to get a particular task accomplished in a particular section.

What You Can Safely Ignore

When you come across a section that contains the steps you take to get something done (marked with the Tootorial icon), you can safely ignore all text accompanying the steps (the text that isn't in bold) if you have neither the time nor the inclination to wade through more material.

Whenever possible, I have also tried to separate background or footnote-type information from the essential facts by exiling this kind of junk to a Technical Stuff section flagged with an icon. You can easily disregard text marked this way. Note, too, that the information you find flagged with a Tip icon, although designed to help you become more efficient with the program, is also extraneous and can be safely skipped over until you're ready for it.

When you see the bomb that signifies the Warning icon, however, it might be a good idea to linger awhile and take some time to read about what might happen if you do something bad.

Foolish Assumptions

I'm going to make only a few assumptions about you (let's see if I'm anywhere in the ballpark):

✔ You have some hands-on experience with Excel 5 for Windows. This may mean that you use the program anywhere from once or twice a week to every day.

✔ You still consider yourself a novice user, even though you may be reasonably familiar with the "basics" of using the program (that is, data entry and editing in cells, saving and printing worksheet data, that kind of thing).

✔ There are still a lot of things in the program that you've never had the need and/or guts to fool around with (charts, databases, pivot tables??!).

✔ You have a feeling (however vague) that there must be easier ways to do some of the things you need to do again and again in Excel, even though you're not sure what they may be.

✔ You own at least one copy of my *Excel For Dummies* title (which you adore and can't re-read often enough).

✔ You bought *MORE Excel 5 For Windows For Dummies* because you can't get enough of my charming prose and need to know more about Excel (even though you still have absolutely no desire to become an expert Excel user).

Well, how close did I get? Regardless of what I scored, you'll find that this book has something for you. In *MORE Excel 5 For Windows For Dummies*, I've endeavored to give you more tips on using the basic Excel feature set as well as a good introduction to some of the more specialized features designed to get fairly specific and sophisticated things done in a short amount of time. Of course, all this information is presented in the same raucous, irreverent style as found in *Excel For Dummies*, following the same old Mary Poppins philosophy that "a spoonful of sugar makes the medicine go down."

How This Book Is Organized

This book is organized in five parts. Each part contains two or more chapters (to keep the editors happy) that more or less go together. Each chapter is divided into loosely related sections that cover the basics of the topic at hand. You should not, however, get too hung up about following along with the structure of the book — ultimately, it matters not at all if you learn how to edit the worksheet before you learn how to format it or learn printing before you learn editing. The important thing is that you find the information — and understand it when you find it — when you need to do any of these things.

Just in case you're interested, a brief synopsis of what you find in each part follows.

Part I: More Everyday Stuff

Part I reviews the fundamentals of using Excel and, at the same time, gives you more information on some of the features you may not have been ready for in *Excel For Dummies*. In this vein, you will learn how to really get in there and use formulas in a worksheet, do editing with workbooks that you didn't design, make your (or someone else's) worksheets as pretty as a picture, and finally get your workbooks organized so that you can locate them and specific information they contain in a heartbeat.

Part II: More Amazing Things You Can Do with Excel

Part II concerns itself with two of the more specialized topics, charts and databases, which were first introduced in *Excel For Dummies*. While *Excel For Dummies* presented you with the barebones facts about creating charts and databases, *MORE Excel 5 For Windows For Dummies* enriches these topics by teaching you how to create great-looking custom charts and do fancy things with your databases, such as sort them on a whole bunch of columns and automatically total and subtotal groups of values that they contain.

Part III: New Fun Stuff

Part III gives you some brand new stuff to chew on. In this section, you learn how to create and use templates to quickly generate worksheets that share the same layout. You also learn how to outline a table of worksheet data so that you can instantly see just the totals or subtotals with or without their supporting data, find and eliminate those nasty worksheet errors, and perform rudimentary "what if" analysis to answer such questions as "how many widgets must I sell next month to be able to comfortably retire in Tahiti?"

Part IV: A Few of the More Advanced Features

Part IV takes you into the wonderful, wacky world of the more advanced features in Excel. In this section, you learn about the weird and wild world of pivot tables, how to edit macros and create custom functions in Visual Basic, and use Excel as part of the suite called Microsoft Office. (Sounds like fun, doesn't it?)

Part V: Tips and Tricks Galore

This books concludes by giving you more tips, tricks, and advice than you can shake a keyboard at. Use this section whenever you want quick answers to such questions as "Isn't there a key I can press to assign the currency format to a cell?" or "What do I do now that I've deleted half of the formulas in my boss's worksheet?"

Conventions Used in This Book

The following information gives you the lowdown on how things look in this book — publishers call these the book's *conventions* (however, no campaigning, flag-waving, name-calling, or finger-pointing is involved).

Keyboard and mouse

Excel is a sophisticated program with lots of fancy boxes, plenty of bars, and more menus than you can count. In Chapter 1, I explain all about these features and how to use them. Be sure to review Chapter 1 if you have any questions about how to get around the program.

Although you use the mouse and keyboard shortcut keys to move your way in, out, and around the Excel worksheet, you do have to take some time to enter the data that you can eventually mouse around with. Therefore, this book occasionally encourages you to type something specific into a specific cell in the worksheet. Of course, you can always choose not to follow the instructions, but you should know what they look like anyway. For example, when you are told to enter a specific function, what you are told to type appears like this:

```
=PROPER(this_is_it)
```

When stuff appears on a screened line like the preceding, you type exactly what you see: an equal sign, the word **PROPER**, a left parenthesis, the text **this_is_it** (complete with underscores), and a right parenthesis. You then, of course, have to press Enter to make the entry stick.

When you are asked to type something that's just right there in the paragraph, the stuff is formatted in **bold type.**

When Excel isn't talking to you by popping up message boxes, it displays highly informative messages in the status bar at the bottom of the screen. This book renders any messages in a special typeface, like this: Ready. (That's the highly informative status message I mentioned.) This special typeface always identifies any on-screen information or messages.

Special icons

The following icons are strategically placed in the margins to point out stuff you may or may not want to read.

This icon alerts you to nerdy discussions that you may well want to skip (or read when no one else is around).

This icon alerts you to shortcuts or other valuable hints related to the topic at hand.

This icon alerts you to information to keep in mind if you want to meet with a modicum of success.

This icon alerts you to information to keep in mind if you want to avert complete disaster.

This icon alerts you to step-by-step tutorial-type information that you can refer to over and over again whenever you really want to get a particular task accomplished.

Where to Go from Here

My suggestion is to first scope out all the great cartoons at the beginning of each part in this book.

After you've had your chuckles, where you go next depends upon what kind of thing you need to do in Excel. If you have an inkling as to which chapter might contain the information you need, go to its opening page and check the "In This Chapter" bullet points for the topic you need to consult. Failing that, you can go to the table of contents and consult the list of major headings in that chapter. If this is no help (as well it might not be unless you've read the section previously), last but never least, you should consult the won-derful index in this book, looking for the particular topic you want to learn about.

Part I
More Everyday Stuff

In this part . . .

This part of the book is like old home week but with a twist. Not only do you get to review some of the fundamentals of using Excel, but you also get more insights, tips, and other pertinent information on how to use it. For example, you'll review how to format your worksheet data and also learn how to create and apply your own custom formats. Also, you'll not only review how to get from one worksheet to another in a workbook, but you'll also learn how to hide worksheets you don't want (others) to see, rearrange worksheets in a workbook, and even how to move or copy the worksheets into a completely different workbook.

Chapter 1

Back to Basics
(Or Déjà Vu All Over Again)

• •

In This Chapter

▶ Starting Excel and choosing commands

▶ Moving around a worksheet and between the sheets of a workbook

▶ Making cell selections of all types and sizes

▶ Entering stuff in a workbook

▶ Editing the stuff you've put in a workbook

• •

*W*ithout a sure grasp of the rock-bottom basics of Excel (such as loading the program, entering information in cells, choosing commands — that kind of stuff), moving on and trying to learn about some of the spiffier Excel features can become not only frustrating but even downright counterproductive. To ensure that this doesn't happen to you as you pick and choose among the many topics in the rest of this book, I have dedicated this first chapter to a "back-to-basics" quick review of Excel fundamentals.

By taking a second to glance over the review material in this chapter, even if you've read every last word in my original *Excel For Dummies* (yeah, right), you can get yourself in a good position to really bail through the exciting new stuff in the rest of this book. By making sure that you're right on the money with the Excel basics, you will have no trouble taking on new features in this spine-tingling program (and, hopefully, even have a great deal of fun with them).

If you're too eager to get on to new things to take the time to review the basics of using Excel right now, I'll understand — just keep in mind that they're here if you should ever get stuck on some little something that I assume you know how to do but in fact have totally spaced or maybe even never really learned in the first place. Suppose that I say that in order to use a certain nifty new feature, you first select all the cell ranges to which you want to apply this nifty feature before you do these "blah-blah-blah" steps. Furthermore, assume (just for the sake of argument, mind you) that you haven't the slightest idea how to go about selecting more than a single block of cells in Excel, which would effectively prevent you from following the blah-blah-blah steps and using this new, nifty feature. Rather than sit there scratching your head in wonder, you can simply turn back to good ol' Chapter 1 and look up the answer in the section called "Building blocks of nonneighboring cells."

Just in case you don't remember how it's possible to select more than one cell range at a time in Excel — and my little hypothetical situation has made you a wee bit curious about how to accomplish this trick — I'll give you a hint: Keep in mind that the Ctrl key magically lets you add to something you've selected, whether it's other filenames in a list or cell ranges in a worksheet.

Sizzling Start-Ups

Excel is simply no fun at all if you can't get the blasted thing to run. So I want to begin the back-to-basics material with a quick review of the many ways to get Excel up and running (then I discuss ways in which you can catch it!).

Starting Excel from DOS

To fire up Excel from that barren C> prompt that DOS (*Dumb Operating System*) is so fond of (this was before the grand arrival of the Windows Program Manager), follow these steps:

1. **Type** `win`.

2. **Press the spacebar once.**

3. **Type** `excel`.

   You should see the following line on your computer screen:

```
C:\>win excel
```

4. **If that's what you see, go ahead and press Enter.** If not, press Backspace until you wipe out your typing errors and then try typing the **win excel** command again.

Assuming that you placed a space between `win` and `excel` and caught all your typos, the computer loads Windows and then, from there, directly loads Excel. On the other hand, if DOS kind of sputters and burps at your command when you press Enter, you have to go back and do it all over again.

What about starting Excel when Windows is already up on your screen? Let's say that your computer is nicely set up so that you *never* have to fool with that old devil DOS. In that case, it's really simple to start Excel from the Windows Program Manager.

Starting Excel from the Windows Program Manager

1. **Locate in the Program Manager the window that contains the Microsoft Excel program icon.** It shows a tiny worksheet with the fancy XL initials in the lower right-hand corner.

   The window containing the Excel program icon is normally the Microsoft Office window, where Excel 5 for Windows always wants to install itself. (However, it could very well be in some other window — you may have to look for it.) If you can't find the Microsoft Office window, open the Window pull-down menu (pressing Alt+W will do the trick) and then type the number that precedes its name in the pull-down list. If the name doesn't appear in the list, choose the More Windows command from the bottom of the list and then double-click its name in the list box in the Select Window window.

2. **After you've located the Microsoft Excel program icon in this program window, double-click on the icon.**

If you're in the Microsoft Office program window but you can't see the XL icon, you can either use the scroll bars on the program window or press the arrow keys.

Pressing the arrow keys to bring the XL program icon into view chooses it at the same time. You can then start Excel by simply pressing Enter — no need to double-click at that point.

Starting Excel and opening a workbook from the Windows File Manager

Here's one more way of starting Excel when you're getting ready to get to work. This method opens an Excel workbook at the same time. To open a workbook document while starting Excel, you have to be in the Windows File Manager rather than in the Windows Program Manager, as shown in these steps:

1. **In the Windows Program Manager, locate the File Manager icon (the one with the picture of a file cabinet) in the Main program window and then double-click on it.**

2. **In the left pane of the File Manager window, locate the name of the directory (or subdirectory) that contains the Excel workbook you want to open and then click on it.** It displays its contents in the pane to the right.

3. **When you locate the name of the workbook you want to open in Excel, double-click on it or click on it and press Enter.**

Windows first opens Excel and then Excel, in turn, opens the workbook you selected in the File Manager. It's all very orderly and efficient.

You can use the Search command from the File Manager's File menu to locate an Excel workbook if you're having trouble remembering which directory it's in. When you choose File⇔Search, Windows opens the Search dialog box. Replace *.* (your friend star-dot-star, which stands for everything in the galaxy and is already chosen in the Search For text box) with the name of the file (or as much of the name as you remember). When you choose OK, Windows searches for the file, starting from the directory that's chosen in the directory tree. If you want to search the entire hard disk, be sure to back up to the top level C:\ before you open the Search dialog box. If you want to see a list of all the Excel documents in the various directories that Windows searches, replace the last * in this line

```
*.*
```

with **.xls** so that this line

```
*.xls
```

appears in the Search For text box. When you see the workbook you want, double-click on it, and you will be transported there.

Around the Screen in 80 Seconds

After you have Excel up and running and your favorite workbook is staring back at you from the screen, you're ready to get down to work. In case there's any doubt about what's what in the Excel window displayed on your screen, I bribed and cajoled my editor into reproducing a picture of the blank Excel screen with descriptions of its various parts (see Figure 1-1). When you start Excel, your screen should look just like this one except, of course, that yours will show some stuff in the worksheet part if you've opened one of your Excel workbooks, and yours won't have all the callouts displayed around it.

The following list gives you a quick rundown of each of the major parts of the Excel window, as shown in Figure 1-1 and on a monitor near you:

  ✔ *Title bar.* At the very tippy-top of the screen, this shows the name of the program (Microsoft Excel — surprise, surprise!) followed by a dash and the name of the workbook shown in the document window below it. A temporary name, such as Book1, Book2, and so on, appears when you start Excel without opening an existing workbook or when you open a new workbook.

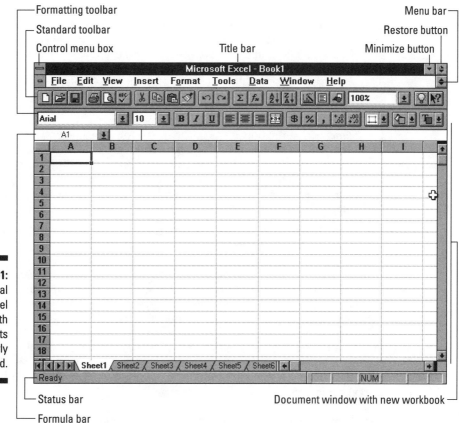

Formatting toolbar

Standard toolbar

Control menu box

Title bar

Menu bar

Restore button

Minimize button

Figure 1-1:
The typical
Excel
screen with
all its parts
clearly
delineated.

Status bar

Formula bar

Document window with new workbook

- ✔ *Menu bar.* Just below the title bar, this contains the pull-down menus for Excel. To open a menu, click on its name or press Alt plus the command (underlined) letter. To choose a command *from* a pull-down menu, click on it or type *its* command letter.

- ✔ *Standard toolbar.* Underneath the menu bar, it contains a number of buttons that perform the most common spreadsheet tasks — such as creating new workbooks, saving the current workbook, and printing — when you click on the buttons.

- ✔ *Formatting toolbar.* Below the Standard toolbar, this contains a bunch of buttons that perform many of the most common formatting tasks — such as changing the font and font size and adding bold, italic, and underlining effects — when you click on the buttons.

- ✔ *Formula bar.* Right beneath the Formatting toolbar, this shows the address of the current cell in addition to the contents of the cell, if any. The current cell is the one with the cell pointer, which is the heavy border surrounding one of the cells in the document window, as shown in cell A1 in Figure 1-1. Keep in mind that the cell contents shown on the formula bar match what's displayed in the cell *only when you have entered text,* such as Hi Mom! or The Big Profits. When you enter a formula in the cell, such as =A2*B2 or =SUM(C1:C40), you see the calculated values, such as 1400 or 5,000.00, in the cell of the worksheet, and the underlying formula shows up on the formula bar.

✔ *Status bar.* At the bottom of the heap, it shows the current condition of the program or activity you've begun in addition to which *locking keys* are active (it displays NUM when Num Lock is engaged or CAPS when Caps Lock is turned on) or which special modes are active (OVR when you turn off Insert mode or ADD when you're adding different ranges to the current selection). Go back and look at Figure 1-1 to see where it is.

✔ *Document window.* Shows you as much of the current worksheet as your monitor and latest zoom size allow.

Of all the Excel screen elements, the most pervasive is the document window. The reason is probably that the document window is the place where almost all the action takes place in Excel. Figure 1-2 gives you a quick rundown of the components in a typical document window.

The most interesting items in the document window are the various sheet tabs and scroll box thingies that you use to move from worksheet to worksheet in a workbook (more on that later) and to bring new regions of the current worksheet into view.

Keep in mind that you can resize the document window in the area between the formula and status bars. When the document window is less than maximum size (as it is in Figure 1-2), the name of the workbook document (its filename) no longer appears *only* after Microsoft Excel in the tippy-top title bar. It also appears in the document title bar. This is very helpful when you have more than one workbook file open and are attempting to keep straight which one is current (the answer is the one whose document title bar is highlighted).

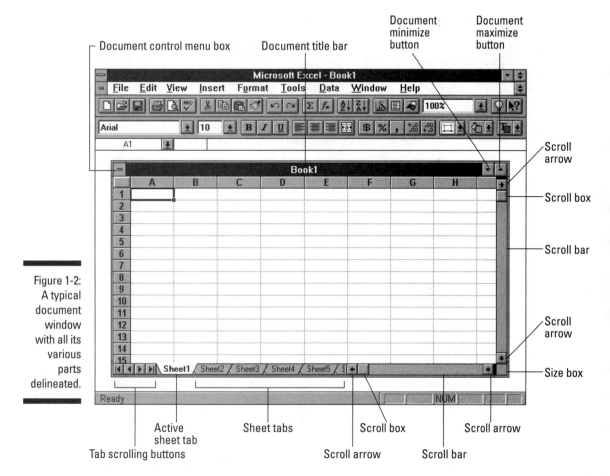

Figure 1-2:
A typical
document
window
with all its
various
parts
delineated.

Icon, Can You?

Excel, like all other Microsoft programs for Windows, makes heavy use of icons. Nowhere is this truer than in the case of the toolbars. The Standard and Formatting toolbars are only two of many you can display. See Tables 1-1 and 1-2 for a run-down of the tools in these two toolbars.

TIP

An easier way of seeing the names of the buttons on a particular toolbar is to position your little mouse pointer on the button in question and hold it still for a second or so (without, for heaven's sake, *clicking* the mouse button — just hold it there). As if by magic, Excel suddenly displays the name of the button in a sickly little yellow box. This trick is known by the stupid name of *tooltips*.

TIP

If you find that you don't use the Standard and Formatting toolbars all that much, you may want to get rid of them in order to make room to display more of the current worksheet. Space is at *such* a premium on standard 14-inch monitors. To remove the display of the toolbars, choose View⇨Toolbars, remove the Xs from the Standard and Formatting check boxes in the Toolbars dialog box, and then choose OK.

Table 1-1	The Cool Tools on the Standard Toolbar	
Tool	*Tool Name*	*What the Tool Does When You Click on It*
	New Workbook	Opens a new workbook with 16 blank worksheets
	Open	Lets you open an existing Excel workbook
	Save	Saves changes in the active workbook
	Print	Prints the workbook
	Print Preview	Lets you preview how the worksheet will appear when printed
	Spelling	Checks the spelling of text in your worksheet
	Cut	Cuts the current selection to the Clipboard
	Copy	Copies the current selection to the Clipboard
	Paste	Pastes the contents of the Clipboard into the current worksheet
	Format Painter	Lets you apply all the formatting used in the current cell to any cell selection you choose
	Undo	Undoes your last action
	Repeat	Repeats your last action
	AutoSum	Sums a list of values with the SUM function
	Function Wizard	Steps you through creating a formula by using one of Excel's many built-in functions (see Chapter 2)
	Sort Ascending	Sorts data in a cell selection in alphabetical order and/or numerical order, depending upon the type of data in cells
	Sort Descending	Sorts data in a cell selection in reverse alphabetical order and/or numerical order, depending upon the type of data in cells

Tool	Tool Name	What the Tool Does When You Click on It
	ChartWizard	Steps you through the creation of a new chart in the active worksheet
	Text Box	Creates a text box that you can use to add notes to a worksheet
	Drawing	Displays the Drawing toolbar that lets you draw various shapes and arrows
100%	Zoom Control	Lets you change the screen magnification to zoom in or out on your worksheet data
	TipWizard	Gives you tips on how to do things quicker in Excel based on whatever actions you've just been performing. You know that Excel has some tips for you when the light bulb icon used by theTipWizard turns yellow (instead of white). Click on the TipWizard tool to display a box containing numbered tips and scroll arrows beneath the Formatting toolbar at the top of the screen. To get rid of the tips after reading them, just click on the TipWizard tool a second time.
	Help	Gives you Help information on the command or region of the screen that you click on with the question mark pointer

Table 1-2   The Cool Tools on the Formatting Toolbar

Tool	Tool Name	What the Tool Does When You Click on It
Arial	Font	Applies a new font to the entries in the cell selection
10	Font Size	Applies a new font size to the entries in the cell selection
B	Bold	Applies bold to the cell selection
I	Italic	Applies italic to the cell selection
U	Underline	Underlines the *entries* in the cell selection, not the cells. (If the entries are already underlined, clicking on this tool removes the underlining.)
	Align Left	Left-aligns the entries in the cell selection
	Center	Centers the entries in the cell selection

Table 1-2 The Cool Tools on the Formatting Toolbar (continued)

Tool	Tool Name	What the Tool Does When You Click on It
	Align Right	Right-aligns the entries in the cell selection
	Center Across Columns	Centers the entry in the active cell across selected columns
	Currency Style	Applies a currency number format to the cell selection to display all values with a dollar sign, commas between thousands, and two decimal places
	Percent Style	Applies a percentage number format to the cell selection by multiplying the values by 100 and displaying with a percent sign and no decimal places
	Comma Style	Applies a comma number format to the cell selection to display commas separating thousands and two decimal places
	Increase Decimal	Adds one decimal place to the number format in the cell selection each time you click on the tool. (Reverses direction and reduces the number of decimal places when you hold down the Shift key as you click on this tool.)
	Decrease Decimal	Reduces one decimal place from the number format in the cell selection each time you click on the tool. (Reverses direction and adds one decimal place when you hold down the Shift key as you click on this tool.)
	Border	Lets you select a border for the cell selection from the pop-up palette of border styles
	Color	Lets you select a new color for the background of the cells in the cell selection from the pop-up color palette
	Font Color	Lets you select a new color for the text in the cells in the cell selection from the pop-up color palette

The Short and Long of the Menus

Talking about toolbars reminds me to remind you about the wonderful world of Excel *shortcut menus.* You know about the standard pull-down menus that are attached to the menu bar, of course, and how they can be used to choose the necessary Excel commands by way of the keyboard with the Alt key and command letters or by clicking the mouse pointer. But don't overlook the shortcut menus and how they can make many of these same commands much more accessible. The following list reviews the shortcuts:

✔ Shortcut menus are attached to particular objects on-screen, such as cells, columns, and rows.

✔ To display the commands on a shortcut menu, click on the object — the cell, row heading, or column heading, for example — with the *secondary* mouse button. (The secondary mouse button is the one you don't normally click — the usual one is called the *primary* mouse button.) Voilà — the shortcut menu appears attached to the object you just clicked on.

✔ To *choose* a command on a displayed shortcut menu, you must click on it with the *primary* mouse button. (Now, if that isn't confusing, I don't know what is.) Alternatively, if you haven't released the secondary mouse button since displaying the shortcut menu, you can drag down until you highlight the command.

Shortcut menu commands don't have command letters like the standard pull-down menus do, so you must be willing to mouse around to use them.

✔ In the standard Excel window, a shortcut menu is attached to each worksheet cell, column (activated by clicking on the column heading), row (activated by clicking on the row heading), toolbar, sheet tab, and — believe it or not — the menu bar itself! (Very strange, if you ask me.)

Don't forget that Excel charts have scads of shortcut menus attached to their individual parts. You can use the commands on these shortcut menus to quickly modify particular chart settings, such as the titles, axes, and so on, when you're creating a custom chart. See Chapter 5 for loads of fun information about creating fancy custom charts.

Getting There Is Half the Fun

As you are no doubt acutely aware by now, very little of the total workbook can be viewed at any one time. Although you may create a few workbooks that utilize only the portion of a single worksheet (the cell range A1:I18 in Sheet1, for example — it varies from monitor to monitor) that comes into view when you start a new workbook, chances are that most of your workbooks will be larger, either in terms of columns and rows of a single worksheet or in terms of multiple worksheets, or both.

Because your average Excel spreadsheet is too large to fit on-screen all at one time, you will do a combination of a great deal of cell pointing and scrolling new parts into view almost any time you sit down to work with this software. For this reason, I suggest that you take a second to review some of the more important shortcuts for moving the cell pointer and scrolling through the worksheet.

Going, going, gone

I assume that you're already proficient at moving the cell pointer one cell at a time with the arrow keys. Using that skill as a starting point, let's look at some larger jumps that can save you oodles of time as you work:

- ✔ Don't forget those little PgUp and PgDn keys. In the current worksheet, they move the cell pointer up and down by one screenful. When you hold down Ctrl and press PgDn, it takes you to the next worksheet in your workbook. You can press this key combination to move down through the sheets (Sheet1 through Sheet16) in a workbook without having to click on the sheet tabs. Likewise, you can press Ctrl+PgUp to move up through the sheets (Sheet16 through Sheet1).

- ✔ When you want to move to the end of a large, continuous block of data, such as the top or bottom of a long column of names or the leftmost or rightmost cell in a long row of dates, hold down Ctrl and then press one of the arrow keys. Press Ctrl+→ to move to the last occupied cell at the end of the current row; press Ctrl+← to move to the first cell. Press Ctrl+↓ to move directly to the last occupied cell at the bottom of the current column; press Ctrl+↑ to move to the topmost cell in the column.

- ✔ If you know the address of the cell to which you want to move the cell pointer, choose Edit⇨Go To (the shortcut key is F5) and then type the cell address and press Enter.

- ✔ If you've named the cell or cell range you want to move to in the workbook (it doesn't have to be in the current worksheet), click on the button with the down arrow on the formula bar next to the current cell address to open an alphabetical list of all the range names in the current sheet. Click on or drag down to the range name you want to move to. When you release the mouse button, Excel moves the cell pointer directly to the named cell, or to the first cell in the case of a named cell range (Excel selects all the cells in the range if the name refers to a bunch of cells). You can also open the Go To dialog box (press Edit⇨Go To or the shortcut key, F5) and then choose the range name in the Go To list box before you choose OK or press Enter.

Moving hither and yon

When you use the Go To dialog box to move the cell pointer, Excel puts in the Reference text box the address of the cell you're moving from at the same time as it moves the cell pointer to the cell address you just typed in this text box. You can then return directly to the cell whence you came by simply pressing F5, Enter (you don't even have to stop to check the cell address in the Go To dialog box). In fact, after pressing F5, Enter to return to the cell from which you originally departed, you can then jump right back to your preceding cell destination by pressing F5, Enter again. Continuing to press F5, Enter creates a kind of Ping-Pong effect, bouncing you between cells, from origin to destination and back again. In and of itself, pressing F5, Enter to jump back and forth in this manner is a colossal waste of time, unless of course, you want to compare very distant parts of a workbook (especially areas in two different sheets of the same workbook) by pressing F5, Enter to flip back and forth from the data in one area to the data in the other.

Slipping through the sheets

One of the biggest differences between Excel 4 and Excel 5 is the way in which each one treats the basic workbook. Although you had access to workbooks in Excel 4, the individual worksheet remained the basic Excel document, saved under its own filename. To create a workbook in version 4, you had to go out of your way by specifically adding each worksheet the workbook was to contain. In Excel 5, the workbook comes automatically equipped with 16 blank worksheets and has taken center stage as the basic document. You no longer have to knit the workbook together from individual worksheets — you can just begin creating the worksheets right within the workbook as you need them.

In keeping with the primary importance of the workbook in Excel 5, you should, at the very least, be proficient in navigating through the workbook by moving from sheet to sheet in Excel 5. (Chapter 4 introduces you to some new sheet tricks for keeping your workbooks organized.) The following list shows a few ways to move from one worksheet to another within the current workbook:

> ✔ One of the most direct ways to move from one sheet to another is to click on its sheet tab at the bottom of the workbook's document window. If the sheet tab for the worksheet you want to move to is not displayed, click on the tab scrolling button that points to the right (left of the tabs) until the sheet tab you want to choose scrolls into view. To scroll the first group of worksheet tabs into view, click on the first sheet tab (the one with the triangle that points to the left and touches the vertical bar). To scroll the last group of sheet tabs into view, you click on the last sheet tab — the one with the triangle that points to the right and touches the vertical bar.

✔ From the keyboard, you can move from sheet to sheet by holding down the Ctrl key as you press PgDn and PgUp. Pressing Ctrl+PgDn moves to the next sheet in the workbook. Pressing Ctrl+PgUp moves you up through the sheets in the workbook. (It positions the cell pointer in cell A1 or whatever was its preceding cell position if you've already visited the sheet and during that visit relocated the cell pointer.)

✔ If you want to move the cell pointer to a named cell or cell range in another worksheet, click on the cell reference button (with the down arrow on the formula bar right next to the current cell address) and then choose the range name in the drop-down list.

Three sheet tabs to the wind

Keep in mind that although Excel normally displays only, at most, about six sheet tabs, this number varies if you've replaced the default sheet names — Sheet1, Sheet2, and so on — with more descriptive sheet names that are longer or shorter. (See Chapter 4 if you've forgotten how to rename sheets.) You can display more sheet tabs if you're willing to shortchange the horizontal scroll bar in the document window. To reveal more sheet tabs, and therefore less scroll bar, position the mouse pointer on the *vertical split bar* between the last visible sheet tab and the left scroll arrow on the horizontal scroll bar. When the mouse pointer changes to a split pointer with a double arrow pointing left and right, click and drag the pointer to the right until you are satisfied with the number of tabs displayed or until you have gotten rid of the horizontal scroll bar. To return to the default arrangement, which gives the horizontal scroll bar about 40 percent of the bar (with the other 60 percent going to the sheet tabs and tab scrolling buttons), simply double-click the split bar when the split pointer appears.

Selective Thinking

Right up there with knowing how to move easily around a worksheet is knowing the most efficient methods for selecting ranges of cells you want to work with. As you probably remember from the original *Excel For Dummies,* our Excel mantra is the following (repeat after me):

Select the cell range and then select the command to apply to cells in the range.

The number of different kinds of commands you can apply to a cell range after it has been selected are legion. Most often, the command has something to do with either formatting the information displayed in the cells or copying or moving that block of information to another place in the workbook.

In addition to recalling the "select first and then act" mantra as you work, you also have to keep in mind that Excel supports two types of cell selections:

✔ The first and most common type is a *single cell range.* A single cell range is made up of just one rectangular block of highlighted cells that is so many columns wide and rows high. (All the cells in the block appear highlighted except the first one, which is still included in the heavy border surrounding the entire range.) Of course, the smallest possible single cell range consists of the current cell alone, and the largest possible single cell range consists of all the cells in the entire worksheet (a mammoth cell range, if ever there was one). Most single cell ranges, naturally, fall somewhere between these two extremes.

✔ The second type is less common but should not be overlooked: It is the *discontinuous* — or what I prefer to call *nonadjacent* — cell selection. The nonadjacent cell selection is made up of at least two or more single cell ranges, all selected at the same time.

Building blocks in the neighborhood (or have you met my cellmates?)

Most of the time, you have to select only a single range of cells for formatting or some such action. When you're making cell selections with the mouse, you should keep the following techniques in mind:

✔ To select a single cell, click on the cell with the plus-shaped mouse pointer.

✔ To select a range made up of a certain number of rows and columns — that is, some type of block formation — click on the first cell (in the upper left-hand corner of the block) and then drag diagonally through to the last cell (in the lower right-hand corner of the block).

✔ To select a range made up of an entire row of cells, click on the gray row number (shown in the far left column). To extend the range so that it includes several complete rows either above or below the one you selected, you simply drag up or down.

✔ To select a range made up of an entire column of cells, click on the gray column letter that appears in the top row of the worksheet. To extend the range so that it includes several complete columns either left or right of the one you selected, you simply drag left or right.

✔ To select all the cells in the entire worksheet, click on the Select All button (the gray, blank button in the upper left-hand corner at the intersection of the row of column letters and column of row numbers).

These techniques work regardless of whether you're selecting blank or occupied cells in a worksheet (remember that you can format cells before or after you put stuff in them).

When you're selecting a range of already occupied cells, such as a table of numbers or a list of names and addresses in a worksheet, you can also select this range with the AutoSelect feature.

Selecting a range of occupied cells with AutoSelect

In case you've forgotten about this little goodie, AutoSelect lets you select a range of occupied cells by following these three simple steps:

1. **Click on the first cell in the range (in the upper left-hand corner of the table of data) to select it.**

2. **Hold down the Shift key as you double-click on the edge of the cell with the arrow head pointer in the direction you want the selection extended.**

   In English, this means that if you want to highlight all the cells in that row of the table, you double-click on the right side of the first cell. If you want to highlight all the cells in that *column* of the table, however, you double-click on the *bottom* side of the cell.

3. **To then extend the range to include the rest of the cells in the table, you double-click on the side of the highlighted cell selection in the direction it next should be extended.**

   In other words, if the top row is selected (by double-clicking on the right side of the first cell), double-click on the bottom side of one of the cells in that selected row to extend the selection down the rest of the last row with occupied cells — presumably the last row in that table. If you selected the first column (by double-clicking on the bottom of the first cell), double-click on the right side of one of the cells in that selected column to extend the selection to the right to the last column in the table.

Just keep in mind that you must keep the Shift key depressed as you do all this double-clicking, or else AutoSelect does no more than move you from corner to corner in the table.

You can use AutoSelect to jump the cell pointer from corner to corner of a table of occupied cells by double-clicking on whatever side of the selected cell you want to move. When the cell pointer is in the first cell of a table, you can go to the last cell in the first row by double-clicking on the right side of the first cell — just be sure that you don't hold down Shift unless you want to select all the cells in between. After the cell pointer is in the top row of the last column in the table, you can return to the first cell in the table by double-clicking on the *left* side of that cell or go to the last cell in the table by double-clicking on the *bottom* of that cell.

You can also select a single range of cells with the keyboard. The most direct way is to move the cell pointer to the first cell in the range and then hold down Shift as you press the cursor-movement keys to move the cell pointer to the last cell in the table.

If you find that holding down Shift with your left hand and holding down the arrow keys or PgUp or PgDn with your right hand is just a little more than you're comfortable dealing with, you can press F8 (Extend) rather than Shift. Here's how: Simply move the cell pointer to the first cell, press F8 once so that you see EXT in the status bar — no need to *hold down* F8, as you do with Shift — and then press the cursor-movement keys to highlight all the cells in the range. What's nice about this method is that you can always reduce the size of the highlighted range by pressing the cursor-movement keys to backtrack your steps. When you have the range properly selected, you then have to remember to press F8 a second time to get out of Extend mode (shown by the disappearance of EXT from the status bar) so that you can again move the cell pointer without also highlighting and selecting more cells.

You can use the keyboard to perform an AutoSelection of a table of data with F8 to get you into Extend mode. Position the cell pointer in the first cell of the table, press F8 to get into Extend mode and then press Ctrl+ → to extend the selection down to the last row of the table — you can also press Ctrl+↓ before Ctrl+→, if you prefer — before you press F8 to get out of Extend mode.

You erstwhile Lotus 1-2-3 users can also press End, ↓ or End, → rather than F8: Just be aware that when you press Shift, you have to be able to hold down the Shift key at the same time as you press Ctrl+→ and Ctrl+↓ or End, → and End, ↓ (if you're an old-time 1-2-3 user), which is not as easy as it sounds.

Building blocks of nonneighboring cells

Every once in a while, you have to select multiple ranges of cells (a nonadjacent selection) in a worksheet. Suppose that you realize that you have to add boldface to all the headings in a table of data, both those that contain the column labels in the top row and those that contain the row labels in the first column. Of course, you can always boldface each range of cells individually by first selecting the row of column headings as a single range, clicking on the Bold button on the Formatting toolbar (or pressing Ctrl+B), selecting the column of row headings as a single range, and then clicking on the Bold button (or pressing Ctrl+B) again. Yeesh! To save some time and what's left of your sanity, you can instead select both ranges with the column and row headings as a nonadjacent selection and then boldface their entries in one operation.

Remember that to create a nonadjacent selection in Excel, you simply select one of the cell ranges (using whatever selection method you prefer) and then add to it either by pressing Shift+F8 to get into Add mode, indicated by ADD on the status bar, before selecting the second range, or by holding down Ctrl as you select the second range. If you press the Shift+F8 key combination, be sure to remember to press Shift+F8 again to get *out* of Add mode when all the ranges you want to work with are selected. If you press Ctrl to add, be sure that you keep it depressed as you select each individual range to be added to the nonadjacent selection.

You Put the Info in . . . .

By now, I assume that you are fairly experienced at doing simple data entry and editing in a worksheet. In fact, you may consider it your forte in Excel. Just in case you missed some of the less-than-obvious hints for entering different types of data in a worksheet and performing straightforward edits offered in the original *Excel For Dummies,* however, please take a quick glance at the bulleted points in the next couple of sections — they may jog your memory or (it's always possible) inform you of something you missed altogether in the first go-around.

Dazzling data entry

Excel tries to make data entry as easy as possible by correctly anticipating which type of information you intend to enter in a cell. Keep these tips in mind:

✔ If you press = (equal sign), Excel expects a formula of some sort. If you disappoint the program by following it with text that doesn't relate to any known cell addresses or range names, the program displays an Error in Formula dialog box the moment you complete the entry.

✔ If you type a string of numbers (such as **3-2-81** or **4/15/95**) or a combination of text and numbers (such as **mar 2, 1981**, or **April 1**) that corresponds to some sort of possible date in some sort of recognizable date format, Excel enters the information as a date. Technically, this means that what you see displayed in the cell is really a front for a horrendous number that represents the number of days that have elapsed between the date displayed in the cell and January 1, 1900.

✔ If you enter only a string of numbers (0 through 9) separated by a period which acts as a decimal point, Excel considers the entry to be a *value,* which is automatically right-aligned in the cell. If you precede a number with – (minus sign) or enclose it within a pair of parentheses, Excel considers the number to be a *negative value.*

✔ If you put such a long number into a cell that it can't fit the current width of that cell, Excel automatically converts the number to scientific notation. You may dimly remember from high school some stuff about *exponents* that raise a *base number* to a particular *power* — and you thought you'd never use it!

✔ Any mishmash of numbers, punctuation, and text that you enter that Excel can't pigeonhole as a formula, date, or value goes in as a *text entry,* which is automatically left-aligned and spills over to any blank cells on the right if all the characters cannot be displayed in the current column width.

When you have a great deal of data entry to do in a worksheet, keep the following helpful pointers in mind:

✔ To speed up data entry when you're creating a table of data, select the range of cells for the table — so many columns over and rows down — and then begin entering the data in the first cell. When you press Enter to complete the first entry, Excel automatically advances the cell pointer to the next cell down in the same column. When you finish entering the last cell in the first column, Excel automatically advances the cell pointer to the first cell at the top of the next column to the right. When you've finished entering all the data in the table, press an arrow key or click a cell outside the table to deselect all the cells.

✔ When you're entering a series of financial figures with various dollars and cents, you can speed things up by having Excel put in the decimal point so that all you have to do is type the digits in each dollar amount. To accomplish this neat trick, choose Tools⇨Options, choose the Edit tab in the Options dialog box, and choose the Fixed Decimal option to put an X in its check box. After you choose OK, Excel automatically adds two decimal places to any number you enter. For example, if you type **12**, Excel enters 0.12 in the cell. If you type **1200**, Excel enters 12 in the cell. If you type **1201**, Excel enters 12.01 in the cell. Just be sure to remember to *deselect* the Fixed Decimal check box in the Edit tab of the Options dialog box when you no longer want Excel to automatically add two decimal places to every number you enter in the worksheet.

✔ To make the same entry in more than one cell in a single operation, select all the cells to hold that entry (even a nonadjacent selection), type the entry in the current cell, and press Ctrl+Enter. Excel puts the entry into all the selected cells. If you mess up and press only Enter, Excel puts the entry into just the *current* cell rather than into all the cells that are highlighted in the nonadjacent selection.

✔ When you're making an entry that is the first in a series of related entries — such as **January** when you want to enter all 12 months across a row, or **Q1** when you want to enter quarters through Q4 down a column — enter the first of the series in the current cell. Then, with the cell pointer in the cell that contains the first entry, position the mouse pointer on the little box that appears in the lower right-hand corner of the cell. When the pointer changes into the *fill handle* (a black cross), click and drag it in the direction in which you intend to extend the series. When you've highlighted all the cells to contain the series of entries, release the mouse button to fill the selection.

The cell pointer's itinerary

Excel normally always moves the cell pointer to the next cell down the current column when you press Enter to complete a cell entry. If you prefer to have Excel do this *only* when you are making entries in a range of cells that you've preselected, choose Tools➪Options, click on the Edit tab in the Options dialog box, and then choose the Move Selection After Enter option to remove the X from its check box. After you choose OK, Excel does not move the cell pointer when you complete an entry with the Enter key unless you are doing data entry in a preselected range; you can still press the ↓ key to complete an entry and move the cell pointer down one row at the same time. Changing this setting makes it really easy to use the AutoFill feature to create a series of dates or numbers because the cell pointer stays in the cell where you make the initial entry, so all you have to do is extend the series by dragging the fill handle through adjacent cells.

Editing made easy

The greater part of your worksheet editing no doubt involves taking care of simple mistakes, such as typos and entering data in the wrong place in the worksheet. When you do this type of simple editing, keep the following pointers in mind:

- ✔ To activate editing in a cell and bring the contents of a cell to the formula bar, double-click on the cell that needs help. If you know approximately where in the cell you want the insertion point to appear, position the cross pointer at about that position within the cell and double-click there.

- ✔ To move the insertion point to the beginning of the cell entry that you're editing, press Home. To move the insertion point to the end of the cell entry, press End. To move the insertion point one word at a time (assuming that you're editing an entry with text), press Ctrl+← or Ctrl+→, depending on which direction you want to be.

- ✔ If you discover, to your horror, that you've begun editing in the wrong cell and are busily in the middle of completely messing up an entry that should have remained exactly as it was, press Esc to remove your edits and restore the entry to its original state.

- ✔ Don't forget to use the spell-check feature to catch any hitherto undetected typos. To restrict the spell checking to just those cells that contain spreadsheet titles and headings, select those cells and then click on the Spelling button on the Standard toolbar or choose Tools➪Spelling or press F7.

✔ To delete a cell or cell selection from the worksheet, select the cells and press Delete (which is the keyboard shortcut for Edit⇨Clear contents). If you ever delete a cell or cell selection in error, choose Edit⇨Undo Clear from the pull-down menus or click on the Undo button on the Standard toolbar or press Ctrl+Z.

Copying and moving

In addition to taking care of mistakes in the entries made in various cells in a worksheet, your basic editing will probably also involve a variety of cut-and-paste operations. When you're relocating cell entries in a worksheet, you should keep in mind the following tips and techniques:

✔ Copy and move operations are restricted to single cell ranges. In other words, don't even *think* about selecting multiple cell ranges in a nonadjacent selection, because you will only end up getting the following error message stuck in your face:

```
Cannot use that command on multiple selections
```

✔ Copying or moving a range of cell entries into an area of the worksheet that already contains cell entries is detrimental to the original entries — so much so that Excel takes out the existing entries to make room for the ones you're moving or copying – which can be bad. To help you avoid unintentionally replacing existing entries, Excel displays an alert dialog box with a message that asks you, `Replace contents of destination cells?` Please consider this question carefully and choose Cancel (or press Esc) if you have the *slightest* bit of doubt about whether you want to wipe out the existing entries.

✔ The simplest way to copy and move a range of data with the mouse is with the drag-and-drop method. To move a range, select it and then position the mouse pointer on one of the edges of the range. When the pointer changes to an arrowhead, drag the range (shown by outline only) to its new position. To *copy* a range of entries, follow the same procedure except hold down Ctrl as you drag the range — the mouse pointer changes to an arrowhead with a plus sign on its right when you position the mouse pointer on a side of the selected range with Ctrl depressed.

✔ To move or copy a cell range using the keyboard, select the range and then choose Edit⇨Cut or press Ctrl+X to move the range, or choose Edit⇨Copy or press Ctrl+C to copy the range. Then position the cell pointer in the cell where *the upper left-hand corner* of the about-to-be-moved or copied range should appear and choose Edit⇨Paste or press Enter or Ctrl+V.

✔ To insert the range of cells you're moving or copying in an area that already contains cell entries (and thereby avoid replacing existing cell entries), cut or copy the range and select the cell where the first cell of the copied or moved range is to appear as usual. Then choose Insert⇨Cut Cells (or Copied Cells) from the pull-down menus to open the Insert Paste or Insert Copied cells. By default, Excel most often chooses the Shift Cells Down radio button. To shift existing cells to the right instead, choose the Shift Cells Right radio button before you choose OK.

✔ To insert a range of entries by moving existing entries down or to the right with the drag-and-drop technique, you have to hold down Shift as you drag the selected range. If you're copying a range, you must manage to depress both the Shift *and* Ctrl keys as you drag the cell range — a challenge to anyone's dexterity. When you place the cursor where the first cell of the range that's being moved or copied will be inserted, you can tell whether existing cells will be pushed down or to the right by the *shape* the outline of the range assumes. When the gray cell range outline appears between the column as a *vertical* I-beam shape — in other words, an I-beam standing straight up, the existing cells will be pushed to the right when you release the mouse button. When the outline of the cell range appears between the rows as a *horizontal* I-beam — that is, on its side — existing cells will be pushed down.

Chapter 2

Spreadsheets Like the Hotshots Make 'Em

In This Chapter

▶ Reviewing how to create simple formulas and learning how to group their elements to override the built-in order of precedence

▶ Reviewing the use of the Function Wizard to insert Excel functions into formulas

▶ Learning how to create formulas that return text-type answers

▶ Learning how to convert formulas to their calculated results

▶ Reviewing how to create master formulas and copy them in data tables

▶ Learning more about setting up formulas in data tables that use different types of cell references — relative, absolute, and mixed

*M*ost of the data entry-type work you do when creating a new worksheet consists of a mixture of the following three procedures:

✔ Entering text for the titles in the worksheet and column and row headings, and that kind of thing

✔ Entering values like the number of things sold, the price at which they sold, and the date on which they were sold

✔ Entering formulas that calculate new values, such as a formula that determines the total amount of money the company grosses during each month of a given quarter, one that computes the total sales during that quarter, or one that reckons what percentage each monthly total is of the quarterly total

Of the three procedures — entry of text, entry of values, and entry of formulas — the trickiest by far is the entry of formulas (the only thing the least bit challenging about entering text and values is getting them formatted the way you want, which you'll pick up more pointers on doing in the next chapter).

Because formulas are so central to most worksheets and they can be a bit touchy at times, I thought it would be a good idea to devote this chapter to the techniques for creating and copying formulas. As part of this process, you'll also review how to use the Function Wizard to insert functions in your formulas and learn about creating formulas that work with text.

The Formula for Success

Keep in mind that when talking about formulas, I'm referring to anything that returns a new result after you enter something into a cell (alert dialog boxes with error messages don't count!). Formulas, of course, can run the gamut from really simple ones like

```
=5+3
```

which returns 8 in its cell, to really yucky, complicated ones like

```
=IF(AND(G3>=1500,G3<=10000),F3+(F3*.20),F3)
```

which returns whatever value is currently in cell F3 when the value in G3 is less than 1,500 or greater than 10,000 but returns the F3 value plus 20 percent when the value in G3 is between the target range of 1,500 and 10,000, inclusive (wow, what a mouthful!).

Also, keep in mind that while most of your formulas are set up only to return new values (be they numbers like 120 or dates like 12/25/95, let's open the presents!), you can actually create formulas in Excel that return text-like answers such as Mary Ann or important-sounding terms like Annuities Due (you'll learn how create some text formulas a little later in this chapter).

Formula basics revisited

Because calculations by formula lie at the heart of almost any worksheet, you want to be sure that you're really up on the basics of setting up formulas, both with and without Excel functions, before you go about setting up new worksheets on your own. Remember that Excel functions are simply built-in formulas that you can use by giving their names along with any parameters that the function needs in order to successfully perform its calculations.

So, what's the point of all these arguments?

The parameters supplied to an Excel function are technically known as the *arguments* of that function. Most functions require at least one argument (although a few like NOW() require no arguments), while some of the more complex ones require two or three. Some of the more complex functions even have optional as well as required arguments. Regardless of the number of arguments to a function, keep in mind that you must include the arguments of a function inside a closed pair of parentheses. Even functions with no arguments, like NOW(), still require these back-to-back parentheses (within which its argument goes if it needs one). Also, when a function takes more than one argument, you need to remember to separate each argument with a comma within the confines of these parentheses.

Instead of using the special built-in functions, *simple formulas* rely solely upon a string of values (indicated by actual numbers or references to cells that contain numbers or formulas) separated by any (or all) of the following operators:

- ✔ + (plus) for addition
- ✔ – (minus) for subtraction
- ✔ / (forward slash) for division
- ✔ * (asterisk) for multiplication
- ✔ ^ (caret) for raising a number to a power (you know, like squaring or cubing a number)

Don't get the impression that simple formulas can't be long. In fact, many times they can end up being longer than formulas that use only functions, which makes sense when you stop and consider that functions represent a compact way of indicating longer strings of computations.

Keep in mind that *all* formulas (simple, complex, those that use functions, and those that do not) start with an equal sign. If you're entering a formula that begins with a reference to a value or a cell reference with a value or formula, you need to actually type the equal sign. When your formula consists solely of a function and you're using the Function Wizard to specify it (see "The Function Wizard is your friend" later in the chapter), Excel inserts the equal sign for you, so there's no need to waste time typing it in yourself.

As an example of how formulas can grow, start by considering this formula

```
=A3
```

which is among the shortest and simplest that you can create in Excel. Now, assume that you edit the first sample formula and alter it slightly by adding just one more operation (an addition operation) to it as follows:

```
=A3+B3
```

Finally, assume that you edit the formula again and, this time, add a bunch more operations to the simple addition shown above so that you end up with this monster when you're done:

```
=A3+B3/C3-D3*E3^F3
```

In its first iteration of =A3, the formula merely carries forward whatever happens to be entered in cell A3 to the cell where this formula is entered (assume that you've entered this formula in cell G3 for the sake of argument). So that if you enter **19.25** in cell A3, 19.25 shows up in cell G3 of the worksheet, as well. However, if you then change the value in cell A3 from **19.25** to **128**, presto, changeo, 128 appears almost instantaneously in cell G3 as well.

In the second iteration of the formula (=A3+B3), Excel takes whatever value is in cell A3, adds it to the value found in B3, and puts the sum into cell G3. So, for instance, if you enter **10** in cell A3 and **20** into cell B3, the sum of 30 appears in cell G3. If you then change the value in cell B3 from **20** to **25**, the sum in cell G3 changes immediately to 35.

By order of precedence (or "In a class of my own")

In the sample formula's last incarnation into the long string of different operations (=A3+B3/C3-D3*E3^F3), Excel doesn't just take the value in A3, add it to the value in B3, divide that sum by the value in C3, subtract the value in D3 from the result of that division, then multiply the result by the value in E3, and finally, raise the result of that multiplication by the value in cell F3.

In fact, instead of following the strictly left-to-right series of calculations that I just outlined, Excel follows a very different order (known as the Order of Precedence — which is more like the "Royal" Order of Precedence because it puts the various operations into different orders, some of which are ranked higher than others and, therefore, are taken care of first). At the behest of the Order of Precedence, *exponentiation* (the fancy term for raising a value to a power) is placed into the highest order. Therefore its computation takes place before any of the addition, subtraction, division, or multiplication. Next in the pecking order is multiplication and division, whose computations take place before any of the addition or subtraction.

In the company of my peers

Certain operations, such as division and multiplication and addition and subtraction, are in the same order and are, therefore, treated "equally" in the eyes of the "Royal" Order of Precedence. This means that when Excel encounters both division and multiplication in a formula, it just computes their operations in a good old democratic, first-come, first-served basis (that is, strictly from left to right) because both these operations belong to the same order in the old precedence scheme.

To visualize the impact that the Order of Precedence has on a formula involving lots of different operations (for example, =A3+B3/C3–D3*E3^F3), refer to Figure 2-1. As you can see in this figure, the six cells in row 3 (from column A through F) that are used in the formula in cell G3 all contain values:

Cell Value

A3   10

B3   25

C3   5

D3   4

E3   3

F3   2

After looking over the values entered in cells A3 through F3, take a gander at the result of -21 (that's negative 21) that's displayed in cell G3! How, you may ask, can this formula, with all positive numbers whose values descend dramatically as you move right, yield this result? The culprit is, of course, that old Order of Precedence:

1. Because exponents belong to the highest order, the operation between E3 and F3 is performed first. This means that 3 in cell E3 is squared (raised to the 2nd power because cell F3 contains 2), which results in 9 ($3^2 = 3 \times 3 = 9$).

2. Excel then multiples and divides on a first-come, first-served basis. Because the division is left of the multiplication in the formula, Excel divides 25 in cell B3 by 5 in cell C3, which results in 5 (25/5 = 5).

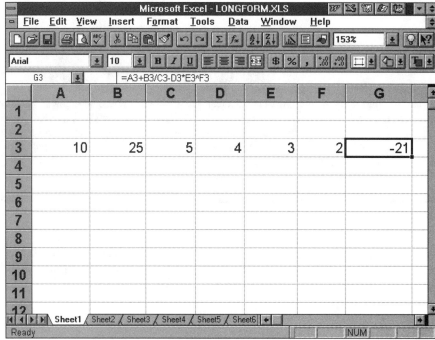

Figure 2-1:
The formula
in cell G3
yields –21 in
cells A3
through F3.

3. Next, Excel performs the multiplication between the value in cell D3 and the result of the first exponentiation operation between cell E3 and F3. Therefore Excel multiplies the 4 in cell D3 by 9 (see Step 1), resulting in 36.

4. Now, Excel is left with only lowly addition and subtraction operations. Because they are both in the same order (low though it may be), Excel first performs the addition at the beginning of the formula (and to the left of the subtraction) by adding 10 in cell A3 to 5 (the result of the division between B3 and C3; see Step 2), which results in 15 (10 + 5 = 15).

5. Last, and certainly least, comes the subtraction between 15 (see Step 4) and 36 (see Step 3), whose result is –21 (15 – 36 = –21).

Whew! I don't know about you, but that was a lot to follow. Catch your breath for a second before you read on to find out how you can alter the Order of Precedence.

Going out of order (or "Moving on up...")

Suppose, for the sake of argument, that you want Excel to calculate the formula

```
=A3+B3/C3-D3*E3^F3
```

in strict left-to-right order instead of slavishly obeying the Order of Precedence (laid out in tedious detail in the section above). This means that you want the calculations to come off as follows:

1. The value 10 in cell A3 is added to the value 15 in cell B3, resulting in 35 (10 + 25 = 35).

2. The result of 35 (see Step 1) is then divided by the the value 5 in cell C3, resulting in 7 ((35/7) = 5).

3. The result of 7 (see Step 2) is then subtracted by the value 4 in D3, which results in 3 (7 – 4 = 3).

4. The result of 3 (see Step 3) is then multiplied by the value 3 in cell E3, which results in 9 (3 x 3 = 9).

5. Finally, the result of 9 (see Step 4) is raised by the power of the value 2 in cell F2 (the same as squaring the value), resulting in a final value of 81 (9^2 = (9 x 9) = 81).

To have this happen, you have to alter the Order of Precedence (in fact, you have to alter it a lot). To move an operation up in the Order of Precedence, you need to regroup it. In order to regroup, you need to enclose the operation in a pair of parentheses. So, for example, if you want to make sure that addition between cell A3 and B3 takes place before the division by C3, you need to edit the formula as follows:

```
=(A3+B3)/C3-D3*E3^F3
```

In this form, the addition between the values in A3 and B3 are now on equal footing with the division and multiplication in the formula. If you want to end up with a strict left-to-right computation of elements, you can't stop here in grouping operations within parentheses. Next, you need to group the subtraction with the addition and division, as follows:

```
=((A3+B3)/C3-D3)*E3^F3
```

In this form, the sum of A3 and B3 is divided by the value in C3 and then the value in D3 is subtracted from this result. Now, only one more grouping is required: this one, to ensure that the exponentiation takes place after the multiplication. To do this, you need to edit the formula to group the multiplication by the value in E3 with all the elements that come before, as follows:

```
=(((A3+B3)/C3-D3)*E3)^F3
```

And that's all there is to it! (See Figure 2-2 for confirmation that in this form, the formula yields 81 rather than –21).

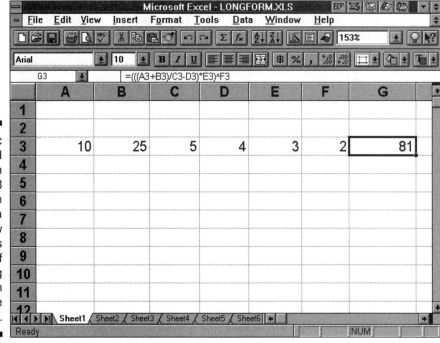

Figure 2-2:
The edited
formula in
cell G3
(shown on
the formula
bar) now
yields 81 as
the result of
the grouping
done with
all the
parentheses.

All right, all right, I'll grant that because of the pile up of parentheses, the edited
version of the formula appears a little (a lot?) more confusing than the original.
However, I'll let you in on a little secret that makes it a great deal easier to
interpret formulas that contain lots of parentheses — always consider the
groups formed by the parentheses from the inside out (which is just the way
Excel does). In our example, the inmost group is

```
(A3+B3)
```

so this is the first calculation (in our example, this calculation results in 35 by
adding 10 in A3 to 25 in B3). The next group you encounter in the formula as
you work your way outward is

```
((35)/C3-D3)
```

After dividing 35 by the value in C3, this result is subtracted from D3 (in our
example, this results in 3 because 35/5=7 and 7–4 is 3). The final group in the
formula as you work outward includes the multiplication by the value in E3 as

```
(((35)/7-4)*E3)
```

The result of 9 (3 x 3) is then subjected to exponentiation ^F2 (not included in any of the groups to ensure that it occurs dead last), which yields the final result of 81 (9^2 = 9 x 9 = 81).

The Function Wizard is your friend

The Function Wizard in Excel 5 takes a great deal of the work out of using functions. I urge you to employ it whenever you need to insert any of the Excel functions into a formula, with the exception of one function. And that function is the SUM function, which is easier to select by clicking on the SUM button on the Standard toolbar (the button with the Σ on it) than via the Function Wizard.

As you may remember from *Excel For Dummies*, the Function Wizard enables you to select any of the Excel functions along with all of its arguments. To insert a function with the Function Wizard when the function is the only thing in the formula, you need to click on the Function Wizard button on the Standard toolbar (the one with the *fx* on it). To insert a function with the Function Wizard when the function makes up only one part of the formula or when you've begun a formula (by at least typing the equal sign), you can also click on the Function Wizard button that appears on the formula bar right beside the Cancel (with the X) and Confirm (with the check mark) buttons.

When you first click on either Function Wizard button, Excel plunks down in the formula bar whatever function is at the top of the alphabetical list of Most Recently Used functions (as this category precedes all others in the Function Wizard – Step 1 of 2 dialog box). The actual function that appears at the top of this list, of course, depends upon how often you use the Function Wizard, what type of functions you choose most often, and where their function names stack up in the alphabet.

When you first start using the Function Wizard, the AVERAGE function is at the top of the alphabetical list of Most Recently Used functions so that

```
AVERAGE(number1,number2,...)
```

is inserted into the formula that appears on the formula bar. You'll also notice that Excel automatically highlights everything from the *A* in AVERAGE to and including the right parenthesis that ends the function. If you then select another category in the Function Category list box or another function in the Function Name list box, the program immediately replaces the highlighted text on the formula bar with the function you've just selected.

For example, if you select Math & Trig in the Function Category list box, Excel replaces the `AVERAGE(number1,number2,...)` function with

```
=ABS(number)
```

on the formula bar because the ABS function is at the top of the alphabetical list of functions in the Math & Trig function category.

After selecting the function you want to use in the Function Wizard – Step 1 of 2 dialog box, click on the Next button (or press Enter) to display the Function Wizard – Step 2 of 2 dialog box, where you specify the function's arguments. As soon as you do so, Excel inserts the selected function in the cell without any functions. In the Step 2 of 2 dialog box, you see text boxes for each of the arguments used by the function. These argument text boxes are displayed in the order in which they would need to be specified in the function if you were typing the whole thing in yourself. After the argument name, the dialog box indicates whether the argument is required or optional. It goes without saying (but I'm saying it anyway) that you have to specify something for each of the text boxes with required arguments (Excel won't let you leave any of them blank), while you can skip all the optional arguments unless you really need them to refine the calculation or change one or more of its default settings.

If you're not sure whether the function you've selected in the Step 1 of 2 dialog box is actually the one you want to use, select the Help button. If you're not sure how to specify the arguments for the function you've selected, choose the Help button in the Step 2 of 2 dialog box. At either time, Excel then displays on-line Help, including what arguments the function uses, some examples, and related functions. If you want a printout of the Help info, choose File Print Topic on the menu bar in the Microsoft Excel Help dialog box. When you're finished with the on-line Help information, you can close the Help dialog box by choosing File Exit. Closing the Help dialog box conserves memory and immediately returns you to Excel and the appropriate Function Wizard dialog box.

When specifying an argument in a particular argument text box, you can either point to the cell that contains the value you want to use or type in its cell reference. When you do either of these, Excel displays the value currently in that cell in the text box to the immediate right (doesn't matter whether the value is something Excel has calculated for you or is something you've entered yourself). However, if you specify the address of a cell that's currently blank or has some text in it, this text box will remain blank. (Note that when you select a cell reference with a date, however, Excel displays the date serial number — that large, weird number specifying the number of days since the date and the dawn of the twentieth century.)

If the value you want to use as a function argument is not displayed in any of the cells in your workbook, you either need to specify the value by actually typing in the number in the argument text box (the very idea!) or by clicking its Function Wizard button and specifying a function (with its arguments) that, in turn, yields the value to be used as the argument.

After you've finished specifying the function's arguments in the Step 2 of 2 dialog box, you may as well check out the value displayed in the Value text box (near the top, in the upper right-hand corner of the dialog box) before you choose the Finish button (or press Enter) to actually insert the function. The Value text box gives you a preview of the calculated value that function returns, given its current arguments. If the result shown in the Value text box seems way off, this probably means that you should recheck and, perhaps, edit one or more of the arguments before you insert the function.

As soon as you select the Finish button, Excel inserts the function into your formula. If you choose the Function Wizard after manually starting the formula or while editing a formula, Excel inserts the function into the formula at the insertion point without completing the entry. If, on the other hand, you choose the Function Wizard first thing before typing the equal sign, Excel goes ahead and completes the formula entry in the cell, which then displays the calculated result.

Text calculations, anyone?

Most formulas refer to numbers and return numbers (even when they are disguised in the form of dates and times). It is, however, possible and, some-times, even desirable to create formulas that return text-like answers.

The simplest text formula is created by calling forward a cell that contains some sort of text label. For example, if you enter the simple little formula

```
=A2
```

in cell A10 of a worksheet, and then you enter the label

```
Alice
```

into cell A2, guess what? Cell A10 will also contain

```
Alice
```

Furthermore, if you edit cell A2 and change Alice to Mary, cell A10 is immedi-ately updated to Mary. Just like that!

In terms of text calculations between cells, you can use the & (ampersand) operator to create simple formulas that join labels from two or more cells together in a third. For instance, suppose that you've got Mary entered in cell A2 and her last name Contrary entered next door in cell B2, and you need to put the first and last names together in cell A10. You can do this by entering the formula

```
=A2&B2
```

The only problem with this formula is that instead of `Mary Contrary` as two words in cell A10, you'll end up with the superword

```
MaryContrary
```

in the cell. To get in that all-important space between *Mary* and *Contrary* in cell A10, you need to join `Mary` in cell A2 with a space and then join Mary-plus-space to `Contrary` in cell B2. To do this, you need to enclose a space in a pair of double quotation marks as you join it to `Mary` and `Contrary`, as follows

```
=A2&" "&B2
```

Excel also includes some very useful Text functions in the form of the PROPER, UPPER, and LOWER functions, which, in case you missed them, are showcased in Chapter 13 of the original *Excel For Dummies*.

Using the ampersand to join text together in different cells can save a lot of typing time. For example, consider the worksheet shown in Figure 2-3. Here, you have a bunch of first names entered in a cell range (A2:A7), with a bunch of last names entered in a cell range right next door (B2:B7). To join the first and last names in a cell range (A10:A15), you simply create the formula

```
=A2&" "&B2
```

in cell A10 and then copy this formula down to cell A15. And that's all there is to that!

Don't confuse the + (plus) operator with the & (ampersand) operator. If you try to join two cells containing labels in a third with a formula that uses the + (plus) as the operator between the cell references, Excel displays the #VALUE! error as the result of the formula (it doesn't know how to sum labels, although it can join them). The same, of course, holds true for all the other math operators lik – (subtraction), / (division), * (multiplication), and ^ (exponentiation).

Converting formulas into the "real thing"

Using ampersand formulas to enter the full names in the cell range A10:A15 shown in Figure 2-3 is pretty slick (especially when you're dealing with a list

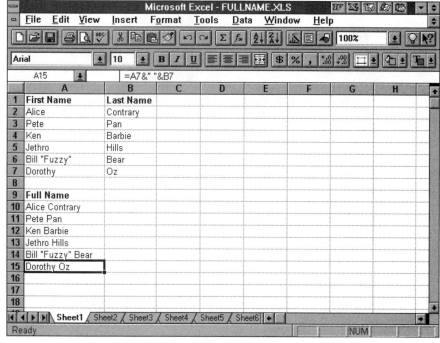

Figure 2-3:
Using text
formulas to
join first and
last names
in one
column of
cells.

with hundreds and hundreds of names). However, I feel it is my duty to point out a potential problem (and its solution) that can arise should you need to do something further with the text, like sort it in alphabetical order.

The problem is that when you sort cells with Excel, the program sorts the contents of the cells in the cell range (and not their display). So if you think about it, the problem is that the range A10:A15 contains a bunch of cells with contents like

```
=A2&" "&B2
```

and

```
=A3&" "&B3
```

but you actually need to sort the calculated results as they appear in the cells, such as

```
Alice Contrary
```

and

```
Pete Pan
```

and so on.

So what's a body to do, short of (yech!) typing the full names in the cell range? The answer is that before you sort, you need to convert the formulas into their displayed values. In other words, tell Excel to replace each formula with its currently calculated result.

There are essentially two methods for replacing a formula with its calculated result:

- ✔ Select the cell with the formula, press F2 (Edit) to get into Edit mode and return the formula to the formula bar. Then press F9 (Calculate) to replace the formula with its calculated result and finally press Enter to complete the edit.

- ✔ Select the cell with the formula, choose Edit⇨Copy (Ctrl+C), and then choose Edit⇨Paste Special followed by the Values radio button in the Paste Special dialog box. Choose OK or press Enter.

The first method is just dandy when you have only a single formula to convert. When dealing with a whole bunch of formulas (as you would be in the example with the full name formulas in the cell range A10:A15), however, you want to be sure to rely upon the second method. You can save oodles of time by converting the entire range of formulas to calculated values in a single operation.

Replacing a bunch of formulas with their results

1. **Select the range of formulas to convert (cell range A10:A15 in your example).**

2. **Choose Edit⇨Copy on the pull-down menu or press Ctrl+C to copy the formulas to the Clipboard.**

3. **Without moving the cell pointer or deselecting the highlighted cell range, immediately choose Edit⇨Paste Special on the pull-down menu to open the Paste Special dialog box.**

4. **Choose the Values radio button under Paste.**

5. **Choose the OK button or press Enter.**

6. **Press the Esc key to remove the marquee (the marching ants) from around the range and to remove the** Select destination and press ENTER or choose Paste **message from the status bar.**

Be careful! In essence, what I'm teaching here is a highly "destructive" editing technique: how to wipe out a bunch perfectly good formulas and replace them with perfectly good calculated numbers or text. So keep in mind that this conversion *from* formula *to* calculated result is a one-way trip. There's no way to convert a calculated result *back* into its original formual short of resorting to Edit⇨Undo⇨Paste Special (Ctrl+Z) right after you complete the operation. So if you're the least bit uncertain as to the necessity of keeping the original formulas around in the workbook (perhaps because their source data may need to be edited, thereby requiring the formulas to be recalculated), you need to be sure to copy the values with the Paste Special command in an uninhabited region of the worksheet, not on top of the range containing the original formulas. To do this, you simply disregard the first part of Step 3 in the preceding Tootorial, replacing formulas with results, and move the cell pointer to the beginning of a blank cell range before you choose Edit⇨Paste Special and select the Values radio button.

After converting the formulas to their calculated values (in this case, their combined text labels), you are ready to sort them (just as though you had entered the little sweethearts by hand). After converting the formulas to text with the Paste Special command, all you have to do is click on the Sort Ascending button (the one with *A* above *Z* and the arrow to the right) on the Standard toolbar (you don't even have to fuss with reselecting the cell range as it remains selected after converting the values). Figure 2-4 shows you the sample worksheet after sorting the names.

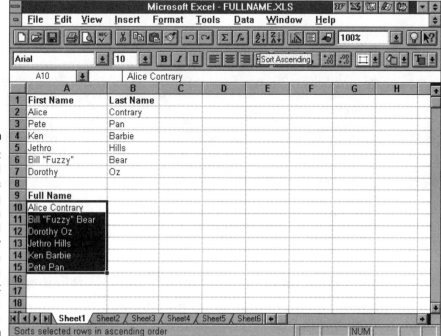

Figure 2-4: Converted full names after sorting them in alphabetical order by first name with the Sort Ascending button.

Follow the Leader

One of the marks of a true spreadsheet "guru" is how he or she handles the creation of original formulas (or *master formulas*) and goes about copying these formulas in the worksheet. By now, you are probably well aware that many worksheets use tables of data that depend upon very similar formulas. The classic example of this is the old sales table. Here, you create a table that normally plots the monthly sales made in each column against the items or services sold in each row. Obligatory in such a table are the SUM formulas for the monthly sales totals in each column of the last row of the table and the SUM formulas for the item totals in each row of the last column.

Regardless of how many months you follow in your table (as few as 3 months for a particular quarter, all the way up to the 12 calendar months or even beyond) and how many items or services sold (to a spreadsheet hotshot), this table requires the creation of two master formulas (using the SUM function) and two copy operations to copy these master formulas throughout the rest of the table.

The first master formula is located at the bottom of the first column of the table, and its SUM function totals the sales for all items and services that occur in the first month included in our mythical sales table. The second (and last) master formula occurs at the top of the last column of the table, and its SUM function totals the sales for the first item or service that occur in all the months tracked by the sales table.

Once the master formulas are in place, all that you have to do is copy them. First, you need to copy the first master formula located at the bottom of the first column over to the columns to its right to total all the columns with monthly sales. Then you need to copy the the second master formula at the top of the last column down the column to the rows beneath it to total all the rows listing items and services.

There are two easy ways to copy a master formula down a column or across a row of a table in Excel. You can either select the cell with the master formula and drag it down or to the right with the fill handle. Or you can select the master formula along with range of blank cells where the copies are to appear and then choose Edit⇨Fill⇨Down (Ctrl+D) or choose Edit⇨Fill⇨Right (Ctrl+R), depending upon the direction you need to go. (See Chapter 4 in *Excel For Dummies* for a complete refresher on copying formulas.)

Relatively speaking, I'm absolutely yours

As every spreadsheet guru can attest, the beauty of copying a master formula down a column or across a row is that Excel automatically adjusts the part of the cell reference that changes as you move down or to the right. For instance, when you copy a master formula down the rows of a column, Excel keeps changing the row number in the cell references of each copied formula without bothering the column references. Likewise, when you copy a master formula to columns to the right, Excel changes the column letters in the cell references in the formulas without touching the row numbers (beautiful, eh?!).

As you learned in *Excel For Dummies*, there are situations where this automatic adjustment of the cell references in copies of a master formula (due to what's called *relative cell references*) doesn't work and needs to be overruled. For example, if you're making copies of a master formula that determines what percentage each monthly total is of the quarterly total, you want the master formula and its copies to be divided by the same cell (the one with the yearly total). To prevent Excel from adjusting some part of the cell with the yearly total to suit the direction of your copying of the master formula, you need to change the cell reference in the master formula for the cell with the yearly total from relative to absolute before you make the copies (a "real" spreadsheet guru would actually make this change when first creating the master formula because she would anticipate the need).

To change a cell reference in a formula from the default of relative cell referencing to absolute cell referencing, press F4 (Absolute) once. So, for instance, if cell G35 contains the yearly total and cell B30 contains the first monthly total, you would enter

```
=B30/G35
```

and then before completing the formula entry with the insertion point at the end of the formula, you would press F4 to change the formula to

```
=B30/$G$35
```

Remember that the dollar signs before the G column reference and 35 row reference indicate that they are absolute and not subject to adjustment in copies of the formula and not that this cell has money in it.

Relative (G35) and absolute ($G$35) cell referencing actually represent the two extremes. In between these two are two types of mixed cell addressing. For example, if you press F4 twice while the insertion point is on the cell reference G35 in the formula, the second cell reference in the formula looks like this

```
=B30/G$35
```

In this mixed cell address, the column reference G is relative (and, therefore, subject to change in copies across a row of columns), while the row reference is absolute (and not subject to change in copies down a column).

If you press F4 again, the second cell reference in the formula changes to this:

```
=B30/$G35
```

In this mixed cell address, the column reference G is absolute (and, therefore, not subject to change in copies across a row of columns), while the row reference is relative (making it subject to change in copies down a column).

Guess what happens if you dare to press F4 again (a fourth time)? Well, you come full circle because the $G35 cell reference changes back to the original G35 reference (if you care to keep playing with F4, you can go around the circle again, from G35 to $G$35 to G$35 to $G35, and back to G35 again).

Often my spreadsheet students are curious to know under what circumstances one may need to use mixed cell addresses like the ones shown in the preceding paragraphs (often they're not, but I tell 'em anyway). To help them see when mixed references are used, I take them through the Loan Payment Schedule exercise. In this exercise, you need to borrow money to buy some new computer equipment for your home. However, you're not actually sure how much money you'll need (depends on what type of system you get and whether or not you buy a printer as well). Also, you're not sure what interest rate you'll get from the credit union when you make the loan (but you are certain you don't have the cash and must get the loan). In fact, there's only one thing you're certain of, and that's how long a loan period you want. In this exercise, you want this computer equipment paid off in five years (heck, the stuff will be obsolete in less than a year!).

To solve the problem, you use Excel to set up a loan payment table that shows you what your monthly loan payments will be for a range of different interest rates and for a range of different dollar amounts if you take five years to pay back the principal and interest. That way, you can base your final computer selection on the monthly loan payment you can afford.

Figure 2-5 shows you the basic setup for the Computer Loan Payment table. To start the exercise, you assume that the least amount you can get away with spending on all this stuff is $7,500 (you need at least a Pentium monster with 16 MB of RAM!!!!). This *base* amount is therefore entered in cell B2. You also assume that ten percent is the lowest interest rate you could get from the credit union (and it could likely be higher than because rates are on the rise). You enter this *base* interest rate in cell B3. Finally, you enter the term of the loan in years (five in this exercise) in cell B4.

As you can see in Figure 2-5, the actual loan table is located beneath the cells containing your basic assumptions in the range A5:G14. Cell A5 at the intersection of the column of possible loan amounts and row of possible interest rates

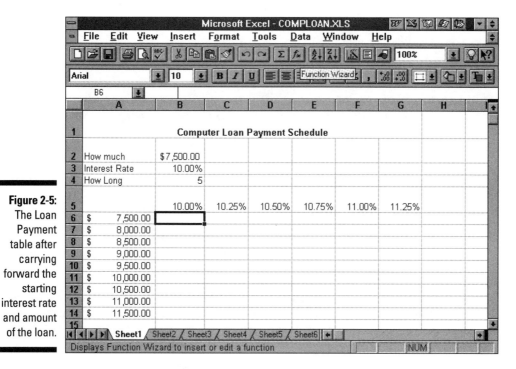

Figure 2-5:
The Loan
Payment
table after
carrying
forward the
starting
interest rate
and amount
of the loan.

remains blank. Cell B5 contains a copy of the base interest rate (10.00% currently). This amount is brought into this cell with the formula

```
=B3
```

You use this formula to actually carry forward the base interest rate rather than copy it from cell B3 because you want to be able to manipulate the range of interest rates in your table simply by changing the value entered in cell B3.

In cell C5, you enter the formula

```
=B5+0.25%
```

to increase the interest rate by a quarter of a percent and then copy this master formula across row 5 to the cell range D5:G5 to end up with a range of interest rates going from 10.00% all the way to 11.25%.

In cell B6, you bring forward the starting loan amount from cell B2 with the formula

```
=B2
```

Then, in cell A7, you create the master formula that increases the base loan amount by $500

```
=A6+500
```

You then copy this master formula in cell A7 down the range A8:A14, creating loan amounts ranging from $7,500 to $11,500 (you're going to have a killer system!).

And the payment is. . .

Now all that you have to do is create the master formula in cell B6 with the PMT function, which finds the monthly loan payment for the base loan amount of $7,500 and base interest rate of 10 percent. Then, to complete the table, you simply copy this master PMT formula across the rows of columns (B through G in row 5) and down the colums themselves (6 through 14).

The trick in creating this master PMT formula (and you know that there has to be a trick) is to determine which cell references have to be relative and which references have to be absolute in order to prevent errors from creeping into your copies of this formula elsewhere in the table.

You begin the process of creating the master formula by clicking on the Function Wizard button on the Standard toolbar and then selecting PMT in the Financial function category in the Step 1 of 2 dialog box.

Figure 2-6 shows the Function Wizard - Step 2 of 2 dialog box, appears when you select the Next button. As you can see from this figure, the PMT function requires three arguments (listed in bold in the dialog box): *rate,* which indicates the interest rate; *nper,* which indicates the number of payment periods; and *pv,* which indicates the present value (the same as the principal or amount loaned).

To specify the *rate* argument, you click on cell B5 (containing the base interest rate of 10.00%) to insert the cell reference B5 in its argument text box. Because this 10.00% represents an annual (yearly) interest rate and you ultimately want the monthly loan payment, you need to divide this amount by 12 to get the monthly interest rate. Before you add the **/12** to do this, however, you need to consider whether or not any part of the B5 cell reference needs changing from relative to absolute.

To determine whether or not any part of the cell reference needs to be relative or absolute, you need to go through a little mental exercise and ask yourself a couple of questions (something like this):

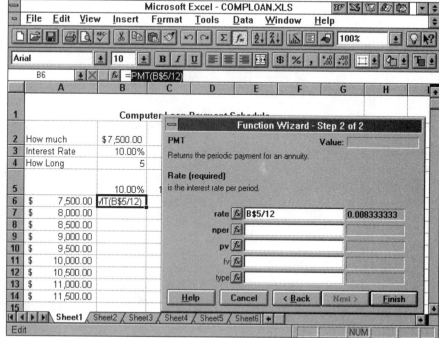

Figure 2-6:
Specifying
the *rate*
argument
for the PMT
function
with the
Function
Wizard.

1. When I copy the PMT formula to columns to the right, does the column reference of B5 need to change (to C, D, and so on)? If the answer is yes, the B reference must remain relative. If the answer is no, the B reference must be changed to absolute or $B.

2. When I copy the PMT formula down the column to the rows below, does the row reference in B5 need to change (to 6, 7, and so on)? If the answer is yes, the 5 reference must remain relative. If the answer is no, the 5 reference must be changed to absolute or $5.

In this case, the answer to the first question is yes. When you copy the PMT formula to the right, you need to adjust B to C, D, and so on, so the copy of the formula uses the correct interest rate (10.00%, 10.25%, 10.50%, and so forth). The answer to the second question is no. When you copy the PMT formula down a column, you want each copy of the formula to use the interest rate values in row 5 of that column. As a result, you press F4 twice (once for $B$5, twice for B$5) then type **/12** to complete the rate argument.

Next, you need to press Tab and specify the *nper* argument for the PMT function. Figure 2-7 shows the Step 2 of 2 dialog box after specifying this argument. In this case, you need to click on cell B4 in the worksheet that contains the number 5 (representing the number of years you want to carry the loan). Because this value expresses years and you are calculating monthly payments, you need to multiply the value in this cell by 12 to get the number of monthly periods in the five-year term of the computer loan.

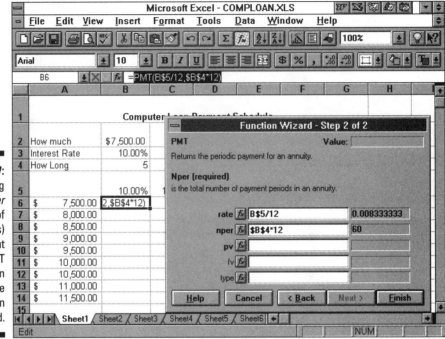

Figure 2-7:
Specifying
the *nper*
(number of
periods)
argument
for the PMT
function
with the
Function
Wizard.

However, before you multiply the cell reference B4 by 12, you need to ask yourself the following two questions:

1. When I copy the PMT formula to the columns to the right, does the column reference of B4 need to change (to C, D, and so on)? If the answer is yes, the B reference must remain relative. If the answer is no, the B reference must be changed to absolute or $B.

2. When I copy the PMT formula down the column to the rows below, does the row reference in B4 need to change (to 5, 6, and so on)? If the answer is yes, the 4 reference must remain relative. If the answer is no, the 4 reference must be changed to absolute or $4.

The answer to both questions is a resounding no. The only "constant" in this entire table is the loan term of 5 years. Each copy of the PMT formula needs to be tied to this cell reference. To do this, press F4 once to change from B4 to $B$4 and then type ***12** to complete the *nper* argument.

The last required argument is the *pv* argument, which indicates the principal of the loan. To specify this argument, you press Tab to move to its text box and then click on cell A6, containing the base loan amount of $7,500. Figure 2-8 shows you the Step 2 of 2 dialog box during the final stage of specifying the *pv* argument.

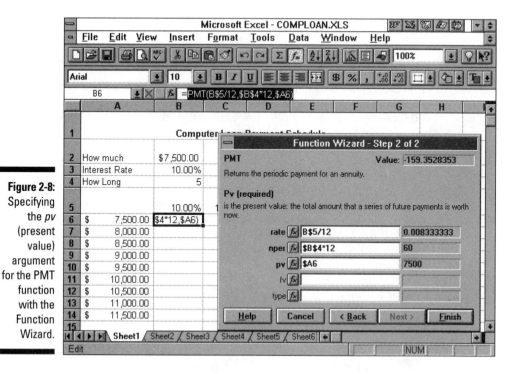

Figure 2-8:
Specifying
the *pv*
(present
value)
argument
for the PMT
function
with the
Function
Wizard.

Before you select the Finish button in the Step 2 of 2 dialog box to complete the PMT function and insert it into cell B6, you need to ask yourself whether or not this cell reference will fly in all the copies of the PMT function if it remains in its pristine, relative state:

1. When I copy the PMT formula to cells to the right, does the column reference of A6 need to change (to B, C, and so on)? If the answer is yes, the A reference must remain relative. If the answer is no, the A reference must be changed to absolute or $A.

2. When I copy the PMT formula down to rows below, does the row reference in A6 need to change (to 6, 7, and so on)? If the answer is yes, the 6 reference must remain relative. If the answer is no, the 6 reference must be changed to absolute or $6.

The answer to the first question is no; the answer to the second question is yes. When you copy the PMT formula to cells to the right, the column reference to A must not change (only column A contains the various loan amounts). Yet, by the same token, when you copy the PMT function down the rows, the row reference must change so that the formula adjusts to pick up the correct loan amount for its row. To change the cell reference from A6 to $A6 so that only the row reference can be adjusted, press the F4 key three times.

Copies below and to the right

After you finish specifying the *pv* argument, you are ready to insert the PMT formula in cell B6 by selecting the Finish button in the Step 2 of 2 dialog box. From there, it's a simple matter of copying this master formula across the columns in row 5 by dragging the fill handle to the right until you reach cell G5 and then copying these copies down columns B through G by dragging the fill handle down to row 14. Figure 2-9 shows the results.

Pretty impressive, if I do say so myself. When you take the time to reason out which parts of a master formula need to be adjusted in the copies and which parts do not, the actual process of copying the formulas and completing the loan table is a snap. Believe me, if you don't take the time to go through the questioning process outlined in this Loan Payment exercise, but, instead, just go with the default of relative cell addresses in a master formula without thinking, you're bound to end up with some very funky (and very wrong) copies of the formula in your worksheet.

There is one more thing to consider before we put aside the subject of formulas, and that is how easy this Loan Payment table is to revise. Imagine, for instance, that upon closer inspection of the monthly payments required for a

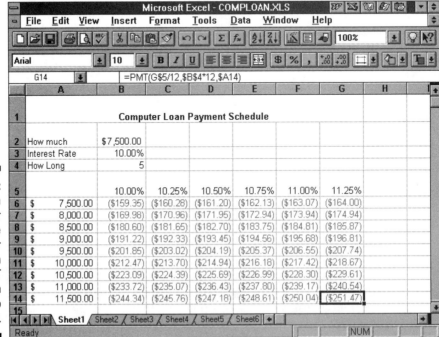

Figure 2-9:
The Loan table after copying the master formula with the PMT function down and to the right.

computer system ranging anywhere from $7,500 to $11,500, you decide to go for something a bit cheaper (how about a fully loaded 486 starting at $4,500 instead of that gold-plated Pentium machine starting at $7,500?). Further, you've learned that the credit union rates are now starting at a minimum of 12 percent. Finally, you think better of a five-year loan on equipment that you're surely going to want to unload in no more than three years.

To see what effect these changes have on the monthly payment, you simply replace **7500** in cell B2 with **4500**, **10%** in cell B3 with **12%**, and **5** in cell B4 with **3**. That's all there is to it. Excel immediately feeds the change to the base interest rate in cell B3 to cell B5 so that the rates run from 12.00% to 13.25%. At the same time, Excel feeds the change to the base loan amount in cell B2 to cell A6 so that amounts range from 4,500 to 8,500.

Figure 2-10 shows you the recalculated Loan Payment table that uses the new range of interest rates, loan amounts, and term. Because of the way this table is set up, you could keep changing the base figures to see what you come up with. But more on this kind of stuff later when you get to Chapter 11.

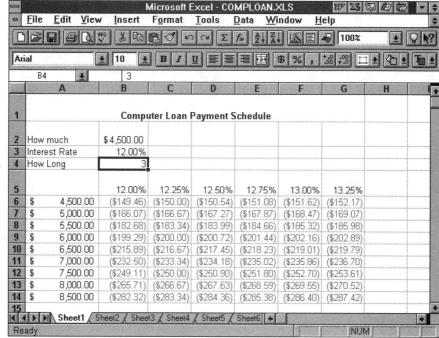

Figure 2-10:
The Loan table after changing the initial loan amount, interest rate, and term.

Chapter 3

Dealing with Someone Else's Creation

••

In This Chapter

▶ How to identify data regions in a worksheet by jumping the cell pointer from data block to data block

▶ How to use the Zoom command to locate and then zero in on a region with data

▶ How to interpret those awful format codes used by Excel's number formats

▶ How to create your own cool number formats using those awful format codes

▶ How to create styles that use your custom formats so that you can reuse them in other workbooks

••

          *L*ike it or not, a great deal of your work in Excel will be done on worksheets that have been designed by others. In this chapter, I cover the most important techniques for editing and formatting the worksheets in workbooks created by others. The emphasis is, of course, on getting in, getting oriented to the layout, and then making your editing changes. Along with this really important "survival" stuff — which builds on the basic information covered in Chapters 3 and 4 of *Excel For Dummies* — I have added information on how to improve the look of the worksheets you're editing with cool editing tricks.

Finding Out Where Everything Is

The first thing to do before you can make any changes to someone else's workbook is to open it up and find out where everything is. If you're unsure about how to open a workbook in Excel or you want to know some tricks for searching for missing files, jump ahead to Chapter 4 before you come back to this point.

These next few sections set out the various techniques for finding out

- ✔ How much stuff the workbook contains
- ✔ How the worksheet's author has arranged the data in the various worksheets in the workbook

Armed with this information, you can safely go about the business of changing some stuff without the danger of mucking up the whole thing.

Looking before you leap

From *Excel For Dummies*, you may remember the technique for jumping the cell pointer from one corner of a data table to another by holding down the Ctrl key while you press one of the arrow keys (↓, ↑, ←, or →). This technique makes it possible to navigate quickly through long lists and wide tables of data.

This Ctrl+arrow key technique also enables you to jump directly from an oc-cupied cell to the next occupied cell in a particular column or row in the work-sheet. If you press Ctrl+arrow key when the cell pointer is in the last occupied cell before a bunch of blanks in a particular column or row, Excel skips over the blank cells and stops only when it reaches the next occupied cell in that direc-tion. (It also stops at the next occupied cell even if the cell pointer is in an empty cell at the time you press Ctrl+arrow key.) If there aren't any more oc-cupied cells in the direction of the arrow key, Excel stops the cell pointer in the last cell on the very border of the worksheet.

You can use this leapfrog capacity of the program to quickly survey an unfamil-iar worksheet by skipping over all blank cells and getting to the important infor-mation. In this way, you familiarize yourself with the worksheet so that you don't remove data tables or cell entries when making your planned modifica-tions.

For example, suppose that you're not sure whether the worksheet author placed any data in the rows below a table that you see when you first open the worksheet. To check out the situation before you begin doing some serious worksheet renovations — such as deleting or inserting new columns in the visible data table — you can press Ctrl+↓ to jump the cell pointer to the cell in the last row of the table and then press Ctrl+↓ again to jump to the next occu-pied cell in the column below. If the cell pointer doesn't stop until it reaches row 16,384 (the last one in the worksheet), you know that there is no more data in that column.

Similarly, if you want to know if there are any occupied cells to the right of the last column of the data table, press Ctrl+→ to position the cell pointer in the last column and then press Ctrl+→ again to jump to the next occupied cell in that row. If the cell pointer ends up in column IV, you know that there are no cell entries between the last one in the data table and the last column of the worksheet.

Of course, if you do use this method to scope out a worksheet and the cell pointer ends up in Timbuktu (that's row 16,384 or column IV to you and me), you can use Ctrl+opposite arrow key (the Ctrl key plus the arrow key going in the opposite direction) to get "right back where you started from."

With this Ctrl+arrow key technique, you are limited to checking the particular column or row that contains the cell pointer. In other words, just because you don't run into any data going in a specific direction in a column or row doesn't mean that there aren't loads of cell entries in columns or rows right next door.

Looking at the big picture

The Ctrl+arrow key shtick works really well when you need to know if something as yet unseen is going to get creamed when you delete its row or column. However, the technique is not that good for getting an overview of the layout of the worksheet. To get an overview, you want to rely on the Zoom Control drop-down button on the Standard toolbar or the Zoom command on the View pull-down menu. Remember that the Zoom feature allows you to select different magnifications for the display of the worksheet.

The drop-down list associated with the Zoom Control button contains all the magnification settings — 200%, 100%, 75%, 50%, 25%, and Selection — available in the Zoom dialog box (except Selection is called Fit Selection). This option is important because it's the one way you can view the entire worksheet in one screen.

Getting the whole thing displayed in one screen

To view the entire worksheet in one screen, follow these simple steps:

1. **Select all the cells in the worksheet by clicking on the button at the in-tersection of the column of row numbers and the row of column letters.**

2. **Choose View⇨Zoom to open the Zoom dialog box.**

3. **Choose the Fit Selection radio button and then choose OK.**

4. **Click on the area of the worksheet that displays some specks (at this magnification, these specks represent cells with data) that you're curious about.**

5. Click on the 100% setting in the Zoom Control drop-down list to restore the worksheet display to normal size.

The cell pointer is now located in the area of the worksheet where you clicked on the specks.

Keep in mind that you can use the Zoom feature to get a handle on the layout of data in a section of the worksheet by choosing a small magnification setting (like 50% or 25%). To view more clearly the information in that particular area, click on one of its cells (represented by itty-bitty squares that you can barely click on) and then select a larger magnification setting (like 75% or 100%).

Remember the shortcuts: Use Ctrl+Home to jump to the first cell in the worksheet and Ctrl+End to jump to the last cell in the active area of the worksheet. Although the first cell (A1) in the worksheet never changes, the last cell in the active area constantly changes as you add more data to the worksheet. The last cell in the active area is the one that falls at the intersection of the last column and row that contains cell entries of some kind. As soon as you enter data in new, previously unoccupied columns, the last active cell changes to the one at the lower right-hand corner of this now enlarged cell range.

Conducting a "bonafide" data search

Sometimes, instead of the general layout, you need to find particular entries in the worksheet (so that you can get right to work changing them). When you don't give a hoot where the data is in the worksheet but are only concerned with getting to them "prontito," you need to turn to the Find feature (Ctrl+F or Edit⇨Find).

With the Find feature, you can locate all the cells in the current worksheet that contain a particular entry, such as a number like *52.75* or text like *New Accounts*. After you open the Find dialog box (shown in Figure 3-1), you enter the stuff to look for in the worksheet in the Find What box. If you're looking for a cell with particular text (rather than a value, such as 105.25), you may want Excel to stop only when the case of the text entered in a cell matches exactly the case of the search text you entered in the Find What box. To specify the case, you need to choose the Match Case check box before you select the Find Next button. For example, to locate all the cells that contain the word *Total* where the word is capitalized, you need to enter **Total** in the Find What text box and then select the Match Case check box.

When searching for text in a worksheet, you may want Excel to locate just those cells that contain only the search text (that is, where the search text is not part of other text). To locate only the search text, select the Find Entire Cells Only check box before commencing the search with the Find Next button. If you take this step, you can search for cells that contain only the word *Total*, for example (and thereby skip cells that contain *YTD Total*, *Total Assets*, and so on).

Don't forget that you can use the Replace button in the Find dialog box if you suddenly decide to change the entry in the cell that Excel has located after selecting the Find Next button. When you choose the Replace button, the program magically transforms the Find dialog box into a Replace dialog box, complete with a Replace With text box, where you enter the new values or text you want to replace in the current cell.

Remember that the Find feature searches the *contents* of the cells in the current worksheet, not the text that is simply *displayed* in a cell. So don't get fooled into trying to search for a *calculated result* — displayed in a cell whose content is a formula — with the Find features 'cause it'll never work. When you search for a value of 1500 that was calculated by the formula =SUM(C3:C11), Excel just gets in your face with the following message:

```
! Cannot Find Matching Data.
```

Because the program searches only for the cell contents, the only way to use the Find feature to locate the cell with the 1500 value is to enter some or all of its formula as the search text in the Find What text box. For example, you can find this cell in one try by entering just this part of the formula in the Find What text box:

```
sum(c3
```

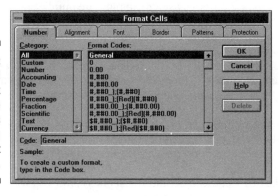

Figure 3-1:
Use the Find
dialog box
to locate
cells
containing
certain text
or values.

Formatting to Suit Every Taste

A good part of everybody's worksheet editing time is taken up with making the darn thing look presentable. This being the case, you're way ahead of the game when you use the most efficient methods for formatting the many kinds of data you're liable to find in a typical workbook.

As you may recall from *Excel For Dummies*, you can format numbers as you enter them by adding the appropriate dollar signs, commas, percent symbols, and so on, along with the digits of the number (although I think this kind of formatting-as-you-go thing is a colossal waste of time if you're adding anything more than one or two numbers to the worksheet). You cannot, however, format numbers placed in cells by formula calculations because you construct the formulas, not the numbers. The only way to format calculated numbers is by selecting their cells and then selecting the desired number formats. You can select the number formats in two ways: by choosing the appropriate style button on the Formatting toolbar (Currency Style, Comma Style, or Percent Style) or by selecting the appropriate number format in the Number tab of the Format Cells dialog box (Ctrl+1).

Formatting dates and times

The BIG exception to my pronouncement against formatting as you go applies to entering dates and times in a worksheet. If you don't enter dates and times with one of Excel's formats, the program treats them as text entries rather than as special date and time serial numbers, thus preventing the entries from being used in calculations. Believe it or not, you may want to use date and time entries in calculations, for such things as determining the number of days between today's date and the date entered or determining the elapsed time between a starting and quitting time, and so on.

Remember, the easiest way to tell whether a date, time, or other entry is accepted in the cell as text versus a value is by checking out how the entry lines up on the left or right side of its cell. Keep these tips in mind:

- ✔ Text entries are automatically left-aligned in their cells. Characters that don't fit into the width of the current column spill over into neighboring columns to the right, provided their cells are empty. If the cells to the right already have something in them, Excel cuts off the extra characters in the cell *display* (they're still there behind the scenes) until you widen the column containing the truncated cell entry.

- ✔ Values are automatically right-aligned in their cells. If the value has too many digits to fit in the cell's current column width, Excel automatically converts the value to scientific notation. If the cell has a number format assigned to it and this format adds too much stuff to display in the current column width, Excel displays a string of number signs (######) across the entire cell until you widen its column sufficiently to accommodate all its digits and extra formatting characters.

Of course, after a cell entry is made as either a text or a value entry, anyone can then change its default alignment (by clicking on the Align Left, Center, or Align Right button on the Formatting toolbar), so you can't totally rely on cell alignment as the indicator of whether existing entries in a worksheet you didn't create are text or value entries.

Text formatting versus value formatting

If you want to enter into a cell as *text* what would normally be a *value* (number, date, or time), you need to preface the entry with an apostrophe ('). For example, suppose that you want to enter *12/56* in a cell as text rather than having it be automatically converted to the date *Dec-56*. To enter it as text, you must enter the following in the cell:

```
'12/56
```

The apostrophe doesn't show up in the cell's display (it only appears on the formula bar when the cell is current or in the cell when the program is in Edit mode). Should you ever run into a situation where you want an initial apostrophe to show up in the cell display, you then need to type in two apostrophes in a row before you enter the rest of the entry. For instance, if you want *'12/56* displayed in the cell (apostrophe and all), you need to enter the following in the cell:

```
''12/56
```

Don't try to cheat by using a double quotation mark entered by holding down Shift as you press the apostrophe key — this is not, I repeat, *not* the same thing as typing two apostrophes in a row.

Formatting options

After you have your entries in the workbook as text or values, you can play around with their formatting to your heart's content. Simply select the cells in question, open the Format Cells dialog box (Ctrl+1), select the appropriate dialog tab, and choose your formatting options. When formatting cell entries, you can do any of the following things to make them all the more beautiful:

✔ Change the alignment of the entries. You can fool with the horizontal (side to side) or vertical (up and down) alignment of the entries in the cell or monkey around with their orientation.

✔ Change the font, font size, or font color of the entries or add some special text enhancements, such as bold, italic, underlining, and so on.

✔ Add borders to the cells with your entries. These borders can be different line weights and/or colors.

✔ Add color and/or patterns (with dots and stripes and that kind of thing) to cells with your entries.

✔ Change the protection status of the entries.

Although formatting changes affect how your data appears in cells of the worksheet, the formatting is really applied to the *cells* containing the entries rather than the entries themselves. The significance of this fact is evident every time you replace one formatted value with another — the new value immediately takes on the formatting of its predecessor. Because the cells — not their entries — retain the formatting, the cells continue to retain formatting even if you delete a cell entry by pressing the Delete key or by choosing the Edit⇨Clear⇨Contents command. (To get rid of the cell entry *and* the format changes, you need to choose Edit⇨Clear⇨All. To jettison the format changes while retaining the cell's current contents, choose the Formats command.)

Fooling with Number Formats

Because so many of the entries in a typical worksheet end up being values (this may have something to do with the "calculating" nature of a spreadsheet program), you must first look at ways to decipher the codes used in the predefined formats that you can choose on the Number tab of the Format Cells dialog box. Then you can move on to learn how to use these codes to create custom number formats of your own design.

Deciphering those awful number format codes

Any time you apply a number format to a cell selection (even if you do so with a button on the Formatting toolbar rather than selecting the format directly from the Number tab of the Cell Formats dialog box), you are telling Excel to apply a format code to those cells. Figure 3-2 shows the Number tab of the Format Cells dialog box as it appears when you first open the dialog box. As you can see, when the Number tab is initially selected, the All category of number formats is displayed with a long list of codes (following the one English word, *General*).

As you move down the list, notice how much more complex this series of codes becomes with the 0s and #s (and other junk). Also notice that as you move down the list, the longer codes are divided into sections separated by semicolons and enclosed within square brackets. Although, at first glance, these codes appear as so much gibberish, you'll actually find that they're quite understandable (well, would you believe, useful, then?).

Figure 3-2:
The Number
Tab of the
Format Cells
dialog box,
with all
those weird
format
codes.

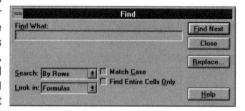

And these codes can be useful, especially after you understand them. You can use them to create number formats of your own design. The basic keys to understanding number format codes are as follows:

- ✔ Excel number formats use a combination of 0, ?, and # symbols with such punctuation as dollar signs, percent signs, and commas to stand for the formatted digits in the numbers you format.

- ✔ The 0 is used to indicate how many decimal places (if any) are allowed in the format. The format code 0.00 indicates that two decimal places are used in the number. The format code 0 alone means that no decimal places appear (the display of all values is rounded up to whole numbers).

- ✔ The ? is used like the 0, except that it inserts spaces at the end as needed to make sure that values line up on the decimal point. For example, by selecting the number format 0.??, such values as 10.5 and 25.75 line up with each other in their cells because Excel adds an extra space after the 5 to push it over to the left so that it's in line with the 7 of 75. If you used the number format 0.00 instead, these two values would not line up on the decimal point when they are right-aligned in their cells.

✔ The # symbol is used with a comma to indicate that you want thousands, hundred of thousands, millions, zillions, and so on in your numbers, with each group of three digits to be separated with a comma.

✔ The $ (dollar sign) symbol is added to the beginning of a number format if you want dollar signs to appear at the beginning of every formatted number.

✔ The % (percent sign) symbol is added to the end of the number format if you want Excel to actually transform the value into a percentage by multiplying it by 100 and adding a percent sign.

Number formats can specify one format for positive values, another for negative values, a third for zero values, and even a fourth for text in the cells. In such complex formats, the format codes for positive values come first followed by the codes for negative values, and each group of codes is separated by a semicolon. Any format codes for how to handle zeros and text in a cell come third and fourth, respectively, in the number format, again separated by semicolons. If the number format does not specify special formatting for negative or zero values, these values are automatically formatted like positive values. If the number format does not specify what to do with text, text is formatted according to Excel's default values. For example, look at the following number format:

```
#,##0_);(#,##0)
```

This particular number format specifies how to format positive values (the codes in front of the semicolon) and negative values (the codes after the semicolon). Because there are no further groups of codes, zeros are formatted like positive values, and no special formatting is applied to text.

If a number format puts negative values inside parentheses, the positive number format portion often pads the positive values with a space that is the same width as a right parenthesis. To indicate this, you add an underscore (by pressing Shift and the hyphen key) followed immediately by a parenthesis, as in _). By padding positive numbers with a space equivalent to a right parenthesis, you ensure that digits of both positive and negative values line up in a column of cells.

You can assign different colors to a number format. For example, you can create a format that displays the values in green (the color of money!) by adding the code [GREEN] at the beginning of the format. A more common use of color is to display just the negative numbers in red (ergo, the saying "in the red") by inserting the code [RED] right after the semicolon separating the format for positive numbers from the one for negative ones. Color codes include

[BLACK], [BLUE], [CYAN], [GREEN], [MAGENTA], [RED], [WHITE], [YELLOW] or [COLOR *n*] where *n* is the number of the color between 1 and 16 that you want to select from the Excel color palette. (To see the palette and its colors, choose Tools⇨Options and then select the Color tab. When assigning a number to a color, count from left to right across each row: 1 – 8 across the top row and 9 – 16 across the bottom row.)

Date number formats use a series of abbreviations for month, day, and year that are separated by characters, such as a dash (—) or a slash (/). The code m inserts the month as a number; mmm inserts the month as three-letter abbreviation, such as Apr or Oct; mmmm spells out the entire month, such as April or October. The code d inserts the date as a number; dd inserts the date as a number with a leading zero, such as 04 or 07; ddd inserts the date as a three-letter abbreviation of the day of the week, such as Mon or Tue; dddd inserts the full name of the day of the week, such as Monday or Tuesday. The code yy inserts the last two digits of the year, such as 95 or 97; yyyy inserts all four digits of year, such as 1995, 2001, and so on.

Time number formats use a series of abbreviations for the hour, minutes, and seconds. The code h inserts the number of the hour; hh inserts the number of the hour with leading zeros, such as 02 or 06. The code m inserts the minutes; mm inserts the minutes with leading zeros, such as 01 or 09. The code s inserts the number of seconds; ss inserts the seconds with leading zeros, such as 03 or 08. Add AM/PM or am/pm to have Excel tell time on a 12-hour clock, and add either AM (or am) or PM (or pm) to the time number depending upon whether the date is before or after noon. Without these AM/PM codes, Excel displays the time number on a 24-hour clock, just like they do in the military. (For example, 2:00 PM on a 12-hour clock would be expressed as 1400 on a 24-hour clock.)

So that's all you really need to know about making some sense of all those strange format codes that you see so often in the Number tab of the Format Cells dialog box.

Creating number formats of your own design

Armed with a little knowledge on the whys and wherefores of how to interpret Excel number format codes, you are ready to learn how to use these codes to create your own custom number formats. The reason for going through all that "code business" is that in order to create a custom number format, you have to type in your own codes for your custom format. Currently, there is no simple way of selecting and inserting the codes from a list. (Where's the Format Code Wizard when you really need it?)

Creating custom number formats

To create a custom format, you go through a series of three simple steps:

1. **Open the Format Cells dialog box (Ctrl+1).**
2. **Choose the Number tab in the Format Cells dialog box.**
3. **Select the Code text box and type in the format codes for the custom format.**

What could be simpler?!! Ah, but Step 3, there's the rub: typing in a whole bunch of weird format codes and getting them just right so that they produce exactly the kind of number formatting you're looking for!

Actually, creating your own number format isn't as bad as it sounds because you can "cheat" by selecting a number format that uses some of the same elements you want. You then simply edit the existing number format to create your own custom format. For example, suppose that you want to create a custom date format to use on the current date entered with the NOW( ) function. You want this date format to display the full name of the current month (January, February, and so on), followed by two digits for the date and four digits for the year, such as January 11, 1995. To do this, select the Date category followed by the mmm-yy format codes and then edit them as follows in the Code text box:

```
mmmm dd, yyyy
```

The mmmm format code inserts the full name of the month in the custom format; the dd inserts two digits for the day (including a leading zero for days like 02 and 03); the yyyy code inserts the year. The other elements in this custom format are the space between the last *m* in mmmm and the dd codes, and a comma and a space between the dd and yyyy codes (these being purely "punctuational" considerations in the custom format).

What if you want to do something even fancier and create a custom format that tells you something like "Today is Wednesday, January 11, 1995" when you format a cell containing the NOW( ) function? Well, you select your first custom format and add a little bit to the front of it, as follows:

```
"Today is" dddd, mmmm dd, yyyy
```

In this custom format, you've added two more elements: Today is and dddd. The Today is code tells Excel to enter the text between the quotation marks verbatim; the dddd code tells the program to insert the whole name of the day of the week. And you thought this was going to be a hard section!

Next, suppose that you want to create a really colorful number format — one that displays positive values in blue, negative values in red (what else?), zero values in green, and text in cyan. Further, suppose that you want commas to separate groups of thousands in the values, no decimal places to appear (whole numbers only, please), and negative values to appear inside parentheses (rather than using that tiny little minus sign at the start). Sound complex? Hah, this is a piece of cake. Open the Format Cells dialog box, select the Number tab and Number in the Category list, and then select the #,##0_);[Red](#,##0) codes in the Format Codes list box and edit them as follows:

```
[Blue]#,##0_);[Red](#,##0);[Green];[Cyan]
```

That's all there is to that.

Before we move on, there's a particular custom format you should know about because it can come in real handy from time to time. I'm referring to the custom format that hides whatever has been entered in the cells. You can use this custom format to temporarily mask the display of confidential information used in calculating the worksheet before you print and distribute the worksheet. This custom format provides an easy way to avoid distributing confidential and sensitive information, while protecting the integrity of the worksheet calculations at the same time.

To create a custom format that masks the display of the data in a cell selection, you simply create an "empty" format that contains just the semicolon separators in a row:

```
;;;
```

(This is one custom format that you probably can type by yourself!)

After creating this format, you can blank out a range of cells simply by selecting them and then selecting this three-semicolon custom format in the Format Cells dialog box. To bring back a cell range that's been blanked out with this custom format, you simply select what now looks like blank cells and then select one of the other (visible) formats that are available. If the cell range contains text and values that normally should use a variety of different formats, first use General to make them visible. After the contents are back on display, format the cells in smaller groups or individually, as required.

The easiest way to find the custom formats that you've created in a workbook is to select Custom as the Category in the Number tab of the Format Cells dialog box.

Creating number formats with a little style

Custom number formats are a great boon to your worksheet formatting needs. However, they are a real pain, too, in that they are workbook-specific. By that, I mean that you can go to all the trouble of creating a whole bunch of really cool custom number formats while editing one workbook, but then you discover that these formats aren't available to you anymore when you switch and start editing another workbook. The way around this little problem is kinda sneaky, so I know you're gonna like it: Simply copy your number formats between workbooks by creating styles that use your custom number format and then merging these styles from the one workbook to another. To apply the custom number formats in the new workbook where they've been merged, you simply select the cells and then choose the style that uses the custom format. (For a refresher on creating styles and merging them between workbooks, see Chapter 3 of the original *Excel For Dummies* book.)

Creating a style that uses a custom format

1. **After creating a custom number format that you want to save in a style, select a cell in the worksheet and then apply that custom style to it.**

2. **With the newly formatted cell still selected, choose Format⇨Style on the pull-down menus.**

3. **Type in a name for the new style you're creating in the Style Name text box in the Style dialog box.**

4. **Look at number style listed after the Number check box in the Style Includes section of the Style dialog box. Make sure that it lists the custom style you want included in the style. If not, click on the Modify button to open the Format Cells dialog box, where you choose Custom as the Category in the Number tab and then select the custom format to use before choosing OK.**

5. **Click on the OK button in the Style dialog box to add the style that uses the custom number format to the workbook.**

6. **Save the workbook containing your new style.**

After creating styles for all the custom number formats that you may want to reuse when editing other workbooks, you can merge these styles into another workbook as you would any other style. And, in case you've forgotten how to merge styles from one workbook to another (or you've lent your copy of *Excel For Dummies* to a coworker in need), here are the steps for merging styles from one workbook to another.

Merging styles from one workbook to another

1. **Open the workbook containing the styles for your custom formats that you want to copy to another workbook.**

2. **Open the workbook in which you would like to copy these styles created from the custom number formats.**

3. **Choose Format⇨Style and then choose the Merge button.**

4. **Select the name of the workbook file containing the styles you want to copy in the Merge Styles From list box of the Merge Styles dialog box and then choose OK.**

   If some of the styles in the current workbook have the same names as styles in the workbook you're merging from, you see an alert dialog box. To replace existing styles with incoming styles, choose the Yes button. To preserve existing styles and copy in only new styles, choose No.

5. **Click on the OK button in the Style dialog box to apply the new style with the custom number formats to a current cell or cell selection. Click on the Close button if you don't want to apply the newly created style at this time.**

6. **Save the current workbook to save the styles with the custom number formats as part of the document.**

After you've done this little procedure, you can then start using your merged styles to apply your custom formats. Simply select the cells to be formatted, choose Format⇨Style, select the name of the style in the Style Name drop-down list box, and choose OK or press Enter.

Chapter 4

Keeping Your Workbooks Shipshape

. . . .

In This Chapter

▶ How to use name cell ranges en masse in existing column and row headings in the worksheet

▶ How to assign range names to your formulas in one operation

▶ How to paste range names into a formula you're building

▶ How to create a list of all the range names in the workbook

▶ How to rename the worksheets in your workbook

▶ How to move and copy worksheets within a workbook and between different workbooks

▶ How to make editing changes in one worksheet that affect a bunch of worksheets in the workbook

▶ How to hide worksheets that you don't want printed or you don't want anyone to see

▶ How to search for workbooks when you can't remember where you saved them or what exactly you called them

▶ How to perform various and sundry file operations, such as copying workbook files, sorting a list of workbook files, or creating a new directory in which to store workbook files within Excel

. . . .

*1*n this chapter, you are going to learn more nifty ways for organizing the massive quantities of data that typically get put in an Excel workbook. In addition to cool tips for ways of organizing and finding information in individual worksheets in a workbook, this chapter also offers some tricks for organizing and working with groups of worksheets in a workbook. Finally, you learn the rudiments of workbook management in Excel so that you can find workbook files even when you don't know exactly what they're called and haven't a clue as to where you saved them on the hard disk!

Range Names Revista

In Chapter 5 of *Excel For Dummies*, I introduced you to the use of range names in a more-or-less straightforward "here's-how-you-do-it" manner. At that time, however, I really didn't get on top of my soapbox (as I am sometimes wont to do) and preach the many virtues of using range names (especially in a large, complex workbook with lots of sheets all full of loads of data).

So, without further ado, let me acquaint you with some of the more important benefits of assigning range names in a workbook:

- ✔ You can select a block of cells anywhere in any worksheet in a workbook just by opening the Go To dialog box (F5) and then selecting its range name. To make this task even easier, you can also choose the range name from a pop-up list just by clicking on the cell-reference drop-down button (next to the cell reference display on the formula bar) and then dragging down to the range name in the pop-up list.

- ✔ You can use range names instead of cell references in master formulas in a worksheet so that people can actually figure out what the formula's function is in the worksheet.

- ✔ If you routinely need to print particular cell ranges in a worksheet, you can print them in a flash by selecting the cells via the range name and then choosing the Selection radio button in the Print dialog box.

- ✔ If you create macros that manipulate blocks of cells and you refer to them by range name rather than by cell range references, the macros won't blow up on you if someone goes and moves the data entries to a new part of the worksheet or even to a different sheet in the workbook. The only way to blow up such a macro is to delete the range name from the workbook (something, I hope you would never even contemplate doing!).

To bring home the point about using range names and make their benefits more concrete, the next couple of sections show you some examples of just how handy these little guys can be.

Using range names in formulas

One of the best ways to keep on top of the ins and outs of the calculations in a worksheet is to name the cells that each formula refers to. For example, suppose that you need to create a master formula that multiplies the number of items ordered by the price of each item in the first row of a table (a common situation). Suppose that cell C7 contains the quantity ordered of the first item, and cell D7 contains the price of the first item. If you want the extended price to appear in cell F7 (as shown in Figure 4-1), you would enter the following formula in cell F7:

```
=C7*D7
```

If however, you assign the range name No._Ordered to cell C7 and the range name Price to cell D7, you can then come up with this formula for cell F7:

```
=No._Ordered*Price
```

The second formula, I think you may agree, is a little bit better description of what's really happening in this cell.

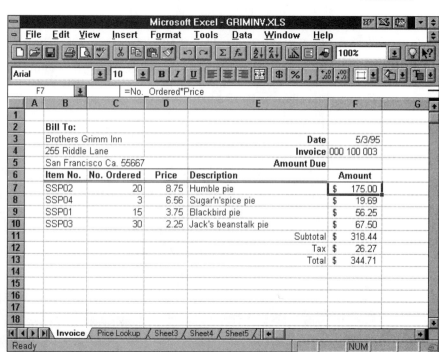

Formula bar

Figure 4-1:
Using range names allows you to make sense of the purpose of a particular formula.

Defining range names from neighboring column and row headings

When you're using range names to document the purpose of formulas in a table, you often can use the already existing column and row headings to create your range names in a jiffy. Normally, when you select a cell and then choose the Insert⇨Name⇨Define command to open the Define Name dialog box, Excel automatically supplies as the suggested name the label in the cell to the immediate left or right above (assuming that one or the other cell contains text rather than some kind of value). If both the cell on the immediate left and the one above contain text, Excel suggests the one on the left as the range name rather than the one above. (Of course, you can always override this or any other suggestion and type in a name of your own. See Chapter 5 of *Excel For Dummies*, if you need a review of the rules for naming a range.)

This propensity for selecting neighboring column and row headings when assigning range names can be applied on a much larger scale with the Insert⇨Name⇨Create command. After you select this command, a Create Names dialog box appears (shown in Figure 4-2) that lets you indicate whether you want the labels in cells in the row immediately above (Top Row), the column on the left (Left Column), the row below (Bottom Row), the column to the right (Right Column), or a combination of some or even all of these options to be assigned as the range names of the neighboring cells.

To see how this technique can save you loads of time, look at the table in Figure 4-2. In this figure, I selected the cell range B6:F10 (which includes the column headings in cell range B6:F6 and the row headings in cell range B7:B10). Then I opened the Create Names dialog box and selected both the Top Row and Left Column check boxes.

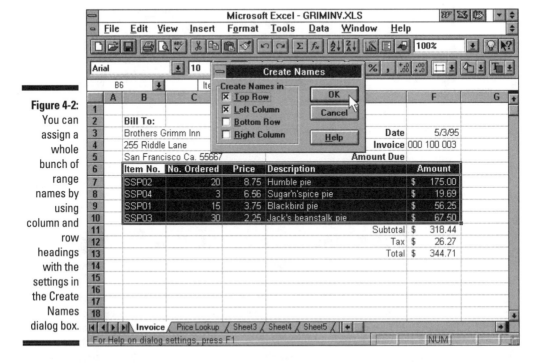

Figure 4-2: You can assign a whole bunch of range names by using column and row headings with the settings in the Create Names dialog box.

As a result of choosing the Top Row and Left Column check box settings, Excel added the following named ranges to the workbook:

Range Name	*Cell Range*
Amount	F7:F10
Description	E7:E10
Item_No.	C7:F10
No._Ordered	C7:C10
Price	D7:D10
SSP01	C9:F9
SSP02	C7:F7
SSP03	C10:F10
SSP04	C8:F8

Note that the program assigned the headings at the top of each column to the range of selected cells in the rows below, just as it assigned the headings at the far left of each row to the range of selected cells in columns to the right.

The most interesting (surprising, perhaps) named range created with the Insert⇨Name⇨Create command using the Top Row and Left Column check box settings is the Item_No. range name for the cell range C7:F10 because this label was entered in cell B6, the one in the very upper left-hand corner of the cell selection. Because this text entry is right above the other text entries that make up the row headings for this table, Excel did not apply the name Item_No. to the cell range B7:B10, as might have been expected. Instead, the program applied the name in cell B6 to all of the table data below the first row of column headings and to the right of the first column of row headings (C7:F10). In this particular example, the name Item_No. entered in cell B6 does not really make an appropriate name for the bulk of the data for this simple invoice. (It would be better named something like Invoice_Data or Grimm_Invoice.)

To rename the Item_No. cell range more appropriately, select it in the cell reference pop-up list to highlight the cell range C7:F10 in the worksheet. Then choose Insert⇨Name⇨Define, type in a new range name (something like **Invoice_Data**) in the Names in Workbook text box of the Define Names dialog box, and click on the Add button. Then select the old range name, Item_No., in the list box and choose the Delete button before you click on OK.

Applying range names to existing formulas

Range names that you create (either individually with the Insert⇨Name⇨Define command or en masse with the Insert⇨Name⇨Create command) for cells used in formulas are not automatically applied to the formulas in which they appear. To have Excel apply a range name to your formula, you must use the Insert⇨Name⇨Apply command as explained in the steps that follow.

Applying range names to your formulas

1. **To replace cell references with range names for a particular group of formulas, select their cells.**

   To replace all formula references with their named counterparts in the entire workbook, make sure that only a single cell is selected.

2. **Choose Insert⇨Name⇨Apply to open the Apply Names dialog box.**

3. **Choose all the names you want to apply in the Apply Names list box.**

   To select multiple range names, hold down the Ctrl or Shift key as you click on the range name. (Note that you can't use the old click, Shift-click method for selecting a continuous list of names in this particular list box; rather, you must select each one individually, even if they all appear in a row).

4. **Click on the OK button to apply the range names selected in the Apply Names list box to the appropriate formulas in the current cell selection.**

Figure 4-3 shows the Apply Names dialog box after you have selected all the range names that pertain to the invoice table (shown selected behind it) in the Apply Names list box. After clicking on OK, Excel then replaces all the cell references in the four formulas in the last column of the selected table (cell range F7:F10).

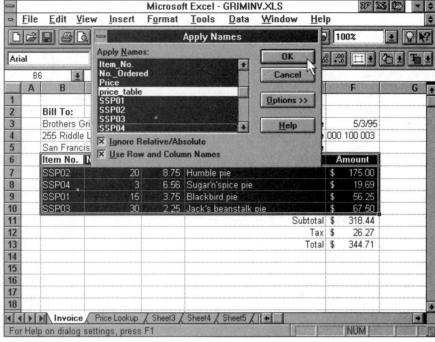

Figure 4-3:
You can
apply range
names to
the formulas
that refer to
them by
using the
Apply
Names
dialog box.

Applying redundant row and column names

When you apply range names to formulas by using the default settings in the Apply Names dialog box, Excel uses the names of row and column ranges that contain the cell references if names for the individual cells can't be found. If you only want specific range names applied, you have to deselect the Use Row and Column Names check box.

Further, when the Use Row and Column Names check box is selected, Excel automatically drops the column-oriented name and uses only the row-oriented range name when the referenced cell is in the same column as the formula and they're both within a row-oriented name. Likewise, the program omits the row-oriented name and uses only the column-oriented range name when the referenced cell is in the same row as the formula and they're both within a column-oriented name. Confused? Let's look at some examples.

In the formula in cell F7, shown earlier on the formula bar in Figure 4-1, you can see the results that these default row and column name settings have on the formulas they're applied to. In cell F7, Excel replaces the cell references

```
=C7*D7
```

in the formula with

```
=No._Ordered*Price
```

Because both of these cell references are in the same row as the formula (row 7) and within the same row-oriented range (SSP02, which encompasses cell range C7:F7), Excel omits this row-oriented cell range name (SSP02) from the references in the formula. The only problem with this omission is that the program does the same thing to all the other row-oriented range names in the subsequent formulas. If you move the cell pointer down one cell to the formula in cell F8, for example, instead of seeing the original cell references

```
=C8*D8
```

you would now see in this cell

```
=No._Ordered*Price
```

In fact, the contents of all four formulas of the table in column F now read `=No._Ordered*Price`. Without the row-oriented range name in the cell references, you literally can't tell one formula from another.

Fortunately, you can easily avoid this situation and have the row-oriented range names show up in the formulas by opening the Apply Names dialog box and choosing the Options button, which expands this dialog box to include some new check box and radio button options as shown in Figure 4-4. Now you can deselect the Omit Row Name if Same Row check box.

If you apply range names to the sample invoice table in this manner, instead of seeing

```
=No._Ordered*Price
```

in cell C7, you would now see

```
=SSP02 No._Ordered*SSP02 Price
```

And, when you move the cell pointer to cell C8, you would now see this slightly different formula:

```
=SSP04 No._Ordered*SSP04 Price
```

Now you have the best of all worlds: formulas with descriptive range names instead of abstract cell references and range names that identify the name of both the row and the column of particular cell references.

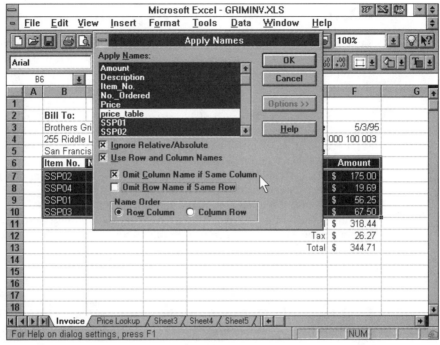

Figure 4-4:
Deselect the
Omit Row
Name if
Same Row
check box.

Everything you never wanted to know about the intersection operator

The innocent-looking little space between the row-oriented and column-oriented range names that appears in the formulas (the space after SSP04) is technically known as an *intersection operator*. This space should help you to interpret the formulas. For example, the formula

SSP04 No._Ordered*SSP04 Price

tells the program to multiply the cell located at the intersection of the SSP04 and No._Ordered range by the cell found at the intersection of the SSP04 and Price range. Keep in mind that if you choose the Column Row radio button instead of the Row Column radio button in the Name Order area of the expanded Apply Names dialog box, Excel reverses the order of the range names (putting the column-oriented name in front of the row-oriented name) while, at the same time, inserting the intersection operator between them.

Pasting range names in formulas

Range names don't have to be applied after the fact to formulas as outlined in the preceding section. You can, in fact, quite easily paste range names right into a formula as you are building it. Figures 4-5 and 4-6 show an example of how this shortcut is done.

In Figure 4-5, you see the start of a formula using the SUM function. In this case, you need to subtotal the amounts in the cell range F7:F10 with a formula in cell F11. Because this cell range has been assigned the name Amount, you can use its name in the argument of the SUM formula by pasting it in. Simply enter **=sum(** in the cell and then choose the Insert⇨Name⇨Paste command, which opens a Paste Name dialog box similar to the one shown in Figure 4-5. After choosing Amount in the Paste Name list box and clicking on OK, you have to type only the right parenthesis and press Enter to complete the formula. Figure 4-6 shows the worksheet with the completed formula in the formula bar and the subtotal in cell F11.

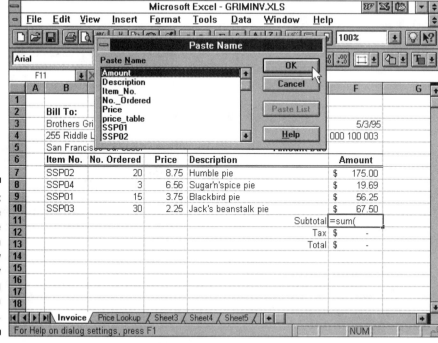

Figure 4-5:
You can use range names in new formulas by pasting them in place.

Microsoft Excel - GRIMINV.XLS						
File Edit View Insert Format Tools Data Window Help						

Subtotal   =SUM(Amount)

	A	B	C	D	E	F	G
1							
2		**Bill To:**					
3		Brothers Grimm Inn			**Date**	5/3/95	
4		255 Riddle Lane			**Invoice**	000 100 003	
5		San Francisco Ca. 55667			**Amount Due**		
6		**Item No.**	**No. Ordered**	**Price**	**Description**	**Amount**	
7		SSP02	20	8.75	Humble pie	$ 175.00	
8		SSP04	3	6.56	Sugar'n'spice pie	$ 19.69	
9		SSP01	15	3.75	Blackbird pie	$ 56.25	
10		SSP03	30	2.25	Jack's beanstalk pie	$ 67.50	
11					Subtotal	$ 318.44	
12					Tax	$ -	
13					Total	$ -	
14							
15							
16							
17							
18							

Invoice / Price Lookup / Sheet3 / Sheet4 / Sheet5 /

Ready   NUM

Figure 4-6:
When you
use a range
name in a
formula, the
result is
calculated
by using the
values in the
named cell
range.

The only drawback to using range names in formulas is that deleting the range name from the workbook will blow up the formula by returning the #NAME? error value in the cell (which of course infects all the other cells that refer to that formula's result). If this error happens to you, the only way to remove the error value is by redefining the range name or rebuilding the formula, this time, with the good old-fashioned cell addresses.

Using range names for values not entered in the workbook

In Excel, you can assign range names to particular values that are required in formulas even when you haven't bothered to enter these values anywhere in the workbook. Figures 4-7 and 4-8 illustrate a situation when you may use this slick little technique. In cell F12 of the sample worksheet (displayed more clearly in Figure 4-8), you need to build a formula that computes the state sales tax. To build this formula, you simply multiply the value in the range named Subtotal (cell F11) by the current tax rate percentage.

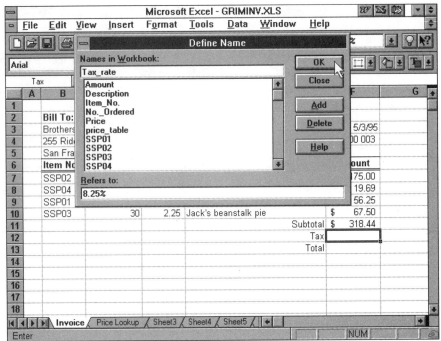

Figure 4-7:
Creating the
Tax_rate
range name
for the value
8.25%.

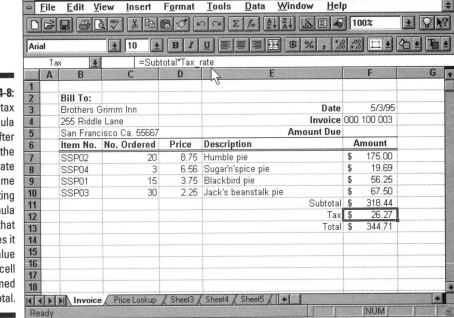

Figure 4-8:
The tax
formula
after
defining the
Tax_rate
range name
and creating
a formula
that
multiplies it
by the value
in the cell
named
Subtotal.

Because the tax rate is not entered anywhere in the workbook, you can create a range name that stores this value so that Excel uses it when you build the following English-like formula in the cell:

```
=Subtotal*Tax_rate
```

To make this formula, you open the Define Name dialog box (see Figure 4-7), type in the name of the range in the Names in <u>W</u>orkbook text box and then replace the current cell reference listed in the <u>R</u>efers to text box with the appropriate value (it's up to 8.25% in my county!) before choosing OK. After you define the formula, you can then use the value in a formula simply by pasting its range name into place. Figure 4-8 shows the worksheet with the completed formula in the formula bar and the tax in cell F12.

The reason for assigning range names to such values as the state tax rate (rather than typing the value over and over again into each of the formulas as you build them) is because the tax rate can change. When the state legislature raises the sales tax rate (and you know it will), you can update all the formulas that use that value in the entire workbook simply by changing the value assigned to the Tax_rate range name. This technique beats the pants off of using the R<u>e</u>place command to find and replace each occurrence of the out-of-date sales tax rate.

Keeping a list of all range names

If you're working in an unfamiliar workbook that contains lots of range names, you may find it quite helpful to generate a list of all the named ranges in the workbook. (You can determine how many range names the workbook has by clicking on the arrow button to the right of the cell reference area of the formula bar.) To generate a list of range names in a workbook, position the cell pointer at the beginning of a clear region in the worksheet (you wouldn't want to overwrite any existing cell entries with the range name table, now would you?), open the Paste Name dialog box (with the <u>I</u>nsert⇨<u>N</u>ame ⇨<u>P</u>aste command), and click on the Paste <u>L</u>ist button.

When you generate a list of range names, Excel lists the name of each range (in alphabetical order) in the first column followed by the range addresses in the second column. Notice in Figure 4-9 that most of the range addresses listed in the second column of this table include the sheet name (or the worksheet number — Sheet1, Sheet2, and so on — if the worksheet is not named) followed by the range address, and that these two items are separated by an exclamation point.

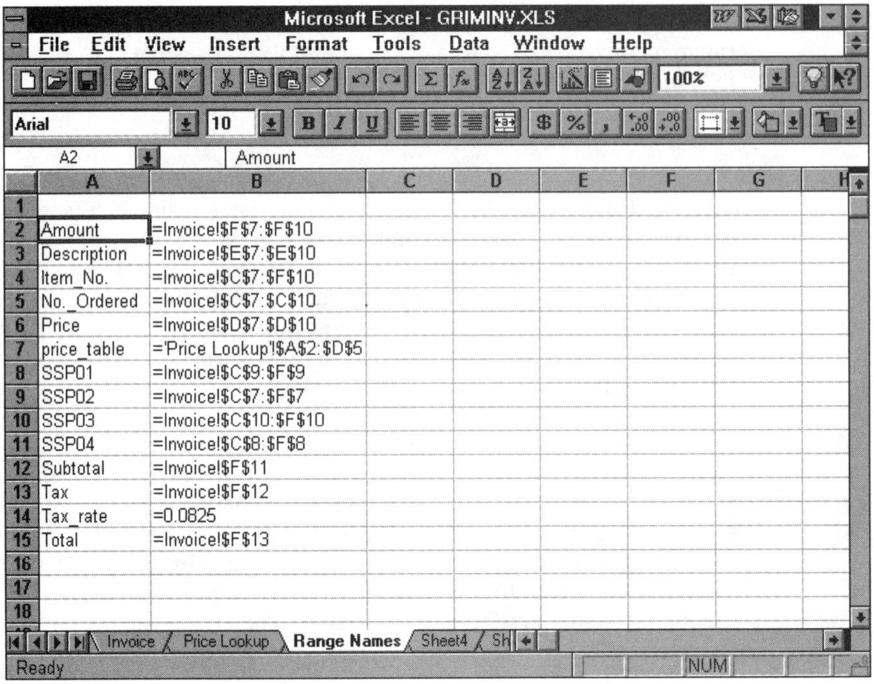

Figure 4-9:
A sample
worksheet
with a list of
all range
names
currently
defined
in the
workbook.

After you have generated a list of range names, the list is not automatically up-dated when you add a couple of new range names to the workbook. The only way that Excel can include the new range names in the list is for you to generate a new list in the workbook with the Paste List button. Most of the time, you can add the range names by pasting the new list right over the old one — the new list automatically and without warning replaces the old one. Just be sure that the new list doesn't wipe out any other existing data as it grows longer. The safest way to generate a range name list so that you can adjust it as required is, of course, to create it on a new blank worksheet in the workbook (as I did in the workbook shown in Figure 4-9).

Workbook Basics: Part Deux

The normal everyday problems related to keeping on top of the information in a single worksheet can easily go off the scale when you begin to use multiple worksheets in a workbook. For this reason, you need to be sure that you are fully versed in the basics of using more than one worksheet in a workbook.

Although each new workbook comes out of the starting gate sporting 16 blank worksheets in a row, you can add more sheets as needed with the

Insert⇨Worksheet command, just as you can remove any extra sheets with the Edit⇨Delete Sheet command. Think of these blank worksheets as blank pages in a new notebook (albeit a very, very big notebook!). Like pages in a notebook, the worksheets lie on top of each other so that each blank cell overlies perfectly its counterpart in the sheet below.

To move to a new sheet in the workbook, you can click on the sheet tab for that worksheet or press Ctrl+PgDn (next sheet) and Ctrl+PgUp (preceding sheet) until the sheet is selected. If the sheet tab for the worksheet you want is not displayed on the scroll bar at the bottom of the document window, use the tab scrolling buttons (the buttons with the left- and right-pointing arrows) to bring it into view. To use the tab scrolling buttons, click on the one with the right-pointing arrow to bring the next sheet into view, and click on the one with the left-pointing arrow to bring the preceding sheet into view.

The tab scrolling buttons with the directional arrows pointing to vertical lines display the very first or very last group of sheet tabs in a workbook. The button with the arrow pointing left to a vertical line brings the first group of sheet tabs into view; the button with the arrow pointing right to a vertical line brings the last group of sheet tabs into view.

When you scroll sheet tabs to find the one you're looking for, don't forget to click on the desired sheet tab to make the worksheet current.

A sheet tab by any other name . . .

The sheet tabs shown at the bottom of each workbook are the keys to keeping your place in a workbook. To tell which sheet is current, you have only to look at which sheet tab appears on the top and matches the background of the other cells in the worksheet. Typically, this means that the active sheet tab's background appears in white in contrast to the nonactive sheet tabs, which sport a gray background.

When you start a new workbook, the sheet tabs are all the same width because they all have the default sheet names (Sheet1, Sheet2, and so on). As you assign your own names to the sheets, the tabs appear either longer or shorter, depending on the length of the sheet tab name. Just keep in mind that the longer the sheet tabs, the fewer you can see at one time, and the more sheet tab scrolling you'll have to do to find the worksheet you want.

In the Rename Sheet dialog box, you can rename a worksheet with a name that has up to 31 characters (including, thank goodness, spaces). To open the Rename Sheet dialog box, double-click on the sheet tab of the worksheet you want to rename, select the Rename command on the sheet tab shortcut menu (there's a tongue twister for you!), or choose the Format⇨Sheet⇨Rename command.

Musical sheet tabs

A worksheet that you add to a workbook is always inserted in front of whichever worksheet is active at the time you choose Insert⇨Worksheet. Because of this positioning, the first thing you may have to do with the new worksheet is move it to a different position in the workbook. To move the worksheet, click on its sheet tab and drag it to the new position in the row of tabs. As you drag, the pointer changes shape to an arrowhead on a dog-eared piece of paper, and you see a black triangle pointing downward above the sheet tabs. When this triangle is positioned over the tab of the sheet that is to follow the one you're moving, release the mouse button.

If you need to copy a worksheet to another position in the workbook, hold down the Ctrl key as you click on and drag the sheet tab. When you release the mouse button, Excel creates a copy with a new sheet tab name based on the number of the copy and the original sheet name. For example, if you copy Sheet1 to a new place in the workbook, the copy is renamed Sheet1 (2). You then can rename the worksheet whatever you want.

In addition to moving a sheet around in the current workbook, you can also move (or copy) sheets between workbooks. You can perform these procedures by using drag and drop or by using the Move or Copy Sheet command on the Edit menu. Although using the pull-down menus and their dialog boxes usually is more complicated than the drag-and-drop method, using the menus is the preferred method in this case.

To use drag and drop to move or copy a worksheet to another workbook, you must have the other workbook open and have resized and repositioned both document windows so that you can see the sheet tabs of both workbooks. Quite frankly, while this procedure is not at all hard to do, it can involve several steps that usually take more time than just opening the Move or Copy dialog box and selecting the workbook and the position in that workbook where you want to move or copy the sheets to.

Using the Move or Copy Sheets command

1. **If necessary, open both the workbook containing the sheets to be moved or copied and the one where the sheets will be moved or copied to. Activate the workbook with sheets to be moved or copied.**

2. **Select the sheet tabs of the worksheets to be moved or copied.**

3. **Choose Edit⇨Move or Copy Sheets to open the Move or Copy dialog box.**

4. **Choose the name of the workbook to move or copy the selected sheets to in the To Book pop-up menu.**

5. **Choose the name of the sheet in the Before Sheet list box that should immediately follow the sheet(s) that you're about to move or copy into this workbook.**

6. **If you want to copy a sheet rather than move it, select the Create a Copy check box.**

7. **Choose OK or press Enter to complete the move or copy operation.**

When copying sheets within a workbook or moving and copying worksheets between workbooks, you don't have to perform the function one sheet at a time. To move or copy several worksheets in one operation, select them all prior to performing the move or copy operation. To select several sheets, re-member to hold down the Ctrl key as you click on the appropriate sheet tabs. To select all the sheets in a workbook, choose the Select All Sheets command on the sheet tab shortcut menu.

Group editing

One of the nice things about a workbook is that is enables you to edit more than one worksheet at a time. Of course, you should be concerned with group editing only when you're working on a bunch of worksheets that share essen-tially the same layout and require the same type of formatting. For example, suppose that you have a workbook that contains annual sales worksheets (named YTD94, YTD95, and YTD96) for three consecutive years. The work-sheets share the same layout (with months across the columns, and quarterly and annual totals, locations, and types of sales down the rows) but lack stan-dard formatting.

To format any part of these three worksheets in a single operation, you simply resort to group editing, which requires selecting the three sales worksheets. Simply click on the YTD94, YTD95, and YTD96 sheet tabs as you hold down the Ctrl key or click on the YTD94 tab and then hold down the Shift key as you click on the YTD96 tab.

After selecting the last sheet, the message [GROUP] appears in the title bar of the active document window (with the YTD94 worksheet, in this case). This message indicates that any editing change you make to the current worksheet will affect all the sheets that are currently selected. For instance, if you select a row of column headings and add bold and italics to the headings in the current worksheet, the same formatting is applied to the same cell selection in all three sales sheets. All headings in the same cell range in the other worksheets will now be in bold and italics. Keep in mind that you can apply not only formatting changes to a cell range but also editing changes, such as replacing a cell entry, deleting a cell's contents, or moving a cell selection to a new place in the work-sheet. These changes also affect all the worksheets you have selected as long as they're grouped together.

After you are finished making editing changes that affect all the grouped worksheets, you can break up the group by choosing the Ungroup Sheets command on the sheet tab shortcut menu or by clicking on a sheet tab that's not currently selected. As soon as you break up the group, the [GROUP] message disappears from the title bar, and, thereafter, any editing changes that you make affect only the cells in the active worksheet.

Now you see them; now you don't

One more technique that comes in handy when working with multiple worksheets is hiding particular worksheets in the workbook. Just as you can hide particular columns, rows, and cell ranges in a worksheet, you also can hide particular worksheets in the workbook. For example, you may want to hide a worksheet that contains sensitive (for-your-eyes-only) material, such as the one with all the employee salaries in the company or the one that contains all the macros used in the workbook.

As with hiding columns and rows, hiding worksheets enables you to print the contents of the workbook without the data in worksheets that you consider either unnecessary in the report or too classified for widespread distribution but which, nonetheless, are required in the workbook. Then, after the report is printed, you can redisplay the worksheets by unhiding them.

To hide a worksheet, make it active by selecting its sheet tab and then choose the Format⇨Sheet⇨Hide command. Excel removes its tab from the row of sheet tabs, making it impossible for anyone to select and display the worksheet in the document window. To redisplay any of the sheets you've hidden, choose the Format⇨Sheet⇨Unhide command, which displays the Unhide dialog box. In the Unhide Sheet list box, choose the name of the sheet that you want to display once again in the workbook. As soon as you choose OK, Excel redisplays the sheet tab of the previously hidden worksheet — as simple as that! Unfortunately, although you can hide multiple worksheets in one hide operation, you can select only one sheet at a time to redisplay with the Unhide command.

Managing Those Pesky Workbooks

Remember that individual files in Excel are actually individual workbooks, with all their worksheets; therefore, one of the larger management tasks that you encounter is keeping track of all the workbook files you create. Never underestimate how easy it is to misplace a workbook file that you know you've saved (but you can't remember where or under what filename).

Fortunately, Excel includes with its File⇨Find File command some nifty facilities for locating lost files. You can search for files by filename, location on the hard disk, file summary information, or the date the file was last saved. After you've completed a file search, you then can preview the results to determine which of the workbooks is the one you want to work with. In addition to opening up a workbook, you can copy, print, or delete a file without having to switch to the Windows File Manager.

Playing hide and seek with files

Excel offers you two ways to search for files by bringing up the Search dialog box (see Figure 4-10): You can choose the File⇨Find File command on the pull-down menus, or you can bring up the Open dialog box (choose File⇨Open or click on the Open button on the Standard toolbar) and then choose its Find File button. The Search dialog box is the place where you can search for your lost workbook files.

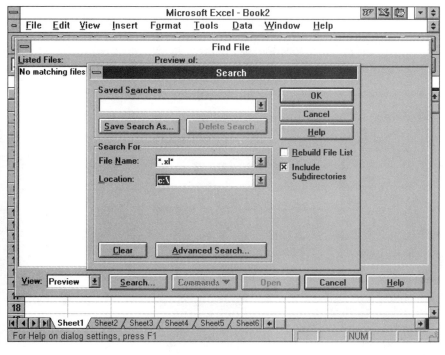

Figure 4-10: This Search dialog box is your key to finding misplaced files as well as performing all sorts of file-related tasks.

You can initiate a search for a workbook file from the Search dialog box in the following ways:

   ✔ Specify the type of file to look for in the File Name text box in the Search For area. Go with the *.xl* default pattern in this text box when you want to search for any and all Excel workbooks or template files because all

Excel workbook files use the *.xl-something-or-other* file extension. If you actually know the name of the workbook file, replace the asterisk (*) with the filename. If you know part of the filename, add the part of the name you're sure of to the *.xl*. For example if you're sure the filename begins with *Sales*, add **sales** to the default pattern so that sales*.xl* appears in the File Name text box.

✔ Specify which disk to search in the Location text box. To search the hard disk for files, choose c:\ from the pop-up list. To search a floppy disk, choose either a:\ or b:\ (depending upon which drive holds the disk you want searched) from the pop-up list.

✔ If the disk you've chosen contains directories and subdirectories with files that should be searched (as is always the case with a hard disk drive like C or D), choose Include Subdirectories.

After specifying this stuff, you can start the search by choosing OK or pressing Enter. Excel then searches the specified location for files whose names match the specified pattern. The results of the search are then displayed in the Find File dialog box (similar to the one shown in Figure 4-11). If no files are found in the specified location matching the filename pattern you used, the message No matching files found appears in the Listed Files box. Otherwise, you see an alphabetical list of files, arranged by directory, if you had Excel search the subdirectories on the specified disk.

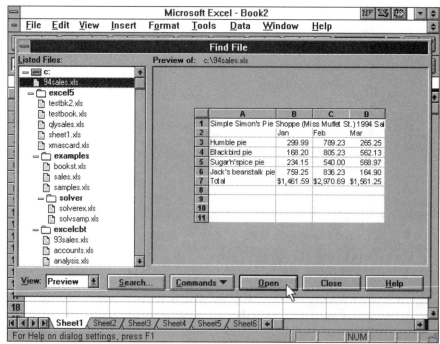

Figure 4-11:
The Find File dialog box shows you the results of any search you undertake with the Find File command.

If no matching files are located, you can then choose the Search button in the Find File dialog box to return to the Search dialog box, where you can change the search criteria before undertaking the search again.

Deciding which file to use

Many times, a file search results in a long list of files that match your search criteria. To help you figure out which of the listed files is the one you want to use, the Find File dialog box lets you choose between three different types of views for the located files:

✔ Preview shows a tiny bit of the upper left-hand corner of the first worksheet in a workbook file (see Figure 4-11). Only workbook files created in Excel 5 or saved as Excel 5 files have previews available for them. Worksheet files created with other spreadsheet programs or earlier versions of Excel do not have a preview available.

✔ File Info shows the filename, the title of the workbook (as entered in cell A1 of the first worksheet), the (Kbyte) size of the file, the author of the workbook (as listed in the User Name text box on the General tab of the Options dialog box), and the date the workbook was last saved (which is the same as the creation date, when you've only saved the workbook once).

✔ Summary shows all the information you've filled out in the Summary Info dialog box (see Chapter 2 of *Excel For Dummies* for information on adding summary information to a workbook when saving it).

To open a particular file in the list, select its name in the Listed Files box and then choose the Open button. For more ideas on what you can do to a file, see "Doing file management stuff right inside Excel" at the end of this chapter.

Keep in mind that it's never too late to add summary information to a workbook file. If you passed up the opportunity the first time you saved the file, you can still add a summary by choosing the Summary Info command on the File menu and then filling out the necessary information in the Summary Info dialog box.

Doing advanced searches

Use the Advanced Search button in the Search dialog box to refine the types of file searches you need to do. When you choose this button, Excel opens the Advanced Search dialog box shown in Figure 4-12.

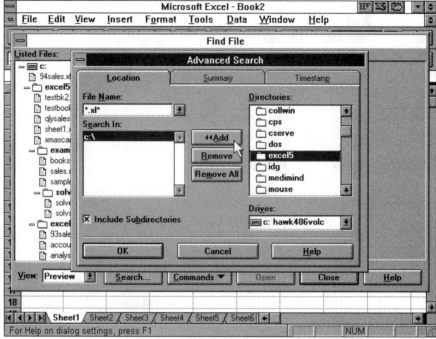

Figure 4-12:
In the
Advanced
Search
dialog box,
you can
search for
files by
location,
summary
information,
or dates.

As you can see from Figure 4-12, the Advanced Search dialog box contains the Location, Summary, and Timestamp tabs, which help you do the following tasks:

✔ The settings on the Location tab let you restrict the search on the selected disk to particular directories on that disk. To specify particular directories, select each one in the Directories list and then choose the Add button. Note that Excel searches any subdirectories of the specified directories unless you deselect the Include Subdirectories check box.

✔ The settings on the Summary tab let you search for files by particular summary information (such as title, author, keywords, subject, and so on). If you want to search for certain text in the Comments section of the summary, type this search text in the Containing Text box.

✔ The settings on the Timestamp tab let you search for files by the date last saved. To search for files saved between a range of dates, enter a date in both the From and To text boxes. To search for files saved on or after a particular date, just enter the date in the From box. To search for files saved on or before a particular date, just enter a date in the To box.

After entering all the required search criteria in a particular tab of the Advanced Search dialog box, click on its OK button to return to the Search dialog box, where you can start the search using the advanced criteria by clicking on OK again.

If you need to search just one directory on the hard disk, and you feel confident in your DOS directory-path skills ("Do you feel lucky, kid?"), go to the Search dialog box. In the Location text box, simply replace the drive letter in the directory path with the correct directory path. This shortcut saves the time it takes you to go through the rigmarole of adding the directory from the Directories list box on the Location tab of the Advanced Search dialog box.

Saving searches

As you get experience with doing simple and advanced searches with the Find File command, you may find yourself doing a certain kind of search on a regular basis. Rather than go through all the trouble of setting up the required search criteria each time you want to do this type of search, you can save the search under a unique name. To have Excel select all requisite search criteria for a particular search, all you have to do is select that particular search name.

To save a search, first set up the necessary search criteria in the Search and Advanced Search dialog boxes and perform the search. Assuming that you get the results you want, you can then save the search by choosing the Search button in the Find File dialog box to reopen the Search dialog box. Then choose the Save Search As button, enter a name for the saved search in the Search Name text box, and choose OK.

After saving a search, you can conduct a search using its search criteria simply by opening the Saved Searches pop-up list, selecting the desired search name in this list, and then choosing the OK button.

If you keep workbook files mixed in with other types of files (such as word processing documents) in your own personal directory, you may want to create a saved search that searches for all the workbooks in your personal directory. For example, if your personal directory is called C:\JOHN, you would enter ***.xls** in the File Name text box and enter **c:\john** in the Location text box in the Search dialog box (making sure that the Include Subdirectories check box is selected). To save this search, you would then choose the Save Search As button and enter a name for the search (such as **All Excel workbooks in c:\john**) in the Save Search As dialog box.

Doing file management stuff right inside Excel

Most of the time, the only thing you want to do with the file you've finally hunted down is open it up in Excel with the Open button in the Find File dialog box. You can, however, do a number of other things to the selected files by choosing the Commands pop-up button in the Find File dialog box. The Commands pop-up list contains the following possibilities:

- ✔ *Open Read Only.* Opens the file in read-only mode (indicated by [Read-Only] after the filename on the title bar), meaning that Excel doesn't allow you to save any changes that you make in the file under the original name. You have to use the File➪Save As command to save changes to the workbook under a new filename.

- ✔ *Print.* Opens the files that you've selected in the Listed Files box and then prints them, using whatever page layout and print settings are currently in effect.

- ✔ *Summary.* This command is not available in Excel.

- ✔ *Delete.* Deletes the files you've selected in the Listed Files box upon confirmation in an alert message dialog box.

- ✔ *Copy.* Copies the files you've selected in the Listed Files box to the disk and directory you specify in the Copy dialog box. To copy the file(s) to a new directory on the selected disk, choose the New button in the Copy dialog box and then type in a name for the new directory in the Create Directory dialog box that appears.

- ✔ *Sorting.* Lets you sort all the files displayed in the Listed Files box of the Find File dialog box. You can sort the files by the Author, Last Saved Date, Name (the default), or Size, and you can have the sorted files listed either by File Name or by Title.

Of all the commands on the Commands pop-up list, the Copy and Sorting commands are probably the most useful. In fact, you can combine these commands with a saved search so that creating backup copies of your workbook files is a virtual breeze.

Using a saved search with the Sorting and Copy commands to back up your workbooks

1. **Choose File➪Find on the pull-down menus.**

2. **If the Find File dialog box shows the files from the last file search you did, choose the Search button to open the Search dialog box.**

3. **Open the Saved Searches pop-up list and select the name of the search that finds all the workbook files in your personal directory. Then choose**

the Rebuild File List check box and click on the OK button to conduct
the search.

(If you haven't yet created such a saved search, go back to the Tip at the
end of the "Saving searches" section in this chapter and make one, for
heaven's sake!)

4. **Choose the Sorting command in the Commands pop-up list in the Find
   File dialog box and then choose the Last Saved Date and the File Name
   radio buttons in the Options dialog box and select OK.**

5. **Put a formatted floppy disk with enough space for backups of today's
   work in your disk drive (A or B).**

6. **Select all the files in the Listed Files box that need backing up.**

   Because they are sorted by date last saved, these files appear in a cluster
   at the very top of the list for your personal directory. To select a range of
   files, use the click, Shift-click method. To select individual files, hold down
   Ctrl while you click.

7. **Choose Copy in the Commands pop-up list in the Find File dialog box. In
   the Drives pop-up list box, select the letter of the drive (A or B) that
   contains your formatted floppy disk and click on OK.**

8. **After Excel finishes copying all the selected files onto your backup disk,
   choose the Close button to close the Find File dialog box and return to
   Excel.**

   If there's not enough room for all the files on your floppy disk, you'll be
   prompted for a new disk. You will also be prompted to overwrite a file if an
   earlier version already resides on the backup floppy disk. Your work is
   saved in two locations: on your personal directory on the hard disk and on
   the backup floppy disk.

9. **Remove the backup floppy disk from its drive and put it in a safe place
   before you shut down your machine. Then take a break — you deserve
   it!**

Part II
More Amazing Things You Can Do with Excel

The 5th Wave   By Rich Tennant

DANGER
HIGH VOLTAGE
POWER LINES

"Hurry, Stuart!! Hurry!! The screen's starting to flicker out!!"

In this part . . .

*P*art II reunites you with two old friends: charts and databases. In Chapter 5, you learn about a million things you can do to customize a chart to get it to look exactly like you want it to. In Chapter 6, you learn new ways of sorting, filtering, and subtotaling data in a database. Of these topics, the automatic subtotals are the most exciting. With this feature, you can get all kinds of totals for a list of data with-out all the muss and fuss of creating and copying SUM formulas or any of that nonsense. Of the new features in Excel 5, I rank this among the highest because it's so fast and easy!

Chapter 5

Creating Custom Charts with No Sweat

- -

In This Chapter

▶ How to create a chart on its very own chart sheet

▶ How to change charted values

▶ How to select particular items in a chart so that you can change them

▶ How to add grid lines to a chart

▶ How to format the chart's axes

▶ How to format the chart area and the plot area

▶ How to format the chart's titles

▶ How to format the chart's legend

▶ How to add your own graphics to a chart

- -

*E*xcel's ChartWizard has made charting worksheet information so easy that it's not enough anymore to create "plain vanilla" charts. To really dazzle the boss nowadays, you have to a go a step farther and add some sparkle and flash to the plain charts that the ChartWizard spits out. And that's exactly what you learn to do in this chapter. After a quick look at creating a chart in a separate chart sheet — as an alternative to plunking down the chart smack dab in the middle of a worksheet (more elegantly known as "embedding" the chart) — you get to learn all sorts of cool ways to add new wrinkles to the charts you create in Excel. You will also learn how to custom format all the parts of the chart as well as how to add graphics (those that you draw yourself and those that you borrow from other sources).

Using Chart Sheets (Or "To Embed or Not to Embed," Is That a Question?)

In *Excel For Dummies*, you learned how to use the ChartWizard to create a chart as part of the worksheet that contains the values that you're actually graphing. If you're an organized type, you may prefer to add your charts to separate chart sheets in the workbook. In this way, the charts always stay separate from the values they represent. This arrangement not only makes for a neater workbook (that would make any mother proud) but also makes it easier to print just the charts in the workbook. (All you have to do is select the tab of the sheet containing the chart before you choose the Print command or button.)

Creating a chart in its own chart sheet

1. **Select the sheet tab of the worksheet that has all the data you want to chart.**

2. **Choose Insert⇨Chart⇨As New Sheet.**

   Excel responds by displaying the ChartWizard – Step 1 of 5 dialog box.

3. **Select the range of data that you want to chart (including column and row headings that you want to do) and then choose the Next button.**

4. **Continue building your chart with the ChartWizard by going through all five steps.**

   Refer to the detailed steps in Chapter 7 of *Excel For Dummies* if you get stuck.

5. **After you finish building your chart, click on the Finish button.**

   Excel draws the new chart in its own chart window (see Figure 5-1) and inserts this new chart sheet in front of the worksheet.

6. **If you want to rename the chart sheet (to something more intelligible than Chart5 or whatever), double-click on the chart sheet tab, type in the new name in the Rename Sheet dialog box, and choose OK or press Enter.**

7. **If you want to locate the chart sheet somewhere after the worksheet whose data are represented in the graph, click on the chart sheet tab and then drag it to the right to its new position in the workbook before you let go of the mouse button.**

When you create a new chart in its own chart sheet, the Chart toolbar automatically appears, floating in the upper left-hand part of the screen. This toolbar contains the following five buttons:

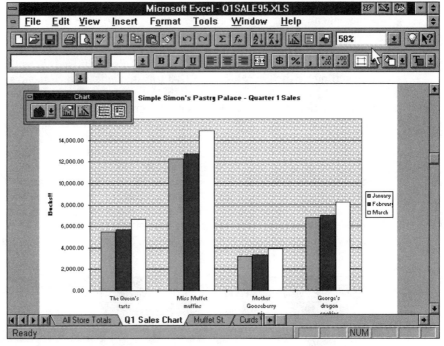

Figure 5-1:
Use the
ChartWizard
to create
charts in
their very
own chart
sheets.

✔ *Chart Type.* Clicking on this button produces a drop-down list that you can use to change the type of chart.

✔ *Default Chart.* If you mess up your chart design, use this button to reinstate the original chart type you created with the ChartWizard.

✔ *Revise Chart.* If you suddenly realize that you chose the wrong cell range or are representing time periods when you wanted categories (or vice versa), use this button to revise the data that's represented in the chart.

✔ *Horizontal Grid lines.* Use this button to add or remove grid lines extending across the chart from the tick marks on the y-axis (that's the vertical one on the left that usually indicates how much moola you've made or spent).

✔ *Legend.* Use this button to make your chart's legend disappear or to select the legend for some type of editing.

If this Chart toolbar gets in your way, remember that you can always put it away by choosing Chart on the toolbar's shortcut menu or by double-clicking on its control menu box.

When you first create a new chart in a separate chart sheet, Excel tries to select a magnification setting that enables you to see the whole chart. This percentage is displayed in the Zoom Control box on the Standard toolbar. Sometimes, however, Excel doesn't quite get everything in the screen. For example, when I created the sample chart shown in Figure 5-1, Excel chose 58% as the magnification setting for the new chart sheet. At this magnification, you can see almost everything in the chart, but some of the category labels are truncated, and the x-axis title *Goodies!* isn't visible at all. To retrofit the chart so that all of it is visible (as shown in Figure 5-2), you simply click anywhere on the chart area (somewhere within the white area around the plotted part of the chart) to select the whole thing. Then choose the Selection option on the Zoom Control pop-up list on the Standard toolbar. This technique causes Excel to resize the entire chart so that it all fits on-screen (at 53% in this particular example).

Of course, you can also use the Zoom Control settings to zoom in on the chart whenever you need to see some part in greater detail (as you may need to do when you customize some of its parts, such as the legend or the chart titles).

Figure 5-2:
Click on the chart background to select it and then choose Selection in the Zoom Control pop-up list to resize it.

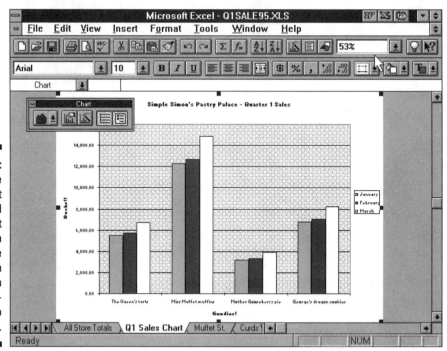

Changing the Charted Values (Or "Be True to My Chart")

Normally, when I teach spreadsheets to unsuspecting students at the college, I make a big deal about how the values that are represented in a chart are dynamically linked to the data they represent. To prove my point, I even make the poor babies go to the underlying worksheet and change the first charted value (such as 5,507.46 in cell B3) to some improbable and humongous number (such as 25,507.46). Then I have them switch over to the chart sheet to see the results of this little change on their work of art. Figure 5-3 shows the results in my sample chart of monkeying around with this first value in the All Store Totals worksheet.

Because the graphic elements of a chart — the bars in a column chart, the lines in a line chart, or the segments of a circle in a pie chart — are directly linked to the worksheet data, you can modify what is and is not represented in a chart simply by changing which range of worksheet cells is being drawn. The easiest way to make this kind of change is to select the part of the chart that you want to change and then redefine the cell range that this part represents.

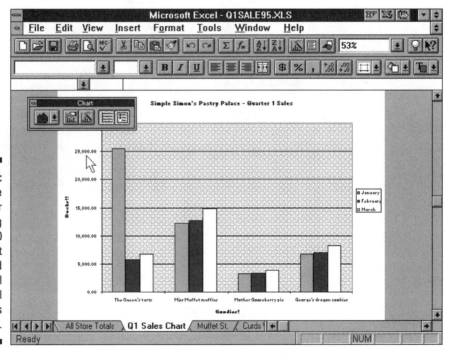

Figure 5-3: The sample chart after increasing by $10,000 the first charted value in cell B3 of the All Store Totals worksheet.

Adjusting a chart by changing the range of the worksheet cells

Suppose that you want to change the worksheet references for the last group of bars (the lightest color) in the column chart in Figure 5-3, representing the total sales made in March, 1995. Simply follow these steps:

1. **Select the chart sheet.**

2. **Click on one of the bars representing the March sales to select all four (indicated by the black selection handles on each bar, as shown in Figure 5-4).**

3. **Choose Format⟳Selected Data Series or choose Format Data Series on the bar's shortcut menu or press Ctrl+1 to open the Format Data Series dialog box, with the Name and Values tab displayed, as shown in Figure 5-5.**

4. **To change the label used in the legend that identifies the data represented in this part of the chart, select the Name (Alt+N) text box and then select the cell in the worksheet that contains the new label you want to use.**

   You may have to drag the Format Data Series dialog box out of the way to see what you're doing.

5. **To change the values that are graphed by this part of the chart, select the Y Values (Alt+Y) text box and then select the new cell range in the worksheet that contains the values you want graphed.**

   Again, you may have to drag the Format Data Series dialog box out of the way to see what you're doing.

6. **Click on OK or press Enter to close the Format Data Series dialog box and have Excel redraw the chart.**

Keep this technique in mind for those times when you need to redefine some of the ranges of data that were selected for the chart when you first created it with ye olde ChartWizard.

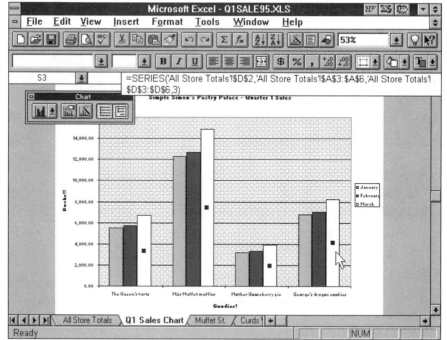

Figure 5-4:
Selecting
the part of
the chart
you want to
change (the
last set of
bars in this
example).

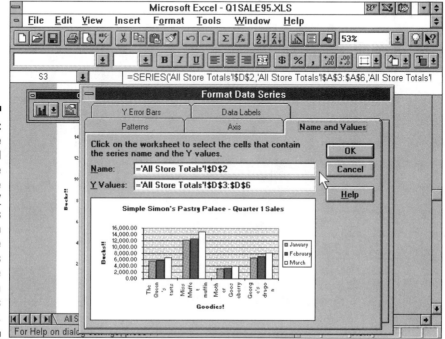

Figure 5-5:
To change
the graphed
values, use
the Name
and Y
Values
options in
the Name
and Values
tab of the
Format Data
Series
dialog box.

Getting serious about the SERIES function

Each element represented in a chart is created by a SERIES function that tells Excel what worksheet information to use. For instance, the last group of bars in the column chart shown in Figure 5-3 contains the following SERIES function (which is displayed on the formula bar when you select this part of the chart):

=SERIES('All Store Totals'!$D$2,'All Store Totals'!$A$3:$A$6,'All Store Totals'!$D$3:$D$6,3)

The first argument in the SERIES function is the cell reference to the name of the data series. This name is used in the chart legend, if there is one, to identify the data series. The second argument is the cell range containing the x-axis labels (sometimes called the *category labels*), which tell Excel where to plot each bar, line, dot, or segment along the x-axis of the chart. The third argument is the cell range containing the y-axis values, which tell Excel where to plot each bar, line, dot, or segment along the y-axis of the chart. The last argument in the SERIES function indicates the plot order, which is the order in which the graphed element appears in the chart. If you know what you're doing, you can change which data are plotted in a chart simply by editing its SERIES function on the formula bar.

The Old Gray Chart Just Ain't What It Used to Be

Most of the time, instead of fooling around with changing the values that are represented in the chart, you are interested only in fooling around with how the graphed values look in the final chart. For example, you may find it necessary to add different patterns to the bars in a column chart in addition to the colors that Excel picks so that the chart prints well on your black-and-white printer. Or you may find it necessary to pick a new font for the chart titles so that they read better on-screen. Or you may find it necessary to change the background of the plotted area so that the plotted data show up better both on-screen and in the printed version. (Excel uses some kind of ugly gray pattern when left to its own devices.) All these things and more can be customized in a jiffy — if you know what to do.

Selecting each part of a chart

The key to being able to adorn what would otherwise be a plain chart is to select the part of the chart you want to embellish *before* you select the command to embellish it. One of the primary differences between working with an embedded chart (one that's been created in the same worksheet as the data it represents) and a chart placed on its own chart sheet is in selecting charts and their associated parts:

✔ When working with an embedded chart, you must first double-click somewhere on the chart area in the worksheet to select the chart. When it is selected, a heavy line appears around the entire chart area. Then you can select the various parts of the chart, such as the titles, axes, legend, or data series, by clicking on them.

✔ When working with a chart on its own chart sheet, you have only to click on its sheet tab to display the chart. After it is displayed, you can then select its various parts (titles, axes, legend, or data series) by clicking on them.

With either type of chart, you can always tell which of its parts is selected because you will see selection handles (black squares, essentially) around the perimeter of the selected object or, in the case of a set of graphic elements represented in a particular data series, in each element.

Formatting the data series

When Excel draws your chart, it decides what color and patterns to apply to each of the data points — the different bars, segments, lines, or dots — representing individual values in the data series. You may want to change the color, pattern, or border for each data point in a particular data series, and you may want to add data labels — with the names of the categories or the actual numbers that each data point represents — that identify each point or the entire data series.

Formatting a data series

1. **Click on the chart sheet tab or double-click on the embedded chart to select it.**

2. **Click on one of the data points in the data series you want to format.**

3. **Choose Format⇨Selected Data Series (Ctrl+1) or choose Format Data Series on its shortcut menu.**

4. **To change the color or pattern or to add a border to the selected data series, choose the Patterns tab and then choose the desired border, color, and pattern in this tab.**

   If you want Excel to invert the color scheme for negative values in the chart, select the Invert if Negative check box.

5. **To add data labels to each data point in the selected data series, choose the Data Labels tab.**

Select the Show Value radio button to display the numbers graphed over each data point. Select the Show Percent radio button when formatting a pie or doughnut chart to show the percentages next to each segment. Choose the Show Percent and Label radio button when you want the category labels displayed, as well. Choose the Show Label radio button when you want only the category labels to appear next to each data point. Choose the Show Legend Key next to Label check box when you want Excel to display the little boxes used in the chart legend to represent each data series in the chart (each box uses its own color and/or pattern key).

Figure 5-6 shows the sample column chart after changing the colors (which don't show up in the book) and adding patterns to each data series.

Formatting the plot area

Charts that have an x- and y-axis, such as column and line charts, have a plot area against which the individual data points of each data series are plotted. In the sample column chart shown in this chapter, the plot area shows up as the gray rectangle on which the bars and the horizontal grid lines are drawn.

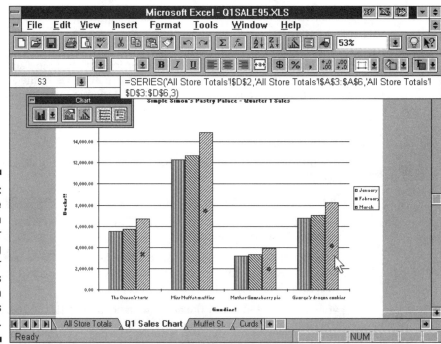

Figure 5-6: The sample column chart after changing the color and patterns for each data series in the chart.

To format the plot area, you select it and then choose Format⇨Selected Plot Area (Ctrl+1) or the Format Plot Area shortcut menu command. Figure 5-7 shows the sample column chart after changing the plot area pattern to none, changing its color to light yellow, and adding a heavy black border around it.

Formatting the chart area

Each chart that you create, whether or not it has a plot area, consists of a chart area that encompasses all the graphics and text shown in that chart. Normally, Excel draws the chart as a borderless white rectangle; however, you can format the chart area by selecting it and then choosing Format⇨Selected Chart Area (Ctrl+1) or the Format Chart Area shortcut menu command. Be sure that you don't click on any other object, such as a title, legend, and so on, when you click on the background of the chart.

Figure 5-8 shows the sample column chart after I changed its chart area color from a borderless white to a dark green color with a slight pattern and a heavy black border around it. Figure 5-9 shows another chart. This time, you see an embedded 3-D pie chart after I changed the borderless white chart area to gray and added a heavy black border with a drop shadow — which, I personally think, really makes the chart stand out next to the worksheet data in the surrounding table.

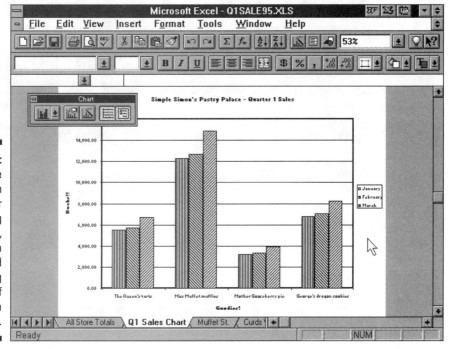

Figure 5-7:
The sample column chart after removing the pattern, adding a border, and changing the color of the plot area of the chart.

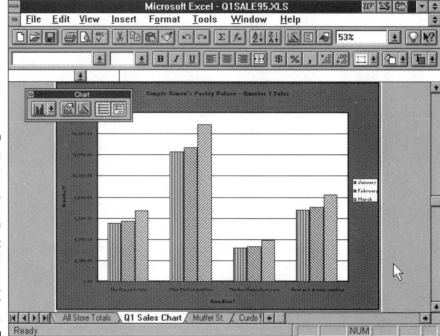

Figure 5-8:
The sample
column
chart after
changing
the color of
the chart
area and
adding a
heavy black
border
around it.

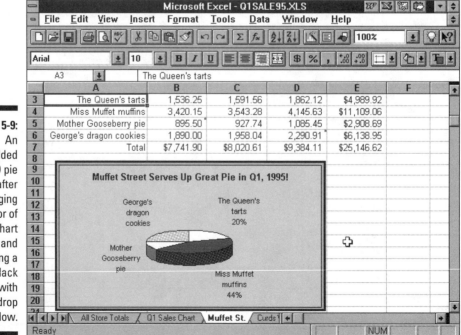

Figure 5-9:
An
embedded
3-D pie
chart after
changing
the color of
the chart
area and
adding a
heavy black
border with
a drop
shadow.

Formatting the chart axes

All chart types, except for the pie and doughnut charts, use two axes: a horizontal x-axis, which normally plots the categories or time across the bottom of the chart; and a vertical y-axis, which plots the values along the left side of the chart. Some charts, such as scatter charts, plot values along the x-axis, too. You can format either (or both) of these axes by changing the pattern, scale, font, number format (if the axis shows values), and alignment.

To format one of the axes, you click somewhere on the axis to select it and then choose Format⇨Selected Axis (Ctrl+1) or the Format Axis shortcut menu command. These commands bring up the Format Axis dialog box that contains Patterns, Scale, Font, Number, and Alignment tabs. Choose the dialog tab you want and then select the new format settings that you want to put in effect.

When formatting the scale of a value axis (in most cases, the y-axis), you can reset the minimum and maximum values used by the value axis. You can also reset the increments (major and minor units) at which tick marks and values appear. You can change these scale settings when you're creating a series of charts that all need to share the same y-axis units so that you (or anyone else for that matter) can successfully compare the chart data.

Figure 5-10 shows the sample column chart after formatting the values on the y-axis and formatting the labels on the x-axis. I chose Bodoni bold as the new font for both the y- and x-axis. I lopped the cents off the dollars shown on the y-axis and added the dollar signs to the numbers by selecting the following Currency format in the Number tab of the Format Axis dialog box:

```
$#,##0_);($#,##0)
```

To change the alignment of the category labels so that they run up the side in line with the columns, I chose this kind of text orientation in the Alignment tab of the Format Axis dialog box.

Formatting the chart titles

As you may recall, in an Excel chart, you can add up to five different titles, including a chart title that appears at the top, up to two Value (Y) Axis titles that appear on the left side with the y-axis, and up to two Category (X) Axis titles that appear along the bottom of the chart with the x-axis. To fancy up any of these titles, you simply click on the title to be formatted and then choose Format⇨Selected Chart Title (Ctrl+1) or the Format Chart Title shortcut menu command. The Format Chart Title dialog box appears, containing Patterns, Font, and Alignment tabs, whose settings you can use as needed to get your various chart titles to stand out in the crowd.

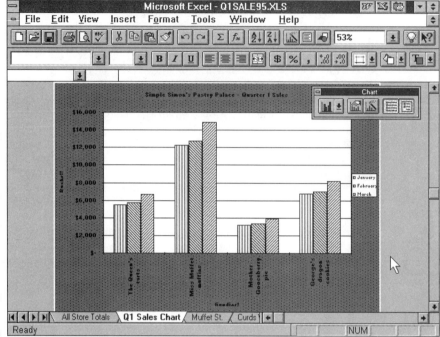

Figure 5-10:
The sample
column
chart after
changing
the number
format and
font of the y-
axis and the
font and
alignment of
the x-axis.

Figure 5-11 shows the sample column chart (yet again), this time after giving facelifts to the chart title, the Value (Y) Axis title, *Bucks!*, and the Category (X) Axis title, *Goodies!*

Formatting the chart legend

Normally, Excel draws a very small chart legend on the right side of the chart. In many charts, you may find that you need to boost the size of the font to be able to make heads or tails of the legend information. In fact, boosting the font size of the legend text is about the only way you can boost the size of the *legend key*, those symbols that correlate the legend text with a particular data series in the chart. Resizing the legend box by dragging the selection handles results only in placing more space in an enlarged legend box, not in increasing the size of the legend key and text.

When formatting a legend, you can change the patterns of the legend box, the font of the legend text, and the placement of the legend in the chart (although you can make this last change manually just by dragging the legend box to the place you want it).

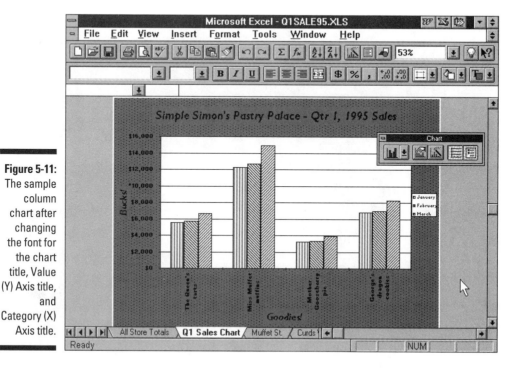

Figure 5-11:
The sample
column
chart after
changing
the font for
the chart
title, Value
(Y) Axis title,
and
Category (X)
Axis title.

In Figure 5-12, you can see the legend for the sample column chart after I made a couple of improvements to it. First, I selected the same color (a light yellow) for the legend box as I had earlier assigned to the plot area. Then I selected a new font in bold and increased its font size. As a result of these font changes, Excel resized the legend key to suit the new font size and gave us a legend that is much easier to read.

Chart Art 100

In addition to the cool enhancements that you can make directly to the various parts of your charts with their shortcut commands, you can also embellish your charts with other graphics. These graphics include those you create in Excel with the Drawing toolbar or those that you import into Excel — whether you create these images in other graphics programs or borrow them from other sources. With the buttons on the Drawing toolbar, you can draw various graphics, create text boxes, and add arrows to your chart. With clip art or images drawn with other graphics programs, you can replace the symbols (bars, dots, lines, and so on) with your graphics to make your charts even more expressive.

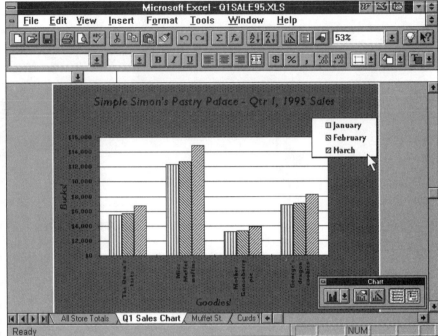

Figure 5-12:
The sample
column
chart after
changing
the color of
the legend
background
and
selecting a
bigger,
bolder font.

Just in case you forgot, the Drawing toolbar can be displayed by choosing it
directly from the shortcut menu.

Drawing your own art

As you learned in *Excel For Dummies*, Excel comes with a Drawing toolbar
equipped with lots of different tools for creating graphics. This Drawing toolbar
supplies you with a palette of simple graphics tools that you can use to beautify
your charts even more. To find out what a particular tool does, just position the
mouse pointer on that tool long enough for the name and a short description of
its function to appear in a little box next to it on the status bar.

Figure 5-13 shows you some of the possibilities offered by the tools on the
Drawing toolbar. In this figure, you see the same embedded 3-D pie chart that
was introduced back in Figure 5-9. In addition to adding a border and a new
color to the chart title to make it stand out — which was done entirely with the
use of its Format Chart Title shortcut menu command — the other major chart
enhancements were all accomplished with the Drawing toolbar, as follows:

✔ First, I physically repositioned the data labels that identify the pie slice and its percentage of the whole. Then, I used the Arc tool in combination with the Arrow tool to create the curved arrows that point from each data label to each pie slice.

✔ To underscore the significance of the largest slice of the pie chart, I used the Text Box tool to create the callout. To tie this text box to the correct area of the chart, I then used the Line and Ellipse tool to draw a circle around the largest pie slice and connect it with the text box.

There are other differences between the 3-D pie chart shown in Figure 5-9 and the one shown in Figure 5-13: In the pie chart in Figure 5-9, Excel placed the largest slice for Miss Muffet Muffins in the lower right-hand corner of the chart. In Figure 5-13, I rotated the chart so that this segment appears on the left side of the chart. I also increased the elevation of the entire pie so that the pie slices are wider. To make these changes, I clicked on the pie itself and then chose the 3-D View command on its shortcut menu. When the Format 3-D View dialog box appeared, I used its rotation and elevation buttons to alter the pie chart's orientation and elevation.

Figure 5-13:
The embedded 3-D pie chart after adding a text box with a circle callout and curved arrows.

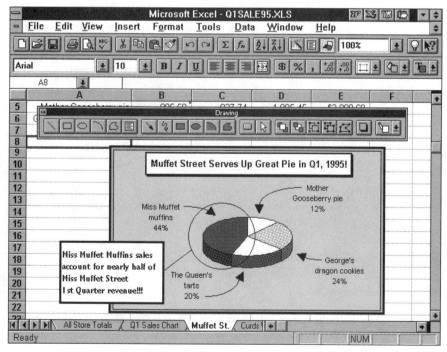

Note that you can also rotate a pie chart by selecting the Format 3-D Pie Group command on the shortcut menu and then changing the number of degrees in the Angle of First Slice text box in the Options tab of the Format 3-D Pie Group dialog box. What's nice about this technique is that as you change the number of degrees, you can see its effect on the pie chart in the thumbnail of the pie chart displayed right on the Options tab.

Borrowing other people's graphics

So what if you're not the artistic type. In fact, you can't even draw a straight line with the Line tool on the Drawing toolbar! Not to worry. For those of you who were not born artists, there's always clip art! And nowadays, you can get your hands on all sorts of ready-made clip art images (for cheap, or in many cases, for free) that you can bring into an Excel worksheet. If you use other Microsoft programs like Word for Windows and PowerPoint (which come with Excel when you purchase or upgrade to Microsoft Office), you already have access to lots of clip art for your Excel worksheets and charts because these programs come with a good number of ready-to-use images.

In Excel, you can replace the symbols representing each data series in the chart with the clip art or, if you're a budding Picasso, with art that you create in other Windows graphics programs. The best way to see how simple this is to do is to follow along with the procedure for replacing the tired old colored bars in a column chart with clip art supplied by Microsoft PowerPoint.

Figure 5-14 shows the original embedded column chart. This chart compares the average salaries for professional men versus professional women in three different age groups. (Please note that I made up all these salary figures. *Any* resemblance between these figures and reality is purely coincidental.) Normally, this type of chart would use a legend that explains to the viewer that blue bars represent the men's salaries and pink bars represent the women's salaries. In this chart, however, I purposely left off the legend because I knew I was going to replace the blue bars with a picture of a typical businessman and the pink bars with a picture of a typical businesswoman.

Inserting graphics into a chart

To replace the bars representing the men's salaries in the column chart, follow these steps:

1. **Double-click somewhere on the column chart to select it (because this chart is embedded in the worksheet with the charted data).**

2. **Click on one of the bars representing the men's average salaries to select this data series in the chart.**

3. **Start PowerPoint or, if it's already running, switch to it.**

   If you use Excel as part of Microsoft Office, Office attaches its toolbar to the Excel menu bar so that you can start PowerPoint by clicking on the Microsoft PowerPoint button, the third from the left in Figure 5-14.

4. **Select Blank Presentation in the PowerPoint dialog box and then choose the AutoLayout that uses Text & Clip Art (the first one in the last row with a cartoon of some guy) in the New Slide dialog box.**

5. **Double-click on the button with the picture of the guy holding up his arms or choose Clip Art on the Insert pull-down menu to open the Microsoft ClipArt Gallery dialog box.**

6. **Choose the picture you want to use in this gallery and then click on OK.**

   For this example, I chose the Man with Briefcase in the People category.

7. **With the picture still selected in PowerPoint (indicated by the selection rectangles all around it), choose Edit⇨Copy or press Ctrl+C.**

8. **Switch back to Excel.**

   If you don't need any more PowerPoint clip art, you can switch back by exiting the program without saving the presentation.

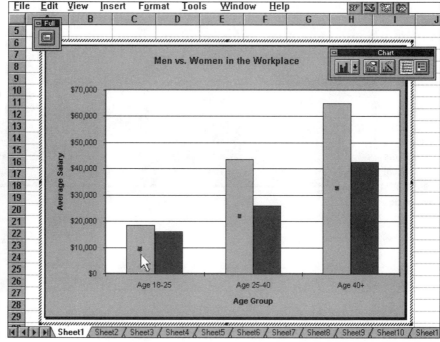

Figure 5-14:
A plain old column chart comparing the average salaries of professional men (the bars on the left) and professional women (the bars on the right).

9. Once back in Excel, with the men's salaries data series still selected in the chart, choose Edit⇨Paste or press Ctrl+V.

As soon as you select the Paste command, Excel replaces those plain old bars in the column chart with the picture of the businessman with a briefcase, as shown in Figure 5-15. Note that Excel automatically stretches the image as required to reach the height of the bars that it replaces.

To replace the bars in the pie chart representing the women's average salaries, I followed the same procedure as described in the preceding Tootorial. This time, however, I copied and pasted the picture called Women with Binder from PowerPoint. Figure 5-16 shows the result.

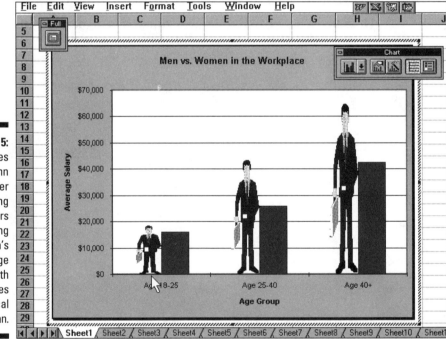

Figure 5-15:
The salaries column chart after replacing the bars representing the men's average salaries with the pictures of a typical businessman.

When you replace a data series with clip art or other graphics copied via the Clipboard, Excel gives you the option of stretching the picture in the chart as required to reach the appropriate places on the value (y) axis or stacking it. Figure 5-17 shows the same 3-D pie chart after switching from stretched to stacked graphics. When you use stacked graphics, Excel represents the values in each data point with the whole graphic or parts of the graphic, depending on what the value is. As you can see in Figure 5-17, making this change results in some headless men and women in the final chart.

To make this change, you need to select each data series in the chart and choose Format⇨Selected Data Series or the Format Data Series shortcut menu. Then choose the Stack radio button on the Patterns tab of the Format Data Series dialog box. If you want Excel to redraw the picture at each major tick mark on the value (y) axis, choose the Stack and Scale to radio button, instead.

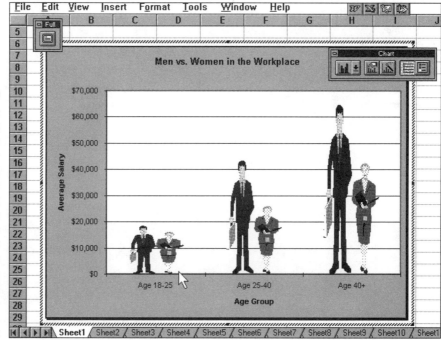

Figure 5-16:
The salaries column chart after replacing the bars representing women's average salaries with the pictures of a typical business-woman.

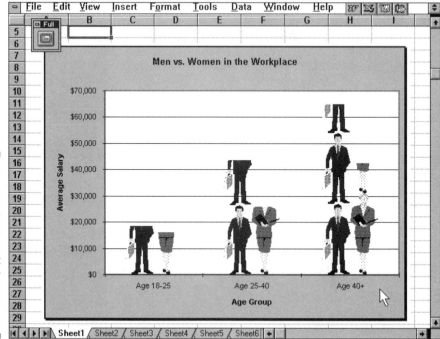

Figure 5-17:
The salaries
column
chart after
changing
the Picture
Format
setting for
the graphics
from Stretch
to Stack.

Chapter 6

Data Sorting, Filtering, and Subtotaling Like the Pros

*T*his chapter takes up where Chapter 8 in *Excel For Dummies* leaves off. After a quick review of the basics of sorting and filtering data in a database, this chapter introduces you to the fascinating subject of advanced filtering. Advanced filtering not only lets you set up complex criteria for filtering records of a database, but it also enables you to copy these filtered records to another place in the worksheet, where you can save them as a new database, print them, or whatever. After you get the lowdown on advanced filtering, you are introduced to a fun new feature in Excel 5: creating automatic subtotals and totals within a list of financial or other types of numerical data.

It Takes All Sorts . . .

Sorting refers to the process of rearranging rows of data — called *records* in a bona fide database — in a worksheet according to the entries in a particular column (or columns, if sorting by more than one key). For example, if you have a list of client names and addresses entered in a first-come, first-served order and you need to sort them alphabetically by company name, you can have Excel sort the list in an ascending (A – Z) order on the column that contains the names of the companies. In sorting the list, Excel actually rearranges the data in the rows of the worksheet as it alphabetizes the company names that are entered in the list.

When sorting a list on a column that contains duplicate entries, you normally designate a second column whose entries determine the final order of the duplicates. (If you don't care, Excel keeps the data with duplicate entries in the order in which they were originally entered.) Should the second column also contain its own duplicates, you designate a third column as the determiner and tiebreaker for those duplicates. In really complex sorts, where three key columns are not sufficient to resolve all the duplicate ordering questions, you are stuck sorting the same data more than once.

Cleaning up a sort

Because sorting actually involves moving around the data that you may have worked so hard to enter in a worksheet, you need to be clear on what to do when disaster strikes. Before undertaking any sorting, save the workbook so that you have an original copy of the file.

Remember that the Undo feature can fix a messed-up list of data (unless the list of data is so humongous that you get a warning that Undo can't undo). To use Undo, however, you can't get so rattled by the mess you've made on-screen that you panic and try to fix the situation by performing some other Excel command, such as sorting the data a second time on some other column or in some other order. If you can't use Undo to restore pristine order to the mangled data you sorted, close the messed-up workbook without saving the changes and immediately open up the original copy of the workbook — the one that you remembered to save before you began all this sorting nonsense.

Some people, including yours truly, also guard against messing up a large database by adding record numbers to the original database before *any* sorting takes place. To add record numbers, just insert a new column at the very beginning of the database by positioning the cell pointer anywhere in the first column and choosing Insert⇨Columns. Then use the AutoFill feature to insert the record numbers in this new column. Remember to enter **1** in the first row and **2** in the second row and then select both cells and drag down with the Fill handle to have AutoFill enter the record numbers.

After adding record numbers, you can then sort the database on any keys that you desire. If you do mess up (or even if you don't, but you prefer using the database in its original order), you can then restore the records to their original order by sorting the database in ascending order (0 – 9, in the case of numbers) on the column containing the record numbers.

Hide the column with record numbers (using the Format⇨Column⇨Hide command) when you don't want to have them appear on-screen or when you don't want to include them in a printed report of the database.

Sorting data on more than one column

1. **Position the cell pointer somewhere in the list (or database) to be sorted.**

2. **Choose Data⇨Sort on the pull-down menus. Excel will automatically select all the cells in the list or database and display the Sort dialog box (like the one shown in Figure 6-1).**

3. **If the list starts with a row of column names (as does a database) that you don't want sorted with the rows below because they identify the data in each column, make sure that the Header Row radio button at the bottom of the dialog box below My List Has is selected.**

   If, however, the list has no such row and you want the entire list sorted, be sure that the No Header Row radio button is selected instead.

4. **In the Sort By drop-down list box, choose the column letter or column name whose entries will determine the new order of the list.**

   If you want the list sorted in descending order (Z–A or 9–0) instead of the default ascending order (A–Z or 0–9), be sure to choose the Descending radio button next to this drop-down list box.

5. **If the column you selected in the Sort By drop-down list box contains duplicates and you want to sort these duplicates by the entries in a second column, choose the Then By drop-down list box and select this column name or column letter.**

   Again, if you want these duplicates arranged in descending order, be sure to choose the Descending radio button next to this drop-down list box.

6. **If the second column you selected in the Then By drop-down list box contains duplicates and you want to sort these duplicates by the entries in yet a third column, choose the Then By drop-down list box and select this column name or column letter.**

   If you want these duplicates arranged in descending order, be sure to choose the Descending radio button next to this drop-down list box.

7. **When you're finished defining the columns to use in sorting the list of data, choose the OK button or press Enter to have Excel go ahead and rearrange the selected rows or records in the list.**

Figure 6-2 shows the sample client database after sorting its records alphabetically first by state, then by city, and finally by the client's last name. As you can see, this means that records with duplicate states (such as AZ) get sorted by city, and records with duplicate cities (such as London, AZ) get sorted by last name.

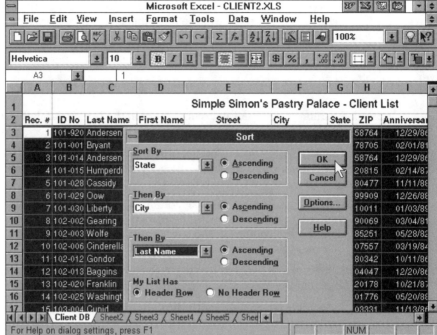

Figure 6-1:
The Sort
dialog box,
where you
choose the
order of
your sort.

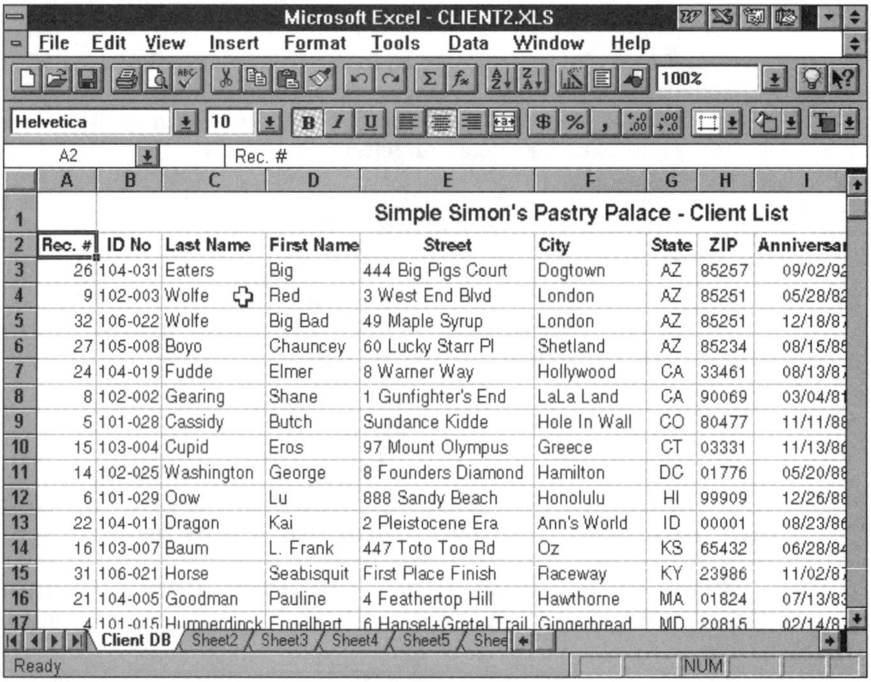

Figure 6-2:
Sorting the
client list
alphabetically
by state,
city, and
last name.

If there are duplicate client last names that need to be sorted in the same city and state — as there are in the sample database (Red Wolfe and Big Bad Wolfe) — you have to sort the database in two operations. To determine which fields (columns) to use in each sort, you first need to determine the order of the key columns from the most general to the most specific. In this example, the order is

State

City

Last Name

First Name

In the first operation, you sort on the three most specific fields (the ones at the end of the list above):

City

Last Name

First Name

Then after sorting the database in ascending order on these three columns, you sort the database again, this time on the most general field (the one at the beginning of this list):

State

Of course, you can use this method of ordering the key columns to determine which column should be used in each consecutive sort operation with more than four key columns (you can use as many as you can keep track of). Always remember to work in groups of three because three is the maximum number of columns you can sort in each operation.

Don't forget the Sort Ascending and Sort Descending buttons on the Standard toolbar when doing the most simple sorting of lists on a single column. To use these buttons, simply position the cell pointer anywhere in the column of data you want to sort and then click on the appropriate sort button.

Filtering Out the Junk

If you ever attended my class on database management, you would have heard my spiel on the difference between data and information in a database. In case you're the least little bit interested, it goes like this: A database consumes vast quantities (à la Coneheads) of *data,* which simply represent all the stuff that everybody in the office wants stored on a given subject (employees, sales, clients, you name it). For instance, suppose that you're keeping a database on the sales transactions made by your customers. This database could very well track such stuff as the customers' identification numbers, names, addresses, telephone numbers, whether or not they have a charge account with the store, the maximum amount they can charge, the purchases they've made (including the dates and amounts), and whether there are accounts due (or overdue).

Now, this vast quantity of data stored in the customer database is not to be confused with the *information* that particular people in the office want out of the database. For example, suppose that you're working in the marketing department and you're about to introduce a line of expensive household items that you want to advertise. You want to limit the advertising to those customers who have a charge account with the store and have purchased at least $5,000 of merchandise in the last six months. Use the *data* provided in the database to supply the *information* you need to weed out the customers from the list.

On the other hand, suppose that you work in the accounting department and you need to send out nasty notices to all the customers who have charge accounts that are more than 90 days past due. Now you want only the data identifying those customers whose accounts are overdue. You could care less about what was actually purchased. All you care about is getting a hold of these folks and convincing them to pay up. You again use the *data* provided in the database to supply the *information* you need to weed out the customers you need from the list.

From these simple examples, it should be clear that the data that supply information to one group in the company at a particular time is often not the same data that supply information to another group. In other words, for most people, the database dispenses information only when you are able to filter out the stuff you currently don't want to see, leaving behind just the stuff you are interested in.

Filtering the database to leave behind only the information you want to work with is exactly the procedure that you follow in Excel. In Chapter 8 in *Excel For Dummies,* you learned how to use the new 5.0 AutoFilter feature to remove the display of unwanted records and leave behind the ones you want to see. Most of the time, the AutoFilter feature is just the thing you need for displaying only the information of interest in the database. There are, however, a couple of limitations to the AutoFilter feature that may force you to learn how to do what

Microsoft refers to as "advanced filtering" in your database. For example, you need to use advanced filtering to filter the database when you use computer criteria (such as when you want to see all the records where the entry in the Sales column is twice the amount in the Owed column), or when you need to save a copy of the filtered database in a different part of the worksheet.

Advanced filtering without fear

When you use AutoFilter, you don't use the drop-down list boxes that appear next to the field names. Instead of selecting the filtering criteria in the drop-down list box or entering it in the Custom AutoFilter dialog box, you need to create a so-called criteria range somewhere on the worksheet containing the database to be filtered (preferably, right above the database so that the filtering criteria can't get in the way of database records).

To create a *criteria range*, you enter the names of the fields whose entries are to be used in the filtering and then enter the values (text, numeric, or formulas) that are to be used in the filtering. When setting up the criteria for filtering the database, you can either create comparison criteria or computed criteria.

Comparatively speaking

Figure 6-3 shows a comparison criteria range (in the cell range B1:C2) that compares the entries in the Daily Sales field (in the cell range A4:G64) by using a formula that filters out the sales that are less than $50 and greater than $70. After you perform the filtering operation, you will be left with a database that gives you daily sales in the $50 – $70 range.

Defining a criteria range

To create a criteria range that includes only the Daily Sales figures between $50 and $70, do the following:

1. **Position the cell pointer on a cell anywhere within the Daily Sales database and choose Data❘Filter❘Advanced Filter.**

   The Advanced Filter dialog box (similar to the one shown in Figure 6-4) appears, with all the data in the Daily Sales list highlighted.

2. **Check the address of the range shown in the List Range text box. If this range includes the entire database (as is usually the case), choose the Criteria Range text box.**

   If the range does not include the entire database, select it first and then choose the Criteria Range text box.

3. **Drag through the cells in the worksheet that contain your filter criteria to select them and enter their range address (in absolute notation) in the Criteria Range text box.**

4. **Click on the OK button or press Enter to filter out all the records that do not meet the criteria listed in the Criteria Range.**

After you select the OK button in the Advanced Filter dialog box, Excel goes through each record in the database and compares the entries in the column (or columns) referred to in the comparison criteria. All records that do not meet these criteria are no longer displayed in the database. Don't worry, the records are merely hidden and can be redisplayed in an instant. Figure 6-5 shows the results of filtering the Daily Sales list with the criteria contained in the Criteria Range text box shown in Figure 6-4.

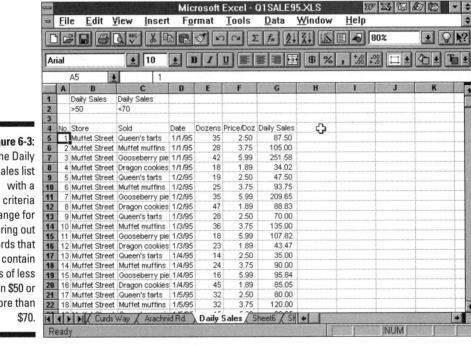

Figure 6-3:
The Daily
Sales list
with a
criteria
range for
filtering out
records that
contain
sales of less
than $50 or
more than
$70.

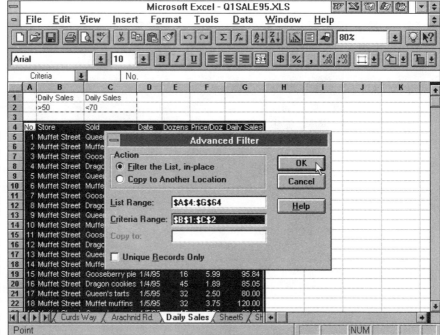

Figure 6-4:
The
Advanced
Filter dialog
box, where
you enter
the criteria
range
($B$1:$C$2)
for filtering
the Daily
Sales list.

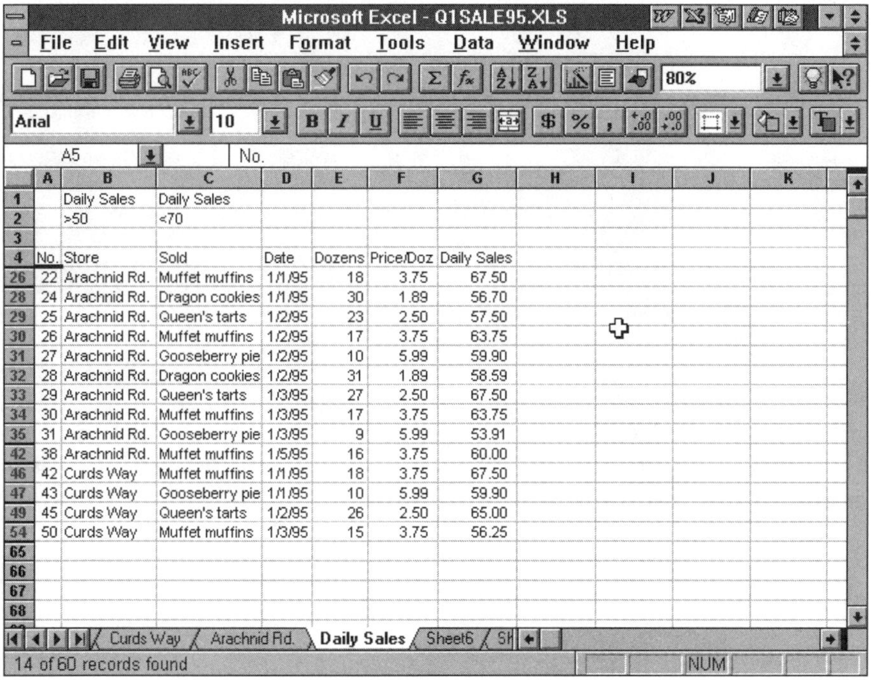

Figure 6-5:
The Daily
Sales list
after
filtering out
records that
contain
sales of
less than
$50 or more
than $70.

Only the unique need apply!

To filter out duplicate rows or records that match your criteria, choose the Unique Records Only check box in the Advanced Filter dialog box before you start the filtering operation. You can remove the display of all duplicate records from a list or database by choosing this check box and also clearing the Criteria Range text box before you choose OK or press Enter.

After filtering a database, you may feel that you haven't gotten the expected results — for example, no records are listed under the field names that you thought should have several. You can bring back all the records in the database by choosing Data⇨Filter⇨Show All. Now you can fiddle with the criteria in the Criteria Range text box and try the whole advanced filtering thing all over again.

QBE made fun (??) and easy

Some folks (none that you would hang out with, I'm sure) refer to the little table that appears after you enter the filtering criteria into a database as QBE (query by example). In the QBE universe, the position of the criteria in relation to the field names in the table determines whether you are looking at an AND or an OR condition.

Multiple criteria in the same *row* form an AND condition. Suppose that you have the following QBE:

City	Sales
Milwaukee	>5000

With this QBE, you have created the following filtering criteria:

City = Milwaukee AND Sales > 5000

If, however, you stack multiple criteria all in the same *column* in succeeding rows, you have created an OR condition. Suppose that you have the following QBE:

City

Milwaukee

Indianapolis

With this QBE, you have created the following filtering criteria:

City = Milwaukee OR City = Indianapolis

And of course, when you have some criteria in the same row and others in the same column, you have created an AND/OR condition.

The real trick to working with a QBE table in Excel is that you must always be sure to include all the cells containing AND or OR criteria when defining the criteria range in the Advanced Filter dialog box. Take it from me, it's easy to forget to increase or decrease the size of the criteria range after fiddling with the criteria by adding or removing an OR or AND condition (I've done this thousands of times). And then, of course, when you use the Data⇨Filter⇨Advanced Criteria command with the wrong criteria range selected, you don't get the expected results.

Computed criteria at your service

Computed criteria are those that evaluate the values in a particular column of a database or list against a value not actually entered in the list or database itself. To create computed criteria, you set up the formula that indicates which column to evaluate (as well as computes the value to be used in the evaluation). When setting up this computed criteria formula, you need to keep the following guidelines in mind:

- ✔ If you enter a label above this computed criteria formula in the criteria range, it must NOT (I repeat, NOT) be the same as any of the column headings or field names used in your database. Use some other text, any other text, for the criteria label.

- ✔ The computed criteria formula must be one that returns a logical value (you know, TRUE or FALSE). In other words, Excel needs to compare some value in the list or database to another computed value either in the formula or in the workbook. To return a logical value, you must use the =, >, <, >=, <=, or <> operators.

- ✔ The computed criteria formula must refer to at least one of the columns in the list or database itself (although the computation that the entries in this column are evaluated against doesn't have to refer to any data in the list). To refer to a column, you select the cell with the very first entry (right beneath the field or column name). Or you can enter its cell address in the formula, using relative cell addresses (such as B15 rather than $B$15). The use of relative cell addresses enables Excel to compare all the entries in that column against the computed value as it performs the filter operation.

Figures 6-6 and 6-7 show an example of how you use computed criteria to filter the Daily Sales list. The only records displayed are those where the Daily Sales entry is greater than or equal to 30 times the price of the particular pastry item. To filter the list based on that criteria, I created the following computed criteria formula in cell B2, as shown in the formula bar in Figure 6-6:

```
=G5>=30*F5
```

This formula begins with the cell reference G5 because it is the one that contains the first daily sales entry in the list. It then uses the greater than operator (>) to compare the value in this cell with a computed value returned by the 30*F5 part of the formula. This part of the formula computes the comparative value by multiplying the first price entry (in cell F5) in the list by 30.

Because the addresses of the cell references — G5 (the first sales entry) and F5 (the first price entry) — in the computed criteria formula are both relative, Excel adjusts them as the advanced filter operation moves down the rows of the sales list. Excel uses this formula to decide which records to hide and which to display. Figure 6-7 shows the result of performing this advanced filter operation on the Daily Sales list.

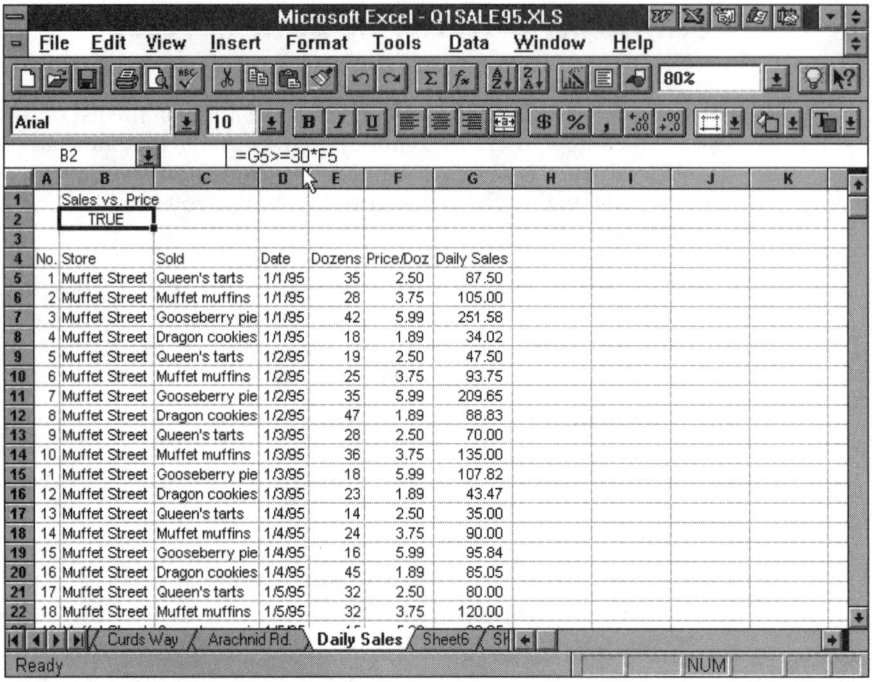
Microsoft Excel - Q1SALE95.XLS
File Edit View Insert Format Tools Data Window Help
80%
Arial 10
B2 =G5>=30*F5
A B C D E F G H I J K
1 Sales vs. Price
2 TRUE
3
4 No. Store Sold Date Dozens Price/Doz Daily Sales
5 1 Muffet Street Queen's tarts 1/1/95 35 2.50 87.50
6 2 Muffet Street Muffet muffins 1/1/95 28 3.75 105.00
7 3 Muffet Street Gooseberry pie 1/1/95 42 5.99 251.58
8 4 Muffet Street Dragon cookies 1/1/95 18 1.89 34.02
9 5 Muffet Street Queen's tarts 1/2/95 19 2.50 47.50
10 6 Muffet Street Muffet muffins 1/2/95 25 3.75 93.75
11 7 Muffet Street Gooseberry pie 1/2/95 35 5.99 209.65
12 8 Muffet Street Dragon cookies 1/2/95 47 1.89 88.83
13 9 Muffet Street Queen's tarts 1/3/95 28 2.50 70.00
14 10 Muffet Street Muffet muffins 1/3/95 36 3.75 135.00
15 11 Muffet Street Gooseberry pie 1/3/95 18 5.99 107.82
16 12 Muffet Street Dragon cookies 1/3/95 23 1.89 43.47
17 13 Muffet Street Queen's tarts 1/4/95 14 2.50 35.00
18 14 Muffet Street Muffet muffins 1/4/95 24 3.75 90.00
19 15 Muffet Street Gooseberry pie 1/4/95 16 5.99 95.84
20 16 Muffet Street Dragon cookies 1/4/95 45 1.89 85.05
21 17 Muffet Street Queen's tarts 1/5/95 32 2.50 80.00
22 18 Muffet Street Muffet muffins 1/5/95 32 3.75 120.00
Curds Way Arachnid Rd. Daily Sales Sheet6
Ready NUM

Figure 6-6: The Daily Sales list with the computed criteria formula for displaying only the records where the sales are greater than 30 times the price of the item.

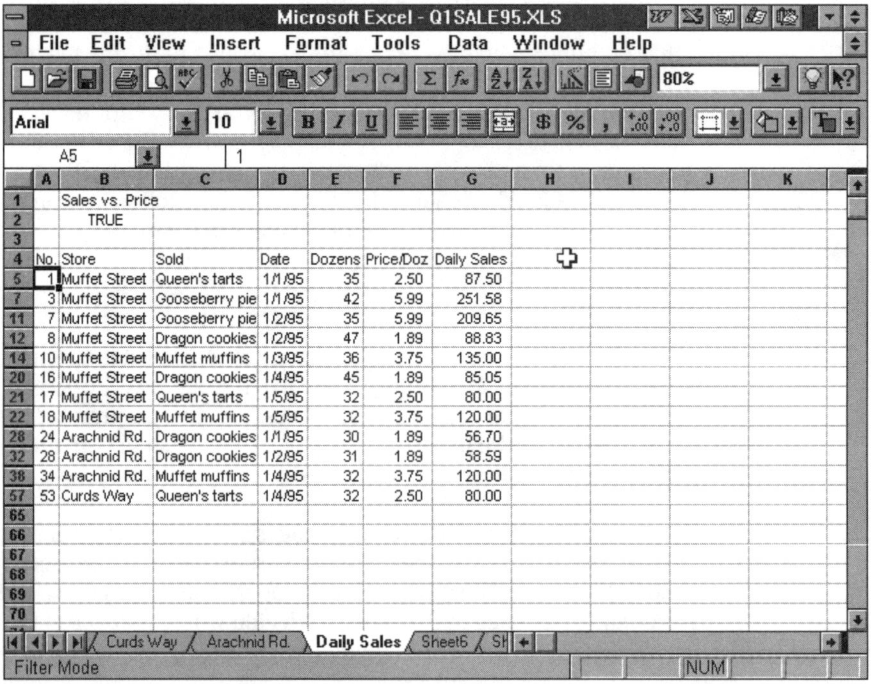
Microsoft Excel - Q1SALE95.XLS
File Edit View Insert Format Tools Data Window Help
80%
Arial 10
A5 1
A B C D E F G H I J K
1 Sales vs. Price
2 TRUE
3
4 No. Store Sold Date Dozens Price/Doz Daily Sales
5 1 Muffet Street Queen's tarts 1/1/95 35 2.50 87.50
7 3 Muffet Street Gooseberry pie 1/1/95 42 5.99 251.58
11 7 Muffet Street Gooseberry pie 1/2/95 35 5.99 209.65
12 8 Muffet Street Dragon cookies 1/2/95 47 1.89 88.83
14 10 Muffet Street Muffet muffins 1/3/95 36 3.75 135.00
20 16 Muffet Street Dragon cookies 1/4/95 45 1.89 85.05
21 17 Muffet Street Queen's tarts 1/5/95 32 2.50 80.00
22 18 Muffet Street Muffet muffins 1/5/95 32 3.75 120.00
28 24 Arachnid Rd. Dragon cookies 1/1/95 30 1.89 56.70
32 28 Arachnid Rd. Dragon cookies 1/2/95 31 1.89 58.59
38 34 Arachnid Rd. Muffet muffins 1/4/95 32 3.75 120.00
57 53 Curds Way Queen's tarts 1/4/95 32 2.50 80.00
65
66
67
68
69
70
Curds Way Arachnid Rd. Daily Sales Sheet6
Filter Mode NUM

Figure 6-7: The Daily Sales list after filtering it so that only the records where the sales are 30 times the price of the item are listed.

Copying the filtered records to another place in the worksheet

When introducing advanced filtering earlier in this chapter, I mentioned that one of the times to use it rather than the AutoFilter feature is when you need to copy the set of records that meet the filter criteria into another place in the worksheet. Normally, the Advanced Filter feature works just like AutoFilter to hide the display of all records that don't match the filter criteria (which can later be redisplayed by choosing Show All on the Filter submenu of the Data menu).

Copying matching records elsewhere

1. **Create the criteria range and then select a cell in the list to be filtered.**

2. **Choose Data⇨Filter⇨Advanced Filter on the pull-down menus.**

3. **Choose the Copy to Another Location radio button (thereby deselecting the Filter the List, in-place radio button).**

4. **Select the range of the list to be filtered and the criteria range to be used in filtering the list in the List Range and Criteria Range text boxes, respectively, as you normally do.**

5. **Choose the Copy to text option and then select the first cell in the range where you want the copy of the filtered data to appear.**

   This cell must be on the same worksheet as the list, and you need to be sure that none of this range contains any data that you wouldn't want overwritten by the copy of the filtered data. The safest place to copy the range is somewhere in the blank rows beneath the list or database, assuming that you never put any other tables of data, charts, graphics, or anything else in these rows.

6. **Click on the OK button or press Enter to filter the database and copy the matching records.**

Figure 6-8 shows the filtered records that have been copied from the Daily Sales list to the area right below the list (starting in row 66). To let you see the criteria used in this filtering operation, I split the workbook window into two panes. In the top pane, you can see the criteria range (cell range B1:B2) that filters out any records where the Daily Sales are less than $100. In the lower pane, you can see the copied filtered records in the cell range A66:G76. When Excel copies records to another part of a worksheet, it copies only the values in the original list, not the formulas (as though you had chosen the Values radio button in the Paste Special dialog box). Therefore, the formulas in the Daily Sales column that multiply the number in the Dozens column by the number in the Price/Doz column do not appear in the copies in the cell range A67:G76.

	A	B	C	D	E	F	G	H	I	J	K	
1		Daily Sales										
2		>=100										
3												
63	59	Curds Way	Gooseberry pie	1/5/95	14	5.99	83.86					
64	60	Curds Way	Dragon cookies	1/5/95	26	1.89	49.14					
65												
66	No.	Store	Sold	Date	Dozens	Price/Doz	Daily Sales					
67	2	Muffet Street	Muffet muffins	1/1/95	28	3.75	105.00					
68	3	Muffet Street	Gooseberry pie	1/1/95	42	5.99	251.58					
69	7	Muffet Street	Gooseberry pie	1/2/95	35	5.99	209.65					
70	10	Muffet Street	Muffet muffins	1/3/95	36	3.75	135.00					
71	11	Muffet Street	Gooseberry pie	1/3/95	18	5.99	107.82					
72	18	Muffet Street	Muffet muffins	1/5/95	32	3.75	120.00					
73	34	Arachnid Rd.	Muffet muffins	1/2/95	32	3.75	120.00					
74	47	Curds Way	Gooseberry pie	1/2/95	18	5.99	107.82					
75	54	Curds Way	Muffet muffins	1/4/95	27	3.75	101.25					
76	55	Curds Way	Gooseberry pie	1/4/95	18	5.99	107.82					
77												
78												
79												
80												
81												

Figure 6-8: Copying filtered records beneath the Daily Sales list.

If you perform an advanced filtering operation by copying the records to another part of the worksheet and then perform another advanced filtering operation by using the same list and new criteria, be sure that you change the cell range in the Copy to text box before you perform the second filtering operation. If you don't change the range, you will replace, and in some cases add to, the records copied during the first filtering operation with the records copied during the second filtering operation.

After you copy filtered records to another part of the worksheet (known in techno-circles as a *subset* of the list or database), you can sort them, chart them, print them, or even delete them when you no longer have any use for them. The easiest way to work on data in a subset is to move it to another worksheet in the workbook.

Moving subset data to another worksheet

1. Select the copied records (the subset).

2. Choose Edit⇨Cut, choose the Cut command on the cells' shortcut menu, click on the Cut button on the Standard toolbar, or you can even press Ctrl+X.

3. Click on the tab of the blank worksheet you want to move the records to.

4. **Select the first cell of the range in the new worksheet where you want the copied records to appear.**

5. **Choose Edit⇨Paste, choose the Paste command on the cells' shortcut menu, click on the Paste button on the Standard toolbar, or for heaven's sake, press Ctrl+V.**

Figure 6-9 shows the records originally copied beneath the Daily Sales list in Figure 6-8 after moving them to a new worksheet (renamed Sales +100). I sorted the records in alphabetical order first on the Sold column and then on the Store column. Finally, the duplicates in the Store column are sorted on the Daily Sales column in descending (highest to lowest) order.

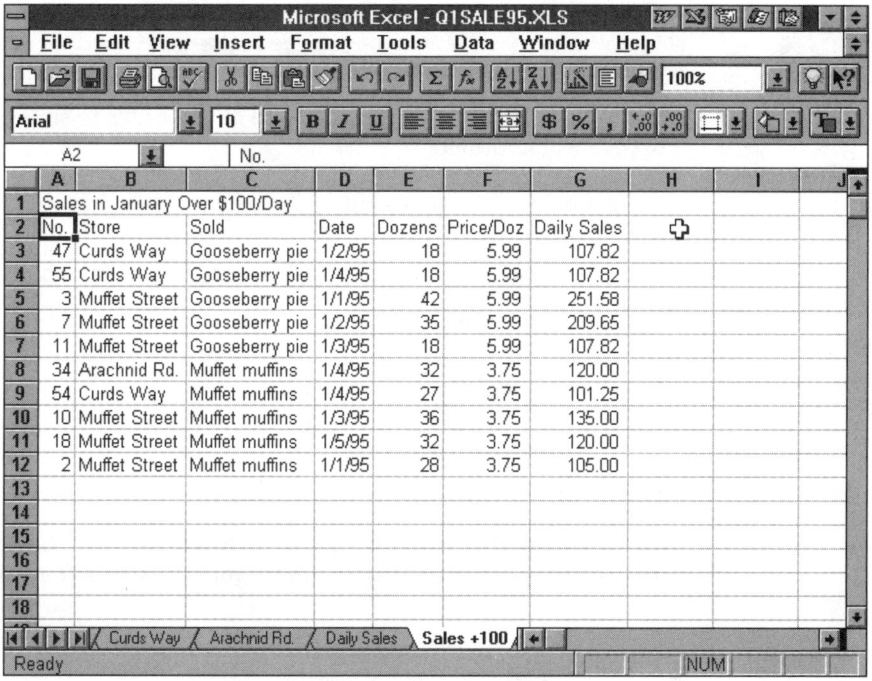

	A	B	C	D	E	F	G	H	I	J
1	Sales in January Over $100/Day									
2	No.	Store	Sold	Date	Dozens	Price/Doz	Daily Sales			
3	47	Curds Way	Gooseberry pie	1/2/95	18	5.99	107.82			
4	55	Curds Way	Gooseberry pie	1/4/95	18	5.99	107.82			
5	3	Muffet Street	Gooseberry pie	1/1/95	42	5.99	251.58			
6	7	Muffet Street	Gooseberry pie	1/2/95	35	5.99	209.65			
7	11	Muffet Street	Gooseberry pie	1/3/95	18	5.99	107.82			
8	34	Arachnid Rd.	Muffet muffins	1/4/95	32	3.75	120.00			
9	54	Curds Way	Muffet muffins	1/4/95	27	3.75	101.25			
10	10	Muffet Street	Muffet muffins	1/3/95	36	3.75	135.00			
11	18	Muffet Street	Muffet muffins	1/5/95	32	3.75	120.00			
12	2	Muffet Street	Muffet muffins	1/1/95	28	3.75	105.00			
13										
14										
15										
16										
17										
18										

Figure 6-9:
Copying
filtered
records to
their own
worksheet.

Instant Subtotals!

Excel 5 makes it really easy to summarize financial and numerical data in a list or database with its new Automatic Subtotal feature. This feature enables you to subtotal categories in a list or database without actually having to go to all the trouble of adding SUM formulas. Before you can use this feature, however, the data in your list must be organized as follows:

- ✔ Organize the data into a list that begins with a row of column labels (like field names in a database).

- ✔ Enter the rows of data (or sort them with Data➪Sort) so that items to be subtotaled are grouped together. For example, to subtotal sales by store, you need to arrange the data in alphabetical order by the store's name. To subtotal sales by salesperson, you need to arrange the data in alphabetical order by the salesperson's name.

To use the Automatic Subtotal command you must be able to supply three pieces of pertinent information:

- ✔ The column for which you want subtotals

- ✔ Whether you want the values to be totaled with the SUM function or you want to use some other function, such as COUNT, AVERAGE, or STDDEV

- ✔ The column containing the values to be summed or averaged

Using the Automatic Subtotal feature

To see how easy it is to use the Automatic Subtotal feature (and I mean *easy*), follow along with the steps for creating summaries with subtotals and the grand total for the Daily Sales list:

1. **Start by sorting the data in the list to be subtotaled with the Data➪Sort command so that the categories you're going to subtotal are all grouped together.**

   For this example, I sorted the list on three columns: Store (ascending), Sold (ascending), and Daily Sales (descending).

2. **Position the cell pointer in one of the cells in the list and choose Data➪Subtotals.**

   The Subtotal dialog box, similar to the one shown in Figure 6-10, opens.

3. **Check over the all the entries in the Subtotal dialog box to make sure that the settings are correct and then choose OK or press Enter.**

   In the At Each Change in list box, make sure that the column containing the groups on which subtotals are to be calculated is selected. In the Use Function list box, make sure that Sum is displayed when you want totals.

In the A̲dd Subtotal to list box, make sure that the check boxes are selected for all the columns whose values you want summed or averaged. To
replace rather than add to existing subtotals, make sure that the Replace
C̲urrent Subtotals check box is selected. To have Excel put a hard page
break after every subtotal, make sure that the P̲age Break Between Groups
check box is selected. To have Excel calculate a grand total for all groups
in the list, make sure that the S̲ummary Below check box is selected.

Figure 6-11 shows the result of selecting the Store column as the one containing
the groups to be subtotaled and the Daily Sales column with the values to be
subtotaled. In Figure 6-11, you can see only the subtotal for sales made at the
first store location at Arachnid Rd. To see the subtotals for the three other
stores, as well as the grand total, you have to scroll down the list.

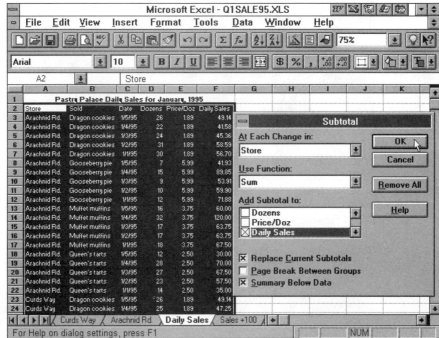

Figure 6-10:
The Subtotal
dialog box,
where you
choose the
settings
for the
Automatic
Subtotal
feature.

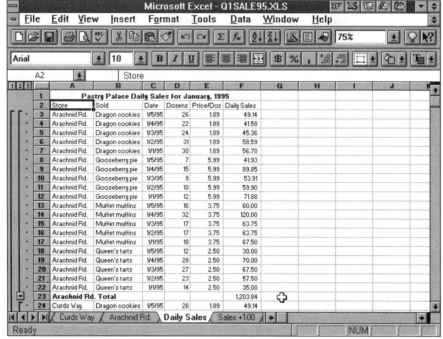

Figure 6-11:
The Daily
Sales list
showing the
subtotals of
the sales
made at the
Arachnid
Rd. store.

When subtotaling a list, you can choose more than one column to summarize and more than one summary function. To choose multiple columns to be summarized, select the check box for each column in the Add Subtotal to list box in the Subtotal dialog box. To use more than one summary function, use the Data⇨Subtotals command multiple times on the same data list, each time selecting a different function in the Use Function drop-down list box in the Subtotal dialog box. Be sure that after summarizing the data list the first time, you deselect the Replace Current Subtotals check box each time you summarize the list with a different summary function.

When you use the Automatic Subtotal feature, Excel outlines your list by adding outline symbols on the left side of the workbook window (see Figure 6-11). You can use these outline symbols — the little [1],[2], and [3] buttons at the top and the [–] button and vertical lines that show what rows are included in the outline — to hide and redisplay certain parts of the outline. (To learn all about outlines in Excel, see Chapter 8.)

Click on the numbered outline buttons to display a particular outline level. In the Daily Sales list, you would click on the [1] button to display only the first level with the row showing the grand total; you would click on the [2] button to dis-play up to the second level with the grand total row and the rows with the sub-totals; and you would click on the [3] button to display up to the third level with all the rows in the list.

Because Automatic Subtotals use outlines and outlines work by hiding columns of the worksheet, make sure that you don't place any data in the same rows as the subtotaled list if you need to be able to see the data at all times when working in that particular worksheet.

Subtotals within subtotals?!

You can use the Automatic Subtotal feature to create subtotals for smaller groups within a list that already contains subtotals. For example, in the Daily Sales list, you may want to have totals for each category of pastry sold at each store location. To create this new subtotal category within the already subtotaled store sections of the list, choose Data⇨Subtotals a second time. This time, however, choose the settings shown in the Subtotal dialog box in Figure 6-12.

The only changes made to the settings in this dialog box this time around are to the At Each Change in text box, which now contains the Sold column rather than the Store column, and to the Replace Current Subtotals check box, which is now deselected. These changes ensure that the subtotals for each category of pastry sold are added to the subtotals for each store location rather than replacing the store subtotals with the category sold subtotals. (Remember that the Daily Sales list was sorted first by Store and then by Sold.)

Figure 6-13 shows the results of subtotaling the Daily Sales list a second time for the Sold column. As you can see from this figure, Excel added totals for each group of goodies (Dragon cookies, Gooseberry pie, and Muffet muffins). Excel also added more outline buttons — several [–] buttons and a[4] button — indicating that another level has been added to the outline. (To verify that these Sold totals were not added at the expense of the store totals, you have to jump ahead and look at Figure 6-14.)

Hide and seek subtotal style

The greatest part of using Automatic Subtotals to summarize the data in your list or database is that you can use its outline symbols to instantly display just the summary stuff. Excel does this feat by hiding all the rows of figures that the totals are based on. And believe-you-me, displaying just the totals on the worksheet makes it a whole lot easier to print and chart this summary information.

When you use the Automatic Subtotal feature to add summary information to a list, Excel adds numbered outline buttons corresponding to the number of levels of subtotals and totals that you've added to the list. For instance, after adding the subtotals for the each type of pastry sold (shown in Figure 6-13) to the subtotals for each store (shown in Figure 6-12), the sample Daily Sales list ends up with four outline levels (and, therefore, four numbered buttons). The buttons produce the following levels:

✔ Choose the [4] button to display level 4, the most general level that shows everything: all the supporting rows of data plus the category sold subtotals, the store totals, and the grand total (partially shown in Figure 6-13).

✔ Choose the [3] button to display level 3, which shows only the category sold subtotals, store totals, and the grand total (shown in Figure 6-14).

✔ Choose the [2] button to display level 2, which shows just the store totals and the grand total (shown in Figure 6-15 along with a 3-D pie chart).

✔ Choose the [1] button to display level 1, which shows only the grand total (not shown).

To display to a particular level in the outline, simply click on the numbered button for the level you want to see. For example, to hide all the supporting data and display just the category sold, store sold, and grand total summary information as shown in Figure 6-14, simply click on the [3] button at the top. To remove the category sold totals from the worksheet, as shown in Figure 6-15, simply click on the [2] button.

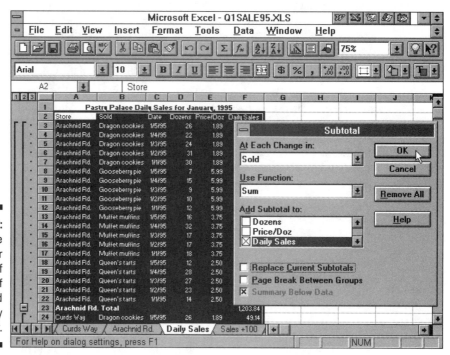

Figure 6-12: Creating the subtotals for the sales of each type of pastry sold in the Daily Sales list.

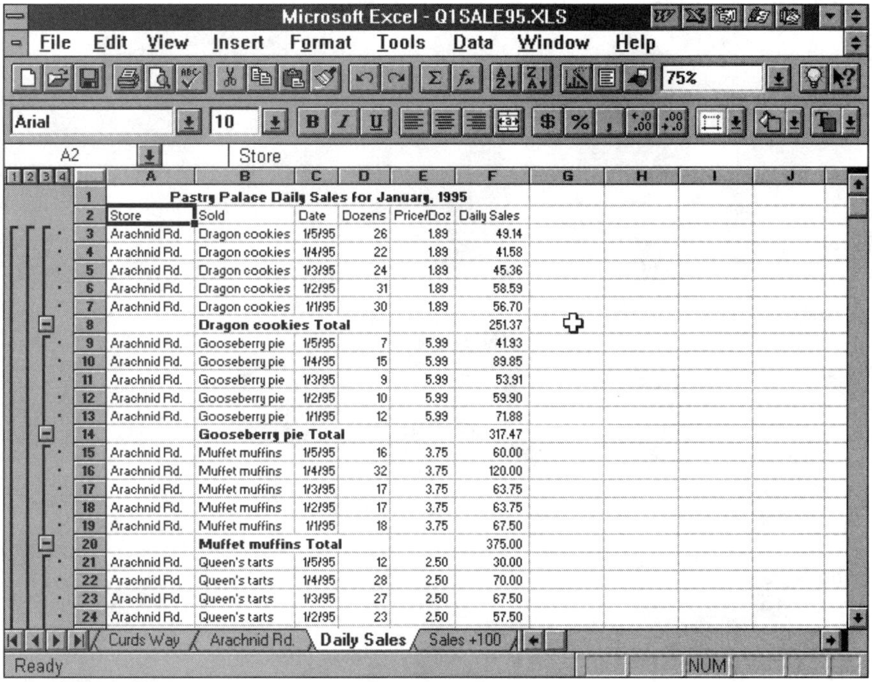

Figure 6-13:
The Daily
Sales list
showing
the Sold
category
subtotals for
Dragon
cookies,
Gooseberry
pie, and
Muffet
muffins.

Note that when displaying level 3 or level 2 of the outline, you see both [+] and
[–] buttons to the side of the various totals. You should also notice that the –
buttons are connected to vertical lines that indicate what rows are under its
control. To expand a particular section of the outline to just the rows of data it
contains, click on (you guessed it) its [+] button. To collapse a particular
section of the outline, click on its [–] button, which is then replaced by a [+]
button that you use to redisplay that section of the outline. (For more on using
outline buttons and collapsing and expanding sections, see Chapter 8.)

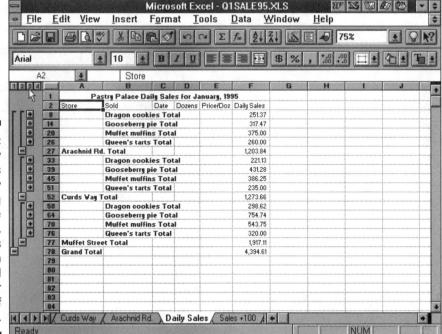

Figure 6-14:
The Daily
Sales
summary
showing
only the
grand total,
subtotals
for each
store, and
subtotals for
each kind of
pastry sold.

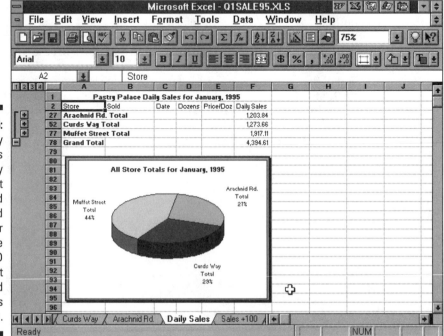

Figure 6-15:
The Daily
Sales
summary
showing just
the grand
total and
subtotals for
each store
with a 3-D
pie chart
created
from this
data.

The vicissitudes of charting a subtotaled list

Figure 6-15 shows a 3-D pie chart that was created from the store totals summary information when the outline level was set to level 2. To create this chart, I selected the three individual cells with the Store total labels (A27, A52, and A77). Then I selected the three individual cells containing the store totals (F27, F52, and F77) as a nonadjacent selection. I selected all these cells by Ctrl-clicking on each of them.

Finally, I selected the ChartWizard button on the Standard toolbar and created the chart as normal. When creating a chart from a subtotaled list, don't get caught in the trap of selecting these cells as ranges in a nonadjacent selection. If you make this mistake, Excel selects not only the displayed cells but all the hidden cells in between, which results in about a million data points in the chart. Then as you display more levels of subtotals in the outlined data, more data points appear on the chart.

The 5th Wave   By Rich Tennant

"Our new program has been on the market for over 6 months, and not one intellectual property lawsuit brought against us. I'm worried."

Part III
New Fun Stuff

The 5th Wave   By Rich Tennant

"YOU'VE PLUGGED YOUR MOUSE INTO THE
ELECTRIC SHAVER OUTLET AGAIN."

In this part . . .

Part III is just for the fun of it. This part starts out with a nifty chapter on creating and using templates to efficiently knock out worksheets that use the same structure. After this bit on cloning worksheets, you get to learn how to outline your worksheet data, a strangely useful feature when you need to be able to quickly look at subtotals and totals for various categories with or without all their supporting values. After that, it's on to a chapter on the ways to find, eliminate, and even prevent errors in your worksheet. Finally, you learn how to consult your spreadsheet crystal ball and see the future by performing "what-if" analysis on data, where you can calculate a whole bunch of different bottom lines based on your best guesses at the time.

Chapter 7

Using Templates to Clone Your Workbooks

*O*h, the monotony of doing the same job over and over again! Thanks to computer programs like Excel, you can cut down on the drudgery involved in creating workbooks and worksheets that do the same thing for different time periods or different departments or divisions within the company. For example, you may be in charge of creating budgets for your department on a quarterly or annual basis, or you may be in charge of keeping track of all the sales made by the account executives in your department on a weekly or monthly basis. Chances are, each time you create a new workbook for the next budget or sales spreadsheet you need to create, you use the same old layout as the preceding workbook, simply changing some of the titles and headings as you enter the new financial or numerical data.

Most people approach the creation of a new workbook as an exercise in deconstructing a copy of the original. In other words, they open the original workbook, use the File⇨Save As command to save a copy of it under a new filename, and then they get busy replacing the old labels and data with the new ones. Although this take-a-copy-of-the-original-apart-to-create-the-new-workbook approach works, Excel offers a better approach: a fill-in-the-form method, if you will, that is safer and ultimately more efficient than the desconstructive method.

This fill-in-a-form method is accomplished by using a workbook template to create each new spreadsheet that shares the same layout so that it is essentially a later generation of the original template. In this chapter, you learn how to create and use such templates. You also learn how to create a special startup template, called the autotemplate, that can serve as the basis for all the different types of new workbooks you create. Finally, you learn how to use Excel's Data⇨Consolidate command to summarize the data in workbooks generated from the same template.

A Template a Day (Keeps the Boss Away!)

In Excel, a *template* is a special workbook that contains all the generic text, graphics, and formulas that are required in any workbook that is generated from it. I liken a spreadsheet template to a blank printed form that you tear off of a tablet and start filling out when you need to create a form for a particular purpose. Excel achieves this kind of blank-form status for the template workbook by saving it in a special file format (indicated by the .xlt filename extension). When you save a workbook in this file format, Excel does not open the original workbook when you choose the File⇨Open command but, instead, opens a copy of the original. This built-in feature of opening a copy rather than the original eliminates the potential problem of messing up the original template file by saving it with data and text that belong only in the particular workbook that you're creating.

Whenever you open an .xlt file in Excel, the program opens up a copy (indicated by a number inserted as the last character in the filename) rather than the original. If you need to make changes to the original template, you must choose the template in the File Name list box of the Open dialog box and then remember to hold down the Shift key as you choose the OK button. Excel then opens up the original .xlt version of the file rather than a numbered copy of it.

Turning workbooks into templates

The easiest way to create a template is to first create an actual workbook prototype, complete with all the text, data, graphics, and macros that it requires to function.

Creating a template from a workbook

After checking out the formulas and making sure that everything is hunky-dory, follow these steps to turn the workbook into a template:

1. **Choose File⇨Save As on the pull-down menus and then give the workbook a new (more generic) filename.**

   For example, if you're creating a budget template from a BDGT95.XLS workbook, rename the template BUDGET.XLT.

2. **Choose Template in the Save File as Type pop-up list.**

3. **If you want to create a new workbook from the template by selecting the template in the New dialog box, choose the C:\EXCEL\XLSTART directory in the Directories list box.**

   (See "Creating a workbook from a template" later in this chapter for more information on this process.)

4. **Click on the OK button or press Enter.**

5. **Replace the actual values for the particular workbook with zeros.**

   You can replace the values quickly by selecting all the cells, typing **0,** and then pressing Ctrl+Enter.

6. **Protect the parts of the worksheet that contain formulas or labels that will never need editing.**

   To protect these parts, select all the ranges where you *do* want to allow editing and then choose Format⇨Cells (Ctrl+1) or the Format Cells command on the cells' shortcut menu. Then deselect the Locked check box on the Protection tab. Next, choose Tools⇨Protection⇨Protect Workbook to turn protection on everywhere in the worksheet (except in the cell ranges you specifically unlocked).

7. **Choose the Save button on the Standard toolbar or choose File⇨Save (Ctrl+S) to save your editing changes and the changes to the protection status of the workbook in the template.**

Figures 7-1 and 7-2 illustrate this process of creating a template from a real live workbook. In Figure 7-1, I created a Pastry Palace invoice for the Brothers Grimm Inn. After getting its formulas to work the way they were supposed to, I decided to convert a copy of this workbook into a template that could generate all future invoices. This template is shown in Figure 7-2.

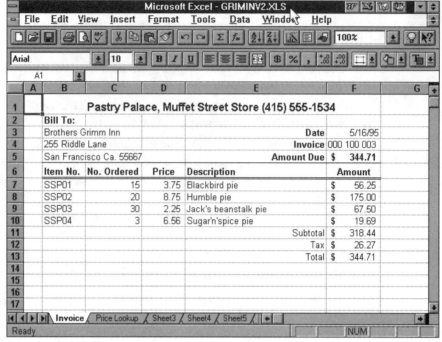

Figure 7-1:
The actual
Pastry
Palace
invoice for
the Brothers
Grimm Inn.

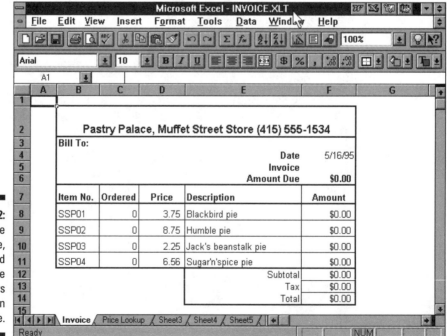

Figure 7-2:
The Invoice
template,
created
from the
Brothers
Grimm Inn
invoice.

To create the INVOICE.XLT template from the GRIMINV2.XLS workbook, I first used the File⇨Save As command to save a copy of the GRIMINV2.XLS workbook as INVOICE.XLT in the C:\EXCEL\XLSTART directory. To do this, I entered **invoice** in the File Name text box and selected Template as the file format in the Save File as Type text box. I then chose the appropriate directory in the Directories list box.

Then I removed the actual address information and invoice number while leaving the date (supplied by the NOW function) and the various item numbers (SSP01 – SSP04). The invoice contains a formula that supplies the prices and descriptions to appropriate cells. This formula looks up the item number in these cells in the lookup table entered on the Price Lookup worksheet (see Chapter 13 in *Excel For Dummies* to see exactly how this was done). Then I replaced the number of items ordered in column C with zeros by selecting the cell range C7:C10, typing **0**, and pressing Ctrl+Enter.

After these steps, I simply removed the display of the grid lines from the worksheet and added borders around the cells in the invoice table to make it look more like a form. (I added the borders with the Borders palette attached to the Border button on the Formatting toolbar.) I also inserted a new row at the very top of the worksheet to create some blank space above the invoice form.

Finally, I selected the cell ranges B2, B4:B6, F4:F5, and C8:C11 (see Figure 7-2) as one big happy nonadjacent selection and unlocked these cells (by deselecting the Locked check box in the Protection tab of the Format Cells dialog box). Then I turned on protection for the Invoice and Price Lookup sheets with the Tools⇨Protection⇨Protect Sheet command and saved the completed template with the File⇨Save (Ctrl+S) command.

Creating a workbook from a template

Creating a new workbook from a template involves nothing more than opening up the template file. Anytime you open up a template file, Excel opens up a copy of the template with a temporary filename (such as Budget1, Budget2, and so forth for the BUDGET.XLT template file).

If you save your workbook templates in the special XLSTART directory (usually located in the C:\EXCEL directory), you can make the job of creating a new workbook from the templates a lot easier. As Figure 7-3 illustrates, any template file that you save in this special directory appears in the New dialog box opened with the File⇨New command on the pull-down menus (or by pressing Ctrl+N). You then simply select the template's name in the New list box and choose OK.

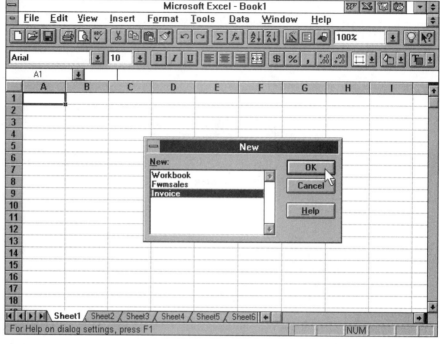

Figure 7-3:
Creating a
new invoice
workbook by
opening its
template in
the New
dialog box.

In the New dialog box shown in Figure 7-3, there are the following three work-book templates to choose from in my XLSTART directory:

✔ The default workbook template, called (you guessed it) Workbook, is created by Excel. This template determines the look and feel of each new workbook you create and assigns such temporary names as Book1, Book2, and so on to the new workbooks. See "Creating your own autotemplate style" later in this chapter for information on how to create your own custom default workbook template.

✔ The Fwmsales workbook template (created by yours truly) generates a new sales workbook for the Fuzzy Wuzzy Media company. (You'll meet up with this template and a series of workbooks created from this template in "Consolidating Workbook Data in a Snap," later in this chapter.)

✔ The Invoice workbook template (also created by yours truly) generates a new invoice workbook for the Pastry Palace (such as the one shown in Figure 7-4).

After I chose Invoice in this New dialog box, Excel opened the Invoice1 work-book, shown in Figure 7-4. I used this blank Invoice workbook to create the INV100-4.XLS workbook for Dave's Greasy Spoon, shown in Figure 7-5.

To create this workbook, I edited the heading in cell B1 and the date in cell F3. Then I entered the new name and address in cells B3 through B6, the invoice number in cell F5, and the number of items ordered in cells C8 through C11. That's all there is to it! And, if the truth be known, this task was made even easier because these are the only unlocked cells in this worksheet. Remember that when a worksheet is protected (as this one is because its template is protected), you can use the Tab key to jump from one unlocked cell to the next (or use Shift+Tab to move to a preceding unlocked cell). In this way, you conveniently avoid all the cells that you can't edit anyway.

Inserting a template worksheet into a workbook

After you've created a workbook template and added it to the XLSTART directory, you can insert its worksheets into whatever workbook you're currently working on. For example, suppose that you've developed a template for creating budgets, and you want to add its worksheet to the current workbook that contains a projected income statement. To put the template

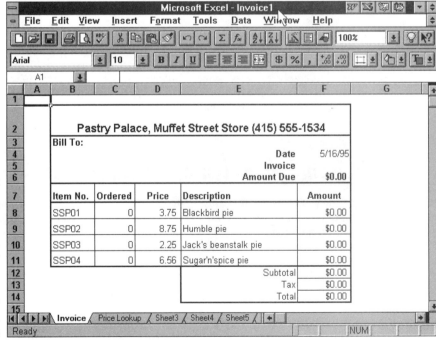

Figure 7-4:
The
Invoice1
workbook,
created by
selecting
Invoice in
the New
dialog box.

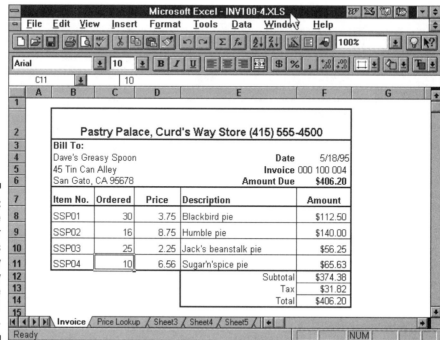

Figure 7-5:
The invoice
created for
Dave's
Greasy
Spoon by
filling in the
Invoice1
workbook.

worksheets into the workbook, simply select the sheet tab where you want the worksheets inserted, open its shortcut menu, and choose the Insert command. An Insert dialog box opens, where you can select the name of the workbook template in the New list box (similar to the New list box in the New dialog box). After you choose OK, Excel inserts copies of all the template worksheets into the current workbook.

Creating your own autotemplate style

As mentioned earlier, Excel automatically uses the template called Workbook as the model for all new workbooks you create. However, you can create a workbook template of your own design, called an *autotemplate*, that replaces the default template each time you open a new workbook. You can create a template, for example, that uses a different font and font size, contains a graphic with the company logo, or contains a special default header and footer to be used when printing reports from your new worksheets.

To create a workbook autotemplate, format a new workbook with all the bells and whistles you want in every new workbook from then on. Then you save this workbook in the template file format by selecting Template in the Save File as

Type pop-up list. Save the autotemplate with the filename BOOK.XLT in the XLSTART directory (usually located in the C:\EXCEL directory). After you create the autotemplate, each new workbook that you open (including the Book1 workbook that appears automatically when you start Excel without opening a workbook) is based on your BOOK.XLT template so that it contains whatever text and formatting this template uses.

Consolidating Workbook Data in a Snap

The natural outcome of creating a series of workbooks from the same workbook template is that the workbooks all share an identical layout. This similarity is just the ticket when you need to summarize their numbers — a process known in spreadsheet circles as *consolidation* — with the Data⇨Consolidate command. For instance, you can use this command to total the data from sales worksheets contained in different workbooks for a particular series of years or find the average of the sales made during these years.

To get a feel for how Excel's consolidation feature works, follow along with the steps for totaling the projected sales data for the Fuzzy Wuzzy Media company for three years, 1996 – 1998. All three of these sales workbooks were created with the Fwmsales template, which was introduced in the New dialog box back in Figure 7-3.

Totaling projected sales data

1. **Open the New dialog box with File⇨New (Ctrl+N) command, select Fwmsales in the New list box, and choose OK.**

   This step creates an Fwmsales1 workbook (shown in Figure 7-6), which will soon contain the totals of the sales from the 1996 Sales, 1997 Sales, and 1998 Sales worksheets.

2. **Open the three workbooks (FWMSALE6.XLS, FWMSALE7.XLS, and FWMSALE8.XLS) containing the 1996 Sales, 1997 Sales, and 1998 Sales worksheets with the File⇨Open (Ctrl+O) command.**

3. **Switch back to the Fwmsales1 workbook from the Window pull-down menu and then position the cell pointer in the first cell that is to contain a consolidated total.**

   In this example, position the cell pointer in cell B4, which will contain the total sales for Fuzzy's Silly Songs on floppy disk for January, 1996; January, 1997; and January, 1998.

4. Choose Data⇨Consolidate to open the Consolidate dialog box (shown in Figure 7-7), where you designate the references of the cells to be totaled by the Sum function.

If you want to use a function other than Sum, such as Average or Count, select it in the Function pop-up list box. To add each reference, I switched to the workbook from the Window pull-down menu, dragged through the cell range to select the cells, and then chose the Add button on the Consolidate dialog box.

5. After adding all the references of the cells to be totaled in the Fwmsales1 workbook, click on the OK button in the Consolidate dialog box.

To create links between the worksheets in these three workbooks and the consolidated workbook so that changes in the sales worksheets are automatically updated in the consolidated workbook, choose the Create Links to Source Data check box before clicking on the OK button.

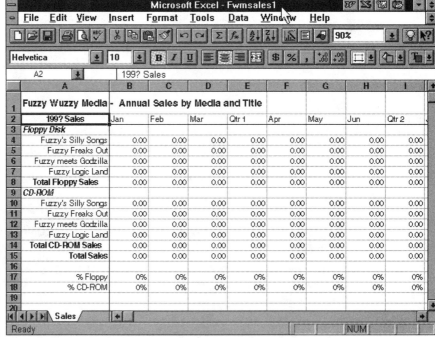

Figure 7-6:
The
Fwmsales1
workbook,
created by
selecting
the
Fwmsales
template in
the New
dialog box.

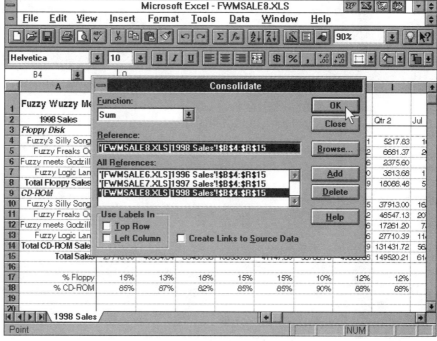

Figure 7-7:
Specifying
the ranges
to be
summarized
in the
Consolidate
dialog box.

Figure 7-8 shows how the first part of the Fwmsales1 workbook appears after Excel completes the consolidation of the projected sales of Floppy Disk and CD-ROM titles for the years 1996, 1997, and 1998. I saved this workbook with the filename FWMCONSL.XLS, renamed the sheet tab, and retitled the worksheet.

To help you visualize what happens when Excel consolidates data from different files, Figure 7-9 shows a small part of the consolidated 96 – 98 Sales worksheet along with each of the three sales worksheets (1996 Sales, 1997 Sales, and 1998 Sales). This view allows you to check that Excel really did correctly total the projected sales for these three years (if you're the suspicious type). I created this view by choosing Windows⇨Arrange and selecting the Tiled radio button in the Arrange Windows dialog box.

Opening up all the workbooks with data you want to consolidate is by far the easiest way to designate the cells to be consolidated because you can actually select the data you want to consolidate. Sometimes, however, your computer may not have enough memory to accommodate all the workbooks open at one time. You can still consolidate the data if you know (in other words, write down) the name of the worksheet and the references of the cell ranges in each workbook to be summarized.

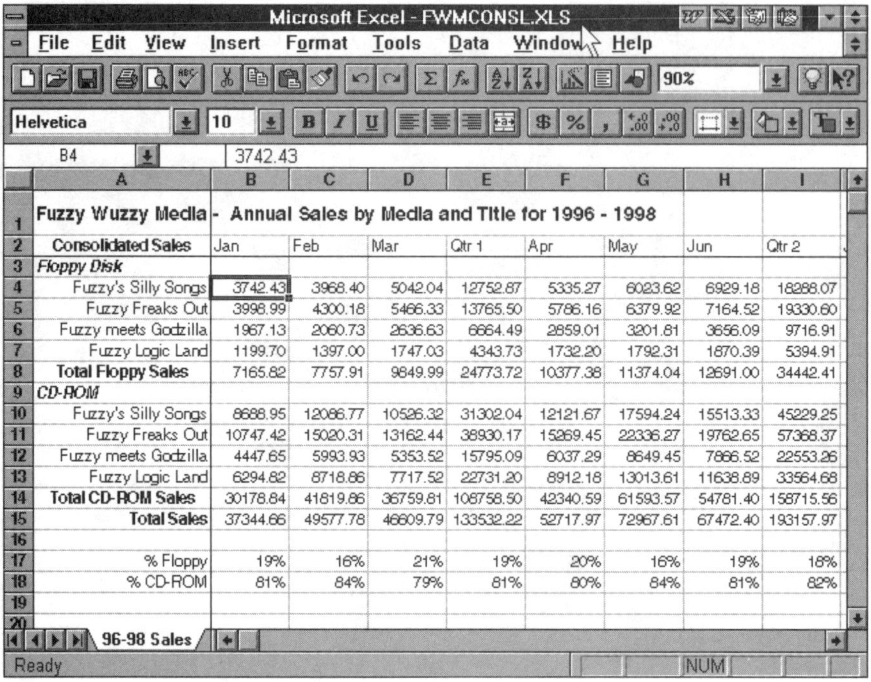

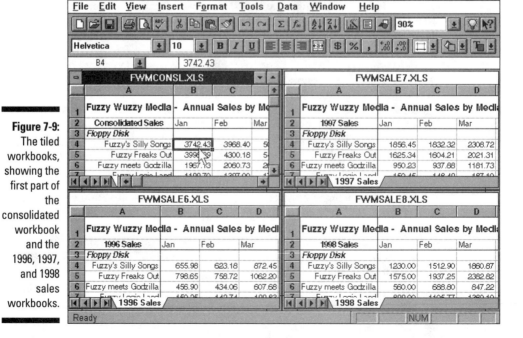

Figure 7-8:
The
consolidated
workbook,
with totals
for the sales
in the 1996,
1997, and
1998 sales
workbooks.

Figure 7-9:
The tiled
workbooks,
showing the
first part of
the
consolidated
workbook
and the
1996, 1997,
and 1998
sales
workbooks.

To help you get started in this process, you can choose the Browse button in the Consolidate dialog box. Then select the workbook file in the Browse dialog box. After you select the filename in this dialog box, Excel inserts the name of the workbook followed by an exclamation point in the Reference text box, as you can see in this example:

```
FWMSALES6.XLS!
```

You can then add to this filename the name of the worksheet and the range address (with absolute cell references) of the cells you want to consolidate, as in this example:

```
FWMSALES6.XLS!1996 Sales!$B$4:$R$15
```

After typing in this additional information, choose the Add button to add this information to the All References list box.

Man does not consolidate by position alone

Most consolidations between worksheets in different workbooks are done by matching the position of the cell ranges to summarize. This is, of course, the method to use when you're consolidating data from workbooks that have all been created from the same template. However, you can also consolidate data from worksheets in different workbooks even when they do not all share an identical layout but do all use the same column and row labels to identify the data. This method of consolidating data by category rather than by position is accomplished by choosing the Top Row and/or Left Column check boxes (depending upon which part of the worksheet contains the identifying labels) after designating the function and references to use.

Chapter 8

Outlining Worksheet Data

● ●

In This Chapter

▶ What is a worksheet outline and why on earth would you ever use it

▶ How to create an outline for a table of worksheet data

▶ How to display and hide different levels of a worksheet outline

▶ How to use grouping to manually change outline levels

● ●

*I*f you read the section called "Instant Subtotals!" in Chapter 6 of this book, you are already familiar with some of the basic principles that Excel uses when outlining worksheet data. (If not, you may want to take a quick peek at this section before coming back here to learn outlining.) There are, however, some important differences between the subtotal outlines created with the Data⇨Subtotals command, as introduced in Chapter 6, and the worksheet outlines created with the Data⇨Group and Outline command introduced in this chapter.

When you create automatic subtotals, Excel not only adds outline levels to the list of data but also adds new rows that contain the summary data — the totals, averages, and so on — for each group in the list. When you create outlines, however, Excel adds to the groups only the outline levels identified within the table of data — it's up to you to put in the formulas that calculate such stuff as subtotals and grand totals in the table. Also, when you create automatic subtotals in a list, Excel assigns outline levels only to the groups identified *down the rows* of the list. When you outline a table of worksheet data, however, Excel assigns outline levels to both the groups identified down the rows and the groups identified across the columns of the table.

The reason for outlining a table of worksheet data is to get instant access to the summary information in the table. When you outline a table of worksheet data, Excel adds outline symbols that enable you to display certain levels of detail in the outline by hiding columns and rows in lower levels. This outline feature makes it possible to see summary information, such as quarterly and annual totals for each division or product down the rows, without the underlying detail information (that is, the individual monthly sales figures) anytime you want at the click of a button. And after the summary information is displayed in the worksheet, you can then print or chart this "bottom-line" information in a snap.

Automatic Outlines at Your Service

Outlining worksheet data — like outlining your ideas for an upcoming business presentation on paper or with a word processor — is based on setting up a hierarchy of levels (a kind of top-down pecking order of ideas). This hierarchy of outline levels always moves from the highest and broadest, or most encompassing, level down to the lowest and narrowest, or most specific, level.

Like the outline levels you would set up for the topics in your business presentation, the levels in an outline created by Excel for a table of worksheet data progress from level 1 (the highest and most inclusive level) to whatever level number happens to be the last one needed for the lowest level. (The lowest level usually contains the data summarized in the levels above.) In a worksheet outline, you can have up to a maximum of eight levels for the rows of data in the table and eight levels for its columns (ranging from levels 1 – 8).

As luck would have it, the layout common to many worksheet tables that summarize numerical and financial data is just perfect for Excel's Outline feature. So perfect, in fact, that you can create an outline for a big table of data simply by selecting the data to be outlined and then choosing the program's Auto Outline command on the Group and Outline submenu of the Data menu.

Figures 8-1 and 8-2 show a typical sales table that is a perfect candidate for automatic outlining. This table contains monthly, quarterly, and annual sales (going across the columns) for the Fuzzy Wuzzy Media company. The various software products are arranged (down the rows) into two major media categories: Floppy Disk and CD-ROM. Down the rows, the table contains a row that calculates the total sales of the floppy-disk programs (in row 7), the total sales of the CD-ROM programs (in row 13), and the total of both types of sales (in row 14). Across the columns, the table contains columns with totals for each quarter (in columns F, J, N, and R) as well as a column with the total sales for the entire year (in column S).

Because this sales table already contains the rows and columns with the subtotals and totals that define each group (and, therefore, each level in the outline), I was able to outline this sales table very easily.

First, I selected all the data to be outlined. In this case, I selected the range C3:S14 because it includes all the sales data except the percentage of total sales for each media category in rows 16 and 17. Figure 8-2 shows how the range looks after it is selected. Then I chose Data⇨Group and Outline⇨Auto Outline on the pull-down menus.

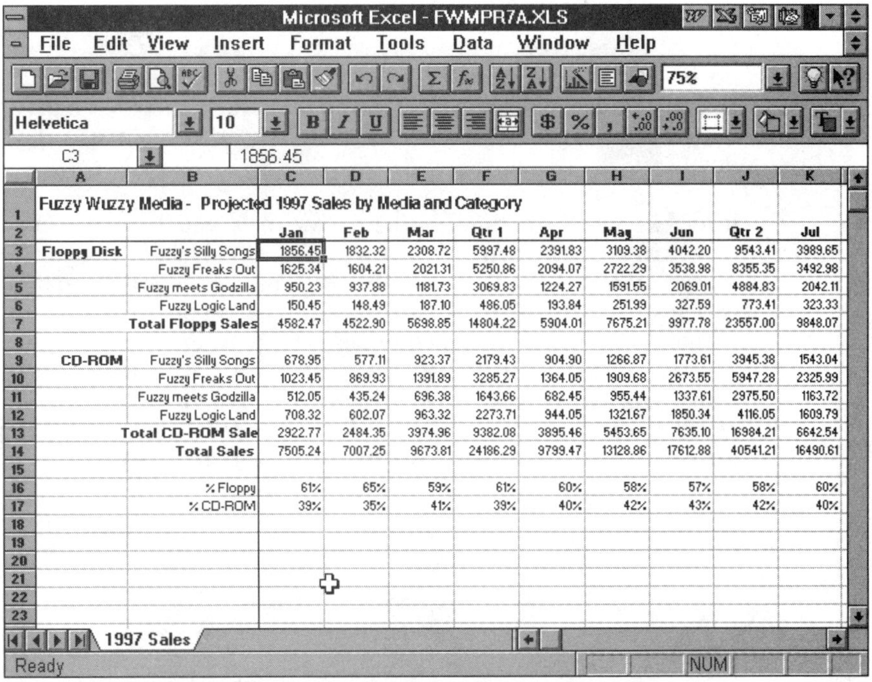

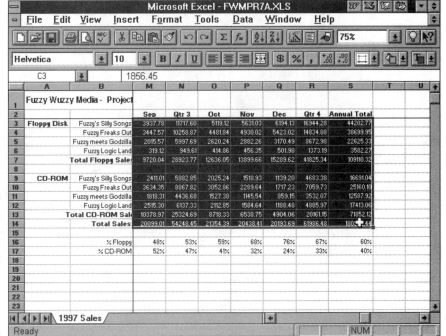

Figure 8-1:
A table of worksheet data arranged by sales category and time period.

Figure 8-2:
Selecting the worksheet table data to be included in the outline.

Figure 8-3 shows the first part of the outline that Excel created as a result of following these two steps. As you can see from this figure, Excel found it necessary to set up three levels for the rows of data and three levels for the columns (indicated by the [1], [2], and [3] buttons, the level bars, and the other outline buttons that appear above and to the left side of the workbook window).

If you examine the outline buttons for the rows, you'll see that level 1 (under the [1] row-level button), as indicated by a row-level bar attached to the [-] button, extends from the row with Total Sales all the way up to the very first row of sales data. Level 2 (under the [2] row-level button), as indicated by two sets of row-level bars attached to the [-] buttons, extends from the row with the Total CD-ROM Sales up to its first row of data and from the row with the Total Floppy Sales up to its first row of data. Level 3 (under the [3] row-level button), as indicated by the dots, consists of the rows of the underlying sales data that are summed by the subtotal and total rows in this table.

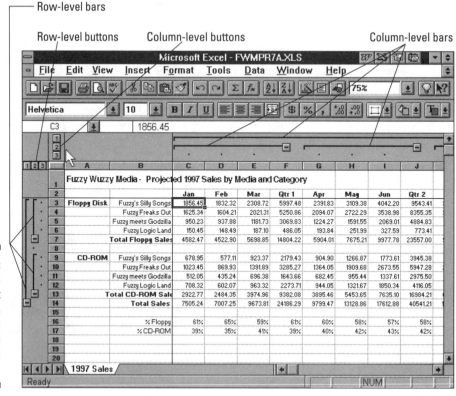

Figure 8-3:
The worksheet outline, created with the Auto Outline command.

Although you can't tell from Figure 8-3 alone (because not all the columns fit in the picture even with the screen magnification set to 75%), the story of the outline levels for columns in this table is mostly the same. Level 1, in the same top row as the [1] column-level button at the top of the window, is indicated by a column-level bar that extends from a [-] button over the last column in the table with the total sales all the way to the first column with the January sales. Level 2, in the same row as the [2] column-level button, is indicated by the column-level bars that extend from a [-] button over each column with a quarterly total all the way to the first column with sales for that quarter. Level 3, in the same row as the [3] column-level button, is indicated by the dots over each of the columns with monthly sales that are summarized by the quarterly and annual totals.

Hide and Seek Outline Style

After you have a created an outline, you can use the outline buttons to display whatever level of detail you see fit. If you're not into clicking on buttons, you can also hide and display different levels of the outline by choosing the appropriate summary column or row in the table and then selecting the Hide Detail or Show Detail command on the Group and Outline submenu of the Data menu.

If you create an outline for a table but none of the anticipated outline buttons appears around it, chances are good that the Outline Symbols check box in the View tab of the Options dialog box is deselected. To check this out quickly, press Ctrl+8 (the number 8 key on the top row of the keyboard, not the F8 key or the 8 key on the numeric keypad). Ctrl+8 is a shortcut toggle that you can use to both hide and redisplay outline buttons. It sure beats the pants off of choosing Tools⇨Options and then choosing the View tab and the Outline Symbols check box.

Figure 8-4 shows the outline after I clicked on the [2] column-level button. Excel collapses the outline down to the quarterly and annual sales columns by hiding all the columns with underlying sales data. Figure 8-5 then shows the outline after I clicked on the [2] row-level button. Now the sales table has been reduced to showing just the subtotals for the floppy and CD-ROM sales along with the grand total for both types of sales (because all underlying sales data have been hidden).

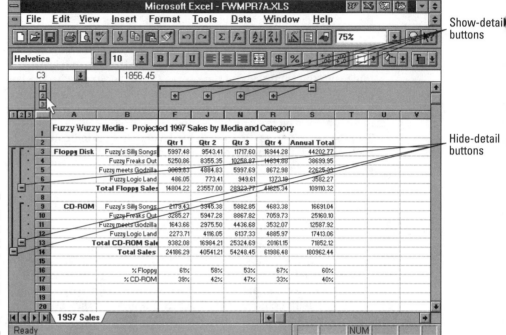

Show-detail buttons

Hide-detail buttons

Figure 8-4: The worksheet outline after clicking on the [2] column-level button.

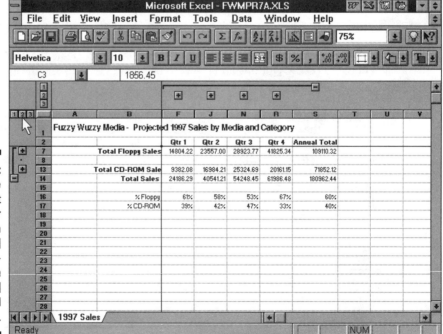

Figure 8-5: The worksheet outline after clicking on the [2] column-level button and the [2] row-level button.

Figure 8-6 shows what happened after I clicked on the [1] row-level button. At this point, only the grand totals of the quarterly and annual sales are displayed. Figure 8-7 shows what happened after I did the ultimate and collapsed the column levels down to the max by clicking on the [1] column-level button. As you can see, after you click on both the [1] row-level and the[1] column-level buttons, you hide all the underlying details, leaving just the granddaddy total of them all, staring you in the face.

In all the figures up to this point, I showed what happens only after you click on a particular combination of row- and column-level buttons. You can, of course, obtain even more views of the outlined data by combining these row- and column-level buttons with the individual hide-detail buttons (the [–] buttons) and the show-detail buttons (the [+] buttons).

In Figure 8-8, for example, you see the sales table after I clicked on the [2] row-level button, the [3] column-level button, and the hide-detail button displayed over column F with the Qtr 1 totals. (After clicking on a [–] button, it immediately turns into a [+] button, as shown in this figure.) In this view, I can see the detail columns for April, May, and June along with the Qtr 1 and Qtr 2 totals for floppy, CD-ROM, and both types of sales.

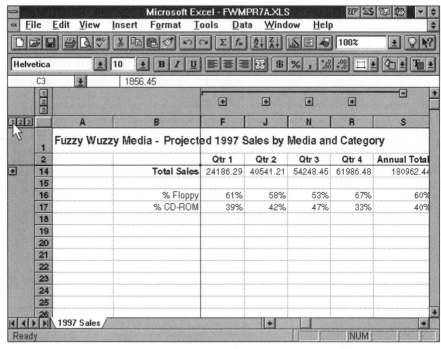

Figure 8-6:
The worksheet outline after clicking on the [2] column-level button and the [1] row-level button.

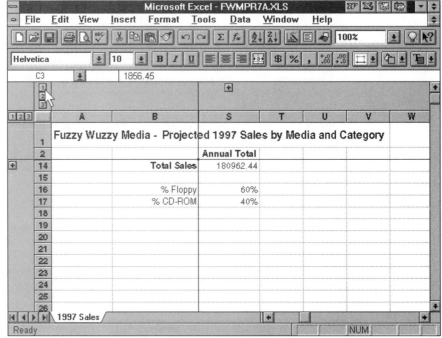

Figure 8-7: The worksheet outline after clicking on the [1] column-level button and the [1] row-level button.

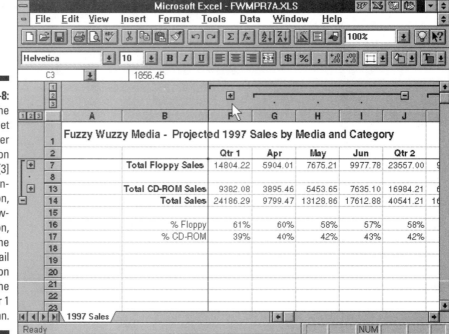

Figure 8-8: The worksheet outline after clicking on the [3] column-level button, the [1] row-level button, and the hide-detail button above the Qtr 1 column.

Figure 8-9 shows a slightly different view of the outlined sales table. To create this view, I clicked on the [2] row-level button, the [2] column-level button, and the show-detail button displayed over the Qtr 3 column (which immediately turned the [+] button into the [–] button, as shown in the figure). Now you can see all the third quarter underlying sales data by product and media type.

After displaying only the part of the outline you want to see, you can select these cells for printing and/or charting. Remember to use Ctrl+click instead of dragging through the cells so that you *don't* select the hidden rows and columns in between the visible cells. When you want to redisplay all the data in the outline, you simply click on the highest row-level and column-level buttons. If you need to hide the outline symbols, press Ctrl+8 or choose Tools⇨Options and then select the Outline Symbols check box in the View tab.

When you need to remove all the outline symbols from the worksheet but you don't want to get rid of the outline, be sure that you press Ctrl+8 or choose Tools⇨Options and then select the Outline Symbols check box in the View tab. Only when you really want to get rid of all traces of the outline (including the outline symbols) do you choose the Data⇨Group and Outline⇨Clear Outline command.

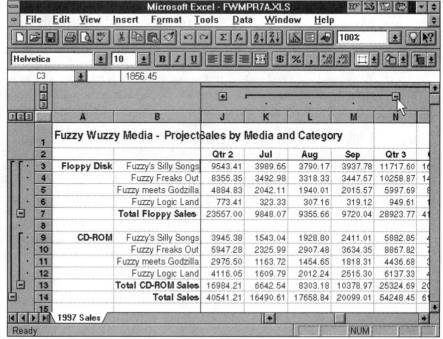

Figure 8-9: The worksheet outline after clicking on the [2] row-level button, the [2] column-level button, and the show-detail button above the Qtr 3 column.

	A	B	J	K	L	M	N
1	Fuzzy Wuzzy Media - Project Sales by Media and Category						
2			Qtr 2	Jul	Aug	Sep	Qtr 3
3	Floppy Disk	Fuzzy's Silly Songs	9543.41	3989.65	3790.17	3937.78	11717.60
4		Fuzzy Freaks Out	8355.35	3492.98	3318.33	3447.57	10258.87
5		Fuzzy meets Godzilla	4884.83	2042.11	1940.01	2015.57	5997.69
6		Fuzzy Logic Land	773.41	323.33	307.16	319.12	949.61
7		Total Floppy Sales	23557.00	9848.07	9355.66	9720.04	28923.77
8							
9	CD-ROM	Fuzzy's Silly Songs	3945.38	1543.04	1928.80	2411.01	5882.85
10		Fuzzy Freaks Out	5947.28	2325.99	2907.48	3634.35	8867.82
11		Fuzzy meets Godzilla	2975.50	1163.72	1454.65	1818.31	4436.68
12		Fuzzy Logic Land	4116.05	1609.79	2012.24	2515.30	6137.33
13		Total CD-ROM Sales	16984.21	6642.54	8303.18	10378.97	25324.69
14		Total Sales	40541.21	16490.61	17658.84	20099.01	54248.45
15							

When Your Outline Levels Need a Nudge

Much as I'd like to tell you different, Excel does make some mistakes, every once in a while, in assigning outline levels to a table of worksheet data when you use the Auto Outline command. The mistakes happen most often after you put labels identifying new groups in the table in places where Excel doesn't expect them.

Figure 8-10 illustrates just such a situation. In this version of the Fuzzy Wuzzy projected sales table for 1997, I placed the Floppy Disk and CD-ROM labels in rows above those with the labels identifying the actual software programs. This organization is different from the one in Figure 8-1, in which the Floppy Disk and CD-ROM labels appear on the same line as the first software program in each category. Actually, the labeling arrangement in Figure 8-10 is more natural than the one in Figure 8-1; however, Excel doesn't associate these labels in Figure 8-10 with the second outline level because they appear in rows above the other data rather than in the same rows in a column to the left.

In Figure 8-11, you can see the result of selecting the cells and then choosing the Data➪Group and Outline➪Auto Outline command. As you can see from the row-level bars, the second level now extends from row 8 up to row 4 and from row 14 up to row 10. Because the second level does not include the Floppy Disk label in row 3 or the CD-ROM label in row 9, these headings do not disappear when you click on the [2] row-level button. Instead, the labels remain visible and separate the subtotals from each other and from the grand totals.

To associate these labels with the second level of the outline, you need to group them with rows containing the detail data and the subtotals. To group the labels, you simply select row 3 and then choose the Data➪Group and Outline➪Group command. Then select row 9 and choose the Data➪Group and Outline➪Group command again. Figure 8-12 shows the result of using the Group command on these two rows. Now the row-level bars for the second level include the Floppy Disk and CD-ROM headings in these two rows. If you clicked on the [2] row-level button now, these rows and their headings would be hidden along with all the rows containing the actual product sales data.

You can use the Data➪Group and Outline➪Group command whenever you need to nudge a wayward row or column up a level in an outline. So, too, can you use the Data➪Group and Outline➪Ungroup command whenever you need to nudge a wayward row or column down a level in an outline.

You also can use the shortcut keys Alt+Shift+→ to group a column or row in an outline and Alt+Shift+← to ungroup a column or row.

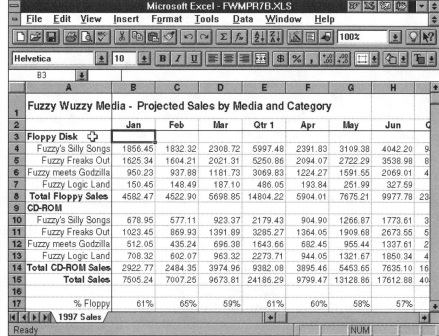

Figure 8-10:
A new
version of
the
projected
sales table,
with the
media labels
in rows
above the
sales rather
than in a
column to
the left.

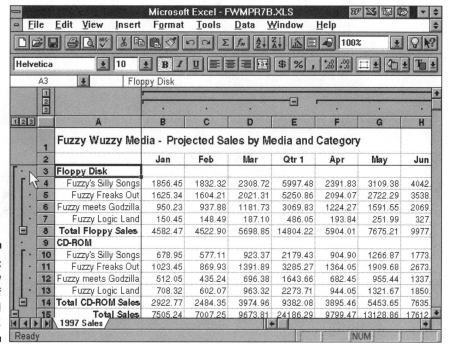

Figure 8-11:
A new
version of
the outlined
sales table.

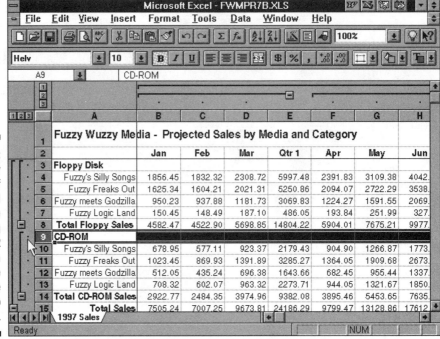

Figure 8-12:
A new
version of
the outlined
sales table
after giving
the level 2
headings a
little nudge
with the
Group
command.

	A	B	C	D	E	F	G	H
1	Fuzzy Wuzzy Media - Projected Sales by Media and Category							
2		Jan	Feb	Mar	Qtr 1	Apr	May	Jun
3	**Floppy Disk**							
4	Fuzzy's Silly Songs	1856.45	1832.32	2308.72	5997.48	2391.83	3109.38	4042.
5	Fuzzy Freaks Out	1625.34	1604.21	2021.31	5250.86	2094.07	2722.29	3538.
6	Fuzzy meets Godzilla	950.23	937.88	1181.73	3069.83	1224.27	1591.55	2069.
7	Fuzzy Logic Land	150.45	148.49	187.10	486.05	193.84	251.99	327.
8	**Total Floppy Sales**	4582.47	4522.90	5698.85	14804.22	5904.01	7675.21	9977.
9	**CD-ROM**							
10	Fuzzy's Silly Songs	678.95	577.11	923.37	2179.43	904.90	1266.87	1773.
11	Fuzzy Freaks Out	1023.45	869.93	1391.89	3285.27	1364.05	1909.68	2673.
12	Fuzzy meets Godzilla	512.05	435.24	696.38	1643.66	682.45	955.44	1337.
13	Fuzzy Logic Land	708.32	602.07	963.32	2273.71	944.05	1321.67	1850.
14	**Total CD-ROM Sales**	2922.77	2484.35	3974.96	9382.08	3895.46	5453.65	7635.
15	**Total Sales**	7505.24	7007.25	9673.81	24186.29	9799.47	13128.86	17612.

Chapter 9

Finding and Zapping Those Pesky Spreadsheet Errors

*T*roubleshooting a worksheet is the topic of this chapter. Here, you will learn how to locate the source of all those vexing formula errors so that you can shoot them down and set things right! As you learned in *Excel For Dummies*, the biggest problem with errors in your formulas — besides how ugly such values as #REF! and #DIV/0! are — is that they spread like wildfire through the workbook to other cells containing formulas that refer to their error-laden cells. If you're dealing with a large worksheet in a really big workbook, you may not be able to tell which cell actually contains the formula that's causing all the hubbub. And if you can't apprehend the cell that is the cause of all this unpleasantness, you really have no way of restoring law and order to your workbook.

Keeping in mind that the best defense is a good offense, you will also learn how to trap potential errors at their source and thereby keep them there. This technique, known affectionately as "error trapping" (just think of yourself as being on a spreadsheet safari), is easily accomplished by adding an IF function skillfully combined with an ISERROR function to the workings of the original formula.

Troubleshooting the Workbook — Thanks to the Auditing Toolbar

Fortunately, Excel offers some fairly effective tools for tracking down the cell that's causing your error woes by tracing the relationships between the formulas in the cells of your worksheet. By tracing the relationships, you can test formulas to see which cells, called *direct precedents* in spreadsheet jargon, directly feed the formulas and which cells, called *dependents* (nondeductible, of course), depend upon the results of the formulas. Excel even offers a way to visually backtrack the potential sources of an error value in the formula of a particular cell.

The easiest method for tracing the relationship between cells is offered by the tools on the Auditing toolbar, shown in Figure 9-1. To display the Auditing Toolbar, choose Tools⇨Auditing⇨Show Auditing Toolbar on the pull-down menus or choose Auditing on the shortcut menu of one of the displayed toolbars. When you first display the Auditing toolbar, Excel automatically makes it a floating toolbar, which you can dock or not, as you see fit.

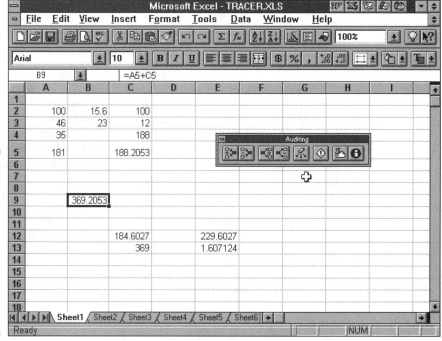

Figure 9-1: The Auditing toolbar, where you can explore cell relationships and hunt down and eliminate nasties.

If you prefer choosing commands from the pull-down menus rather than clicking on toolbar tools, you can select pull-down commands equivalent to most of the tools on the Auditing toolbar. These commands are available on a submenu that appears after you choose the Auditing command on the Tools menu.

This nifty toolbar contains the following eight tools (from left to right) that you can put to good use in your never-ending struggle for truth, justice, and perfection in your Excel workbooks:

- ✔ *Trace Precedents.* When you click on this tool, Excel draws arrows to the cells (the so-called direct precedents) that are referred to in the formula inside the selected cell. By clicking on this tool again, Excel adds "tracer" arrows that show the cells (the so-called indirect precedents) that are referred to in the formulas in the direct precedents.

- ✔ *Remove Precedent Arrows.* Clicking on this tool gets rid of the arrows that were drawn when you clicked on the Trace Precedents tool.

- ✔ *Trace Dependents.* When you click on this tool, Excel draws arrows from the selected cell to the cells (the so-called direct dependents) that use, or depend on, the results of the formula in the selected cell. By clicking on this tool again, Excel adds tracer arrows that identify the cells (the so-called indirect dependents) that refer to formulas found in the direct dependents.

- ✔ *Remove Dependent Arrows.* Clicking on this tool gets rid of the arrows that were drawn when you clicked on the Trace Dependents tool.

- ✔ *Remove All Arrows.* Clicking on this tool removes all the arrows drawn, no matter what tool you clicked on to get them there.

- ✔ *Trace Error.* When you click on this tool , Excel attempts to locate the cell that contains the original formula that has an error. If Excel can find this cell, it selects it and then draws arrows to the cells feeding it (the direct precedents) and the cells infected with its error value (the direct dependents). Note that you can use this tool only on a cell that contains an error value.

- ✔ *Attach Note.* Clicking on this tool opens the Cell Note dialog box, where you can add a text note or — if you have one of those newfangled multimedia computers — a sound note.

- ✔ *Show Info Window.* Clicking on this tool opens the Info window, where you can list a whole bunch of information — such as the formula, value, formatting, and the precedents and dependents — about the selected cell. The Info window also displays the text of any note that you've attached to the list.

Holding down the Shift key while you click on the Trace Precedents or Trace Dependents tool on the Auditing toolbar produces the same results as clicking on the Remove Precedent Arrows or the Remove Dependent Arrows tool, respectively.

"Oh what a tangled web we weave . . ." or genealogy, formula style

Using the Trace Precedents and Trace Dependents tools s on the Auditing toolbar (or the Trace Precedents and Trace Dependents commands on the Auditing submenu of the Tools menu) lets you see the relationship between a formula and the cells that directly and indirectly feed it as well as those that directly and indirectly depend upon its calculation. Excel establishes this relationship by drawing arrows from the precedent cells to the active cell and from the active cell to its dependent cells. If these cells are on the same worksheet, Excel draws solid blue arrows (on a color monitor), extending from each of the precedent cells to the active cell and from the active cell to the dependent cells. If the cells are not located locally on the same worksheet (they may be on another sheet in the same workbook or even on a sheet in a different workbook), Excel draws a black dotted arrow. This arrow comes from or goes to an icon with a picture of a miniature worksheet that sits to one side with the direction of the arrowheads indicating whether the cells on the other sheet feed the active formula or are fed by it.

Setting precedents

You can use the Trace Precedents tool on the Auditing toolbar to trace all the gen-erations of cells that contribute to the formula in the selected cell (kinda like tracing all the ancestors in your family tree). Figures 9-2 through 9-5 illustrate how you can use the Trace Precedents tool to quickly locate the cells that con-ribute, directly and indirectly, to the simple addition formula in cell B9.

Figure 9-2 shows the worksheet after I clicked on the Trace Precedents tool the first time. As you can see, Excel draws trace arrows from cells A5 and C5 that indicate they are the direct precedents of the addition formula in cell B9. In Figure 9-3, you see what happened when I clicked on this tool a second time to display the indirect precedents of this formula (think of them as being a gen-eration earlier in the family tree). The new tracer arrows show that cells A2, A3, and A4 are the direct precedents of the formula in cell A5 — indicated by a border around the three cells. (Remember that cell A5 is the first direct precedent of the formula in cell B9.) Likewise, cells B2 and B3 as well as cell C4 are the direct precedents of the formula in cell C5. (Cell C5 is the second direct precedent of the formula in cell B9.)

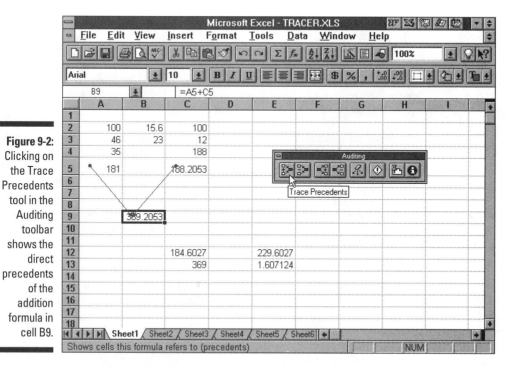

Figure 9-2:
Clicking on
the Trace
Precedents
tool in the
Auditing
toolbar
shows the
direct
precedents
of the
addition
formula in
cell B9.

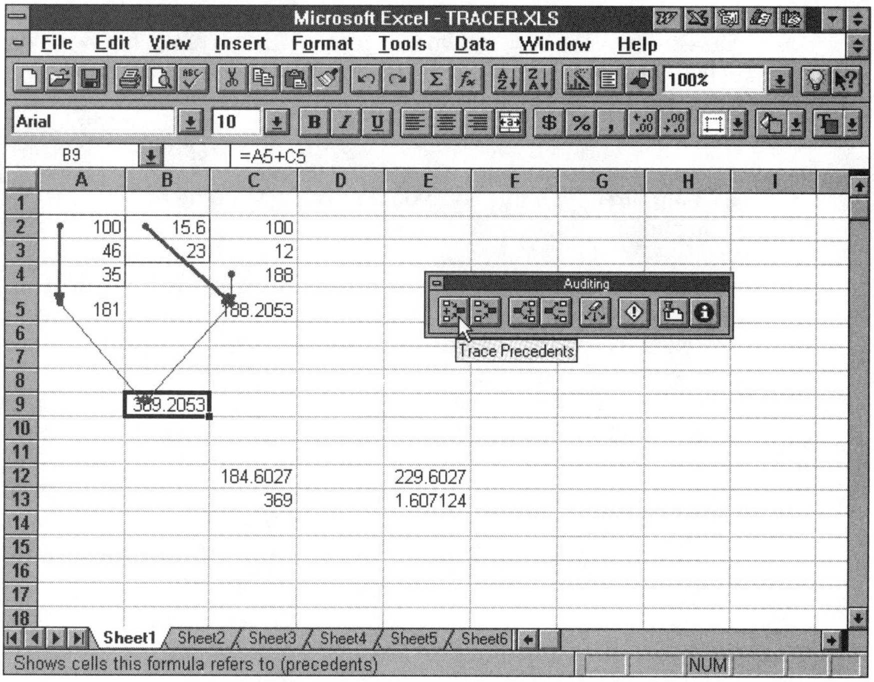

Figure 9-3:
Clicking on
the Trace
Precedents
tool in the
Auditing
toolbar
again to
show the
indirect
precedents
of the
addition
formula in
cell B9.

Each time you click on the Trace Precedents tool, Excel displays another (earlier) set of precedents (until no more generations exist). If you are in a hurry (as most of us are most of the time), you can speed up the process and display both the direct and indirect precedents in one operation by double-clicking on the Trace Precedents tool. To clear the worksheet of tracer arrows, click on the Remove All Arrows tool on the Auditing toolbar (or hold down Shift as you click on the Trace Precedents tool).

Figure 9-4 shows what happened when I double-clicked on the Trace Precedents tool (after single-clicking on it twice before as shown in Figure 9-2 and Figure 9-3). Double-clicking on the tool reveals both the direct and indirect precedents for cell C4. The formulas in cells C2 and C3 are the direct precedents of the formula in cell C4. The direct precedent of the formula in cell C2 (and, consequently, the indirect precedent of the one in cell C4) is not located on this worksheet. This fact is indicated by the dotted tracer arrow coming from that cute miniature worksheet icon sitting on top of cell A3.

To find out exactly which workbook, worksheet, and cell(s) hold the direct precedents of cell C2, I double-clicked somewhere on the dotted arrow (clicking on the icon with the worksheet miniature doesn't do a thing). Double-clicking on the dotted tracer arrow opens the Go To dialog box, which shows a list of all the precedents (including the workbook, worksheet, and cell references). To go to a precedent on another worksheet, double-click on the reference in the Go to list box or select it and click on the OK button. (If the worksheet is in another workbook, this workbook file must already be open before you can go to it.)

The Go To dialog box, shown in Figure 9-5, displays the following direct precedent of cell C2, which is cell B4 on Sheet2 of the same workbook:

```
[TRACER.XLS]Sheet2!$B$4
```

To jump directly to this cell, you double-click on the reference in the Go To dialog box.

You can also select precedent cells that are on the same worksheet as the active cell by double-clicking somewhere on its tracer arrow. Excel selects the precedent cell without bothering to open up the Go To dialog box.

You can use the Special button in the Go To dialog box (see Figure 9-5) to select all the direct or indirect precedents or the direct or indirect dependents that are on the same sheet as the formula in the selected cell. After opening the Go To dialog box (Ctrl+G or F5) and selecting the Special button, you simply choose the Precedents or Dependents radio button and then choose between the Direct Only or All Levels radio button before you choose OK.

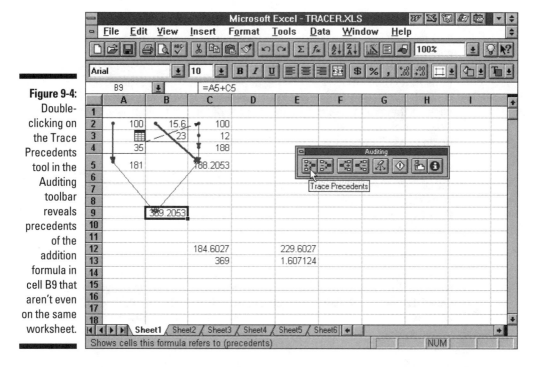

Figure 9-4:
Double-clicking on the Trace Precedents tool in the Auditing toolbar reveals precedents of the addition formula in cell B9 that aren't even on the same worksheet.

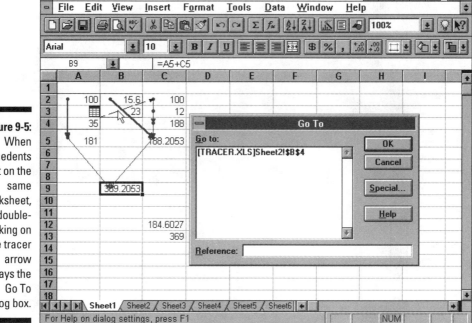

Figure 9-5:
When precedents aren't on the same worksheet, double-clicking on the tracer arrow displays the Go To dialog box.

Getting acquainted with your dependents

You can use the Trace Dependents tool on the Auditing toolbar to trace all the generations of cells that either directly or indirectly utilize the formula in the selected cell (kinda like tracing the genealogy of all your prodigy in the generations that come after you). Tracing dependents with the Trace Dependents tool is much like tracing precedents with the Trace Precedents tool. Each time you click on this tool, Excel draws another set of arrows that show a generation of dependents further removed. To display both the direct and indirect dependents of a cell in one fell swoop, you double-click on the Trace Dependents tool.

Figure 9-6 shows what happens after I selected cell B9 and then clicked on the Trace Dependents tool for the first time. As you can see in this figure, Excel draws tracer arrows from cell B9 to cells C12 and C13, indicating that they are the direct dependents of cell B9. The computations of these two cells depend in some part on the result returned to cell B9.

Figure 9-7 shows what happens after I double-clicked again on the Trace Dependents tool. As you can see from this figure, cells E12 and E13 are shown to be the indirect dependents of cell B9 and, in turn, the direct dependents of cells C12 and C13. In addition, cell E13 is a direct dependent of cell E12, and cell E12 has another direct dependent on some other sheet, either in this workbook or some other workbook (indicated by the dotted tracer arrow pointing to the worksheet icon).

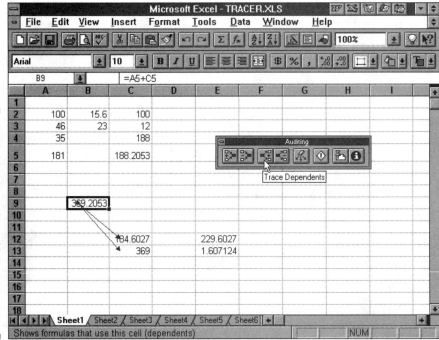

Figure 9-6: Clicking on the Trace Dependents tool in the Auditing toolbar shows the direct dependents of the addition formula in cell B9.

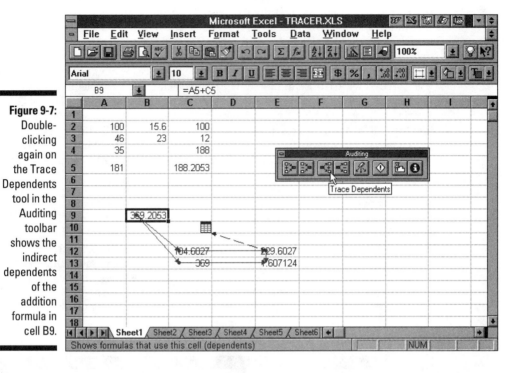

Figure 9-7:
Double-
clicking
again on
the Trace
Dependents
tool in the
Auditing
toolbar
shows the
indirect
dependents
of the
addition
formula in
cell B9.

The Error Tracer to the rescue!

Tracing a formula's family tree, so to speak, with the Trace Precedents and
Trace Dependents tools is fine, as far as it goes. When it comes to a formula that
returns a hideous error value, such as #VALUE! or #NAME!, you need to turn to
the trusty Trace Error tool in the Auditing toolbar (the one with an exclamation
point in a diamond).

Using the Trace Error tool is a lot like using both the Trace Precedents and the
Trace Dependents tools, except that the Trace Error tool works only when the
active cell contains some sort of error value returned either by a bogus formula
or a reference to a bogus formula. In tracking down the actual cause of the error
value in the active cell (remember that these error values spread to all direct
and indirect dependents of a formula), Excel draws blue tracer arrows from the
precedents for the original bogus formula and then draws red tracer arrows to
all the dependents that contain error values as a result.

Figure 9-8 shows the sample worksheet after I made some damaging changes
that left three cells — C12, E12, and E13 — with #DIV/0! errors (meaning that
somewhere, somehow I ended up creating a formula that is trying to divide by

zero, which is a real "no-no" in the wonderful world of math). To find the origin of these error values and identify its cause, I clicked on the Trace Error tool on the Auditing toolbar while cell E12 was the active cell to engage the use of Excel's faithful old Trace Error feature.

Figure 9-8 shows the results (unfortunately, without color, you can't tell which trace arrows were drawn in blue or red). Note that Excel has selected cell C12, although cell E12 was active when I clicked on the Trace Error tool. To cell C12, Excel has drawn two blue tracer arrows (you'll have to take my word for it) that identify cell B5 and B9 as its direct precedents. From cell C12, the program has drawn two red tracer arrows (again, you have to trust me on this) — one that goes from cell C12 to cell E12 and one that goes from cell E12 to cell E13 — that identify its dependents.

As it turns out, Excel's Trace Error tool is right on the money because the formula in cell C12 contains the bad apple rotting the whole barrel. I had revised the formula in cell C12 so that it divided the value in cell B9 by the value in cell B5 without making sure that cell B5 first contained the SUM formula that totaled the values in the cell range B2:B4. The #DIV/0! error value showed up — remember that an empty cell contains a zero value as if you had actually entered a *0* in the cell — and immediately spread to cells E12 and E13 that, in turn, use the value returned in C12 in their own calculations. Thus, these cells were infected with the #DIV/0! virus, as well.

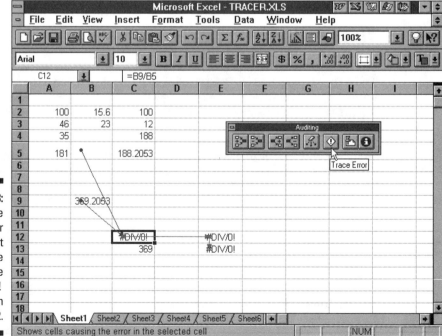

Figure 9-8:
Using the Trace Error tool to hunt down the cause of the #DIV/0! error in cell C12.

When the Error Tracer loses the trail

The Trace Error tool finds errors along the path of a formula's precedents and dependents until it either finds the source of the error or it finds one of the following problems:

It encounters a branch point with more than one error source. In this case, Excel doesn't make a

determination on its own as to which path to pursue.

It encounters existing tracer arrows. Therefore, *always* remove all arrows before you click on the Trace Error tool.

It encounters a formula with a circular reference.

As soon as you correct the problem in the original formula and thus get rid of all the error values in the other cells, Excel automatically converts the red tracer arrows (showing the proliferation trail of the original error) to regular blue tracer arrows, indicating merely that these restored cells are dependents of the formula that once contained the original sin. You can then remove all the tracer arrows from the sheet by clicking on the Remove All Arrows tool on the Auditing toolbar.

Adding your own two cents to a cell

As you may have noticed, the Auditing toolbar contains an Attach Note tool (which is the equivalent of choosing Insert⇨Note on the pull-down menus) to open up the Cell Note dialog box, where you can add your two cents to cells of your choice. I guess that the Attach Note tool was put on the Auditing toolbar just in case you want to leave yourself or a coworker some kind of note, which either documents a problem that still needs fixing or documents the solution that you used to fix the messed up cells.

Figure 9-9 shows that I used the Attach Note tool to add a note to myself so that I wouldn't forget to fix the #DIV/0! error in cell C12 with an error trapping form-ula. To see how I accomplished this neat trick, jump ahead to the section called "Stopping Errors Dead in Their Tracks (Or Errors Go In but They Don't Get Out!)" at the end of this chapter.

After you add a note to a cell, Excel lets you know of its existence by placing a tiny red (on a color monitor) dot in the upper right-hand corner of the cell. (If you don't see the dot after adding a note, you have probably deselected the Note Indicator check box on the View tab of the Options dialog box.) Because these dots are hard to see, the best way to get to a cell with a note is to open the Go To dialog box (Ctrl+G or F5), select the Special button, and then click on OK or press Enter (the Notes radio button is automatically selected in the Go To Special dialog box). Excel then selects all cells in the active worksheet that contain notes. While all the cells with notes are selected, you can move from cell to cell by pressing Tab (to go to the next cell) or Shift+Tab (to go to the preceding cell).

For more information on how to use notes, edit notes, add sound notes, or get rid of notes, see Chapter 5 of *Excel For Dummies*.

Getting the lowdown on a cell

The last tool on the Auditing toolbar is the Show Info Window tool, which opens the Info Window where you can display all kinds of information about the active cell. You can also display the Info Window by opening the Options dialog box and then choosing the Info Window check box on the View tab.

After you first click on the Show Info Window tool on the Auditing toolbar, Excel opens the Info Window to its full size. The window contains only three pieces of information: the address of the active cell, the contents of the cell, and the text of any written note (sound notes don't count) in that cell. If you want to be able to see the worksheet at the same time you review the facts in the Info Window, you need to reduce the size of the Info Window by clicking on its Restore button and then manually resizing and strategically relocating it.

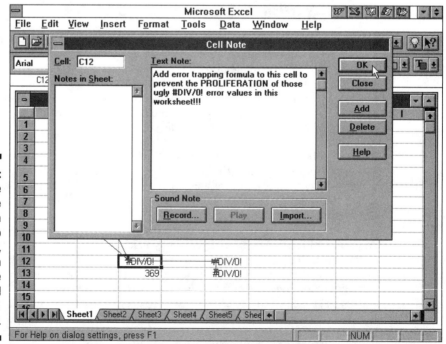

Figure 9-9:
Using the
Attach Note
tool to add a
comment to
cell C12,
which
contains the
original
#DIV/0!
error.

The three pieces of information that Excel puts into the Info Window by default are not the only facts you can dredge up on the selected cell. To display (or hide) other pieces of information about a cell, choose the Info command on the menu bar and select each piece of information you want included on the Info Window (the menus on the menu bar change the moment you open the Info Window). Figure 9-10 shows the Info Window with all the information you can possibly get on a cell after resizing the Info Window and locating it to the right side of the screen.

Keep in mind that the information displayed in the Info Window is in a different document window, just like other windows that contain on-line Help or another workbook file that you may have opened. If the Info Window is active and you click on a new cell in the part of the worksheet that is still displayed, Excel activates the workbook window (by putting it on top), and the Info Window disappears. To bring the Info Window back, select its name near the bottom of the Window pull-down menu. To retain the display of the Info Window on-screen while you select different cells in your workbook, choose the Window➪Arrange command and then select one of the Arrange radio buttons, such as Tiled, Horizontal, or Vertical, in the Arrange Windows dialog box.

When you no longer need the Info Window, you can close it by double-clicking on its control menu box or by choosing the Close command on its File menu.

Figure 9-10:
Using the
Show Info
Window tool
and the
commands
on the Info
pull-down
menu to get
a whole
bunch of
information
about cell
C12, which
contains the
original
#DIV/0!
error.

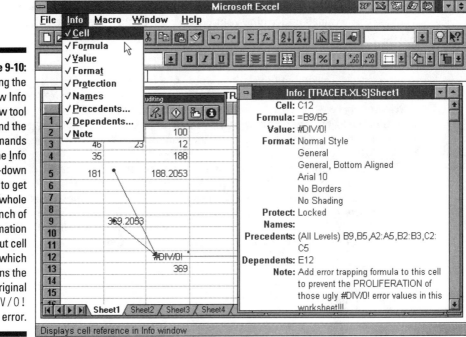

Stopping Errors Dead in Their Tracks (Or Errors Go In but They Don't Get Out!)

Sometimes, you will know ahead of time that certain error values are unavoidable in a worksheet as long as it's missing certain data. The most common error value that gets you into this kind of trouble is our old friend, the #DIV/0! error value. Suppose, for example, that you're creating a new sales workbook from your sales template (see Chapter 7 for details), and one of the rows in this template contains formulas that calculate what percentage each monthly total is of the quarterly total. To work correctly, the formulas must divide the value in the cell that contains the monthly total by the value in the cell that contains the quarterly total. When you start a new sales workbook from its template, the cells that contain the formulas for determining the quarterly totals will contain zeros, and these zeros will put the #DIV/0! error values in cells that have the formulas that calculate the monthly/quarterly percentages.

These particular #DIV/0! error values in the new workbook do not really represent mistakes, as such, because they automatically disappear as soon as you enter some of the monthly sales for each quarter (so that the calculated quarterly totals are no longer 0). The problem you may have is convincing your non-spreadsheet-savvy coworkers (especially the boss) that despite the presence of all these error values in your worksheet, the formulas are hunky-dory. All your coworkers see, however, is a worksheet that is riddled with error values, and these error values undermine your coworkers' confidence in the correctness of your worksheet.

Well, I have the answer for just such "perception" problems. Rather than risk your boss's freaking out over the display of a few little #DIV/0! errors here and there, you can set up these formulas so that whenever they're tempted to re-turn any type of error value (including #DIV/0!), they instead return zeros in their cells. Only when there is absolutely no danger of cooking up error values will Excel actually do the original calculations called for in the formulas.

This bit of sleight of hand in an original formula not only effectively eliminates errors from the formula but also prevents their spread to any of its dependents. To create such a formula, you rely on a powerful combo of functions: the IF function, which operates one way when a certain condition exists and another when it doesn't, and the ISERROR function, which returns a value of TRUE when a formula returns an error value and FALSE when it doesn't.

To see how these functions can be applied to a formula that sometimes gives you a #DIV/0! error, reconsider the original problem child formula in C12. This formula says

```
=B9/B5
```

and because cell B5 is currently empty (the equivalent of zero), it calculates #DIV/0! as the answer. Now, to set a trap for the error in this formula, you first need to create a test to determine when the formula returns an error value and when it doesn't. This is done with the ISERROR function in the following manner:

```
=ISERROR(B9/B5)
```

This ISERROR function returns TRUE when the division returns an error value (such as #DIV/0!) and FALSE when it doesn't.

You can then use this ISERROR function as the *logical_test* argument inside an IF function. If you remember from *Excel For Dummies*, the IF function requires the following three arguments:

```
IF(logical_test,value_if_true,value_if_false)
```

After the *logical_test* argument, you enter the *value_if_true* argument (which is 0 in this example) and the *value_if_false* argument (which is the division of B9/B5). With the addition of the IF function, the final formula looks like this:

```
=IF(ISERROR(B9/B5),0,B9/B5)
```

This formula then puts 0 in cell C12 (as shown in Figure 9-11) when the formula actually returns the #DIV/0! error value (because cell B5 is still empty or has a 0 in it) and returns the result of the division (as shown in Figure 9-12) when the formula doesn't return the #DIV/0! error value (because cell B5 is no longer empty or it contains any other value besides 0).

And there you have it — a foolproof method for masking those ugly error values with zeros until the time that you can eliminate them by supplying the data needed for the final and correct formula calculations in the worksheet.

Some people prefer to remove the display of zero values from any template that contains error-trapping formulas so that no one interprets the 0s as the correct value for the formula. To remove the display of zeros from a worksheet, deselect the Zero Values check box in the View tab of the Options dialog box. By this action, the cells with error trapping formulas remain blank until you give them the data they need to return the correct answers!

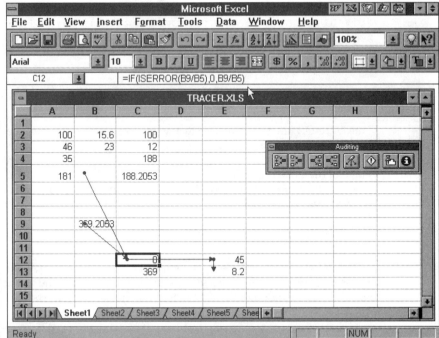

Figure 9-11:
Replacing the original
`#DIV/0!`
error with 0 helps the new version of the formula in cell C12 trap and eliminate all error values.

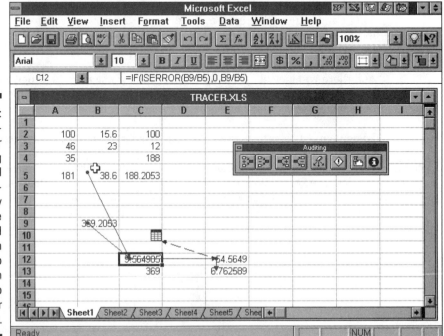

Figure 9-12:
The worksheet after eliminating the potential error condition by adding the SUM formula in cell B5 so that division by zero is no longer possible.

Chapter 10
Let's All Play "What If"

. . . .

In This Chapter

▶ How to use goal seeking to find out how to achieve a predetermined result

▶ How to play "what if" with a single-input data table

▶ How to play "what if" with a two-input data table

▶ How to play "what if" with the Scenario Manager

▶ How to create a summary report of what-if scenarios

. . . .

*B*ecause electronic spreadsheets are so good at updating their results by automatically recalculating their formulas based on new input, they have, from time immemorial, been used (and misused) to create financial projections based on all sorts of assumptions. Under the guise of what-if analysis, you will often find the number crunchers of the company using Excel as their crystal ball for projecting the results of all sorts of harebrained schemes designed to make the company a fast million bucks. As you start dabbling in this form of electronic fortune telling, keep in mind that the projections you get back from this type of analysis are only as good as your assumptions. So when the results of what-if analysis tell you that you're gonna be richer than King Midas after undertaking this new business venture, you still need to ask yourself if the original assumptions on which these glowing projections are based fit in with the real-world marketing conditions. In other words, when the worksheet tells you that you can make a million bucks of pure profit selling your lead-lined boxer shorts, you still have to question how many men really need that kind of protection and are willing to pay for it.

In Excel, what-if analysis comes in a fairly wide variety of flavors (some of which are more complicated than others). In this chapter, I'm going to introduce you to three simple and straightforward methods: goal seeking, which allows you to find out what it takes to reach a predetermined objective (such as how much you have to sell to make $20 million dollars profit this year); data tables, where you can see the effect of changing one or two variables on the bottom line (such as what happens to the net profit if you fall into a 45 percent tax bracket, a 60 percent tax bracket, and so on); and scenarios, which let you set up and test a wide variety of different cases, all the way from the best-case scenario (profits grow by 20 percent) to the worst-case scenario (you don't make any profit).

What's It Take to Reach Your Goal?

In most what-if analysis, you're looking for the effect that changes in various variables (such as revenues, expenses, and so on) have on the bottom line (such as net profits). Well, goal seeking sets this kind of analysis on its ear. When you perform goal seeking, you're looking for what changes you need to make to one of the variables to achieve a particular result.

To do goal seeking, you set up your model complete with its formula and variable cells that hold whatever values sound feasible. Then you select the cell that contains the formula that you want to return the predetermined result (appropriately enough referred to as the *set cell*). Open the Goal Seek dialog box and enter the desired result that you want to show up in the formula in the active cell. Finally, indicate which cell Excel can change to reach this desired result. (A more detailed example follows.)

To see how easy this goal seeking stuff really is, follow along with the example set up in the Goal Seek tab of the WHATIF.XLS workbook shown in Figure 10-1. This sheet contains a simple table for projecting the gross sales to be made in 1996 based on the gross sales actually made in 1995 and an assumed rate of growth. As you can see in Figure 10-1, gross sales in 1995 were $850,000. When a growth rate of 10 percent above that figure is assumed, you can expect gross sales of $935,000 in 1996.

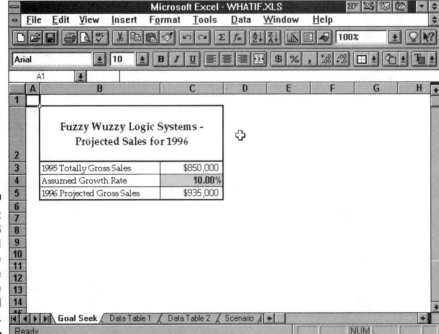

Figure 10-1:
This 1996 projected sales table is a prime candidate for goal seeking.

Now in normal what-if analysis, you would fiddle around with the growth rate (the real variable in the model) to see what happens to the projected sales in 1996 when the growth percentage changes (if the growth rate is less than ten percent or goes well above ten percent). But what if the boss should turn the problem around by coming to you and saying, "Smithers, the company has to have at least a million dollars in gross sales for fiscal year 1996, or heads will roll!"

Put in this way, you will be highly motivated to find out what growth rate is required to meet that all important objective of $1,000,000 in gross sales in 1996 (and retain your job). Fortunately, you can make this kind of calculation in a snap with the goal-seeking feature.

Using the goal-seeking feature

1. **Select the cell that contains the formula for calculating the projected gross sales for 1996.**

   This is cell C5, which currently contains 935,000.

2. **Choose Tools⇨Goal Seek to open the Goal Seek dialog box (similar to the one shown in Figure 10-2).**

3. **Press Tab to advance to the To value text box where you enter** 1000000.

4. **Press Tab to advance to the By changing cell text box where you select cell C4, the cell that contains the anticipated rate of growth.**

   You can select the cell by clicking on the cell or by typing in its cell reference (as an absolute value).

5. **Click on OK or press Enter to have Excel to seek the growth rate necessary to reach the goal.**

When the program finishes solving the problem, it lets you know in a Goal Seek Status dialog box, such as the one in Figure 10-3. When the program is able to find a variable that gives you the desired result, it not only indicates it in the Goal Seek Status dialog box, but it also changes the values in the worksheet. In Figure 10-3, the growth rate in cell C4 is now 17.65%, and the projected gross sales in cell C5 is $1,000,000. If you click on the OK button, Excel replaces the original values in these cells with the new values returned by the goal-seeking operation. If you choose Cancel instead, the program returns these cells to their original values.

When goal seeking pans out and you're happy with the result, click on the OK button in the Goal Seek Status dialog box to change the original values in the worksheet table. Then use the Undo command (Ctrl+U) to flip back and forth between the original values you put in the table and those returned by Excel during goal seeking.

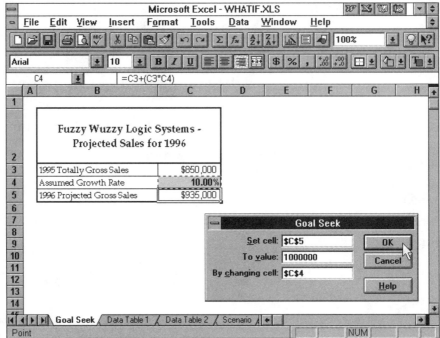

Figure 10-2:
Using the
Goal Seek
dialog box to
find out the
growth rate
required to
sell a million
bucks worth
in 1996.

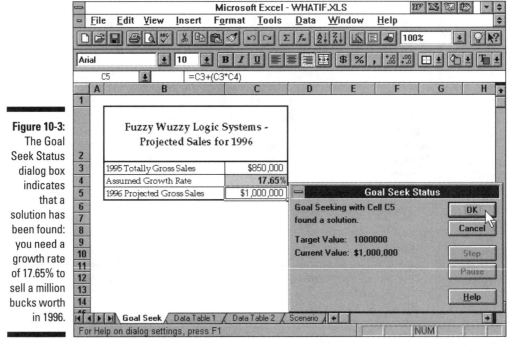

Figure 10-3:
The Goal
Seek Status
dialog box
indicates
that a
solution has
been found:
you need a
growth rate
of 17.65% to
sell a million
bucks worth
in 1996.

Making Wild Projections with Data Tables

The Data⇨Table commands in Excel offer you good old-fashioned what-if analysis so that you can see the effect that changing certain variables has on a particular calculation. There are two flavors of data tables that you can set up in Excel: a single-input data table, in which Excel computes a formula multiple times by changing one variable with a series of different values; and a two-input data table, in which the program computes a formula multiple times by changing two variables, each with its own series of values.

Tables that play with one assumption

You can use a single-input data table to see the effect that changes to one variable in a formula has on the results. Figure 10-4 shows an example of a problem that can benefit from a single-input data table. In this figure, the original projected sales table in Figure 10-1 has been re-created to show the projected sales in 1996 when the annual rate of growth is assumed to be ten percent.

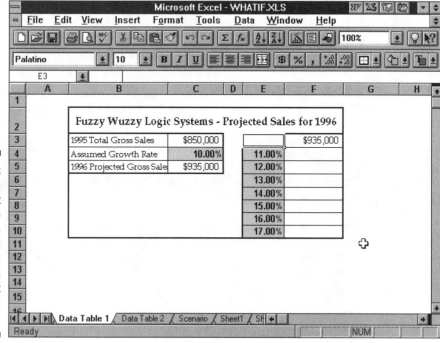

Figure 10-4: Setting up a single-input data table to calculate projected sales based on a series of different growth rates.

Now, suppose that you want to see what effect a series of different growth rates has on the projected sales. To determine this effect, you set up a single-input data table like the one shown in the cell range E4:F10. You enter the series of growth percentages in the first column. In this case, type in **11.00%** in cell E4 and **12.00%** in cell E5, select them, and use the fill handle to extend this series down to cell E10. Then enter the formula where the various percentages are to be substituted at the very top of the second empty column. In this case, bring forward the formula in cell C5 into cell F3.

The percentages in the first column of the data table (cell range E4:F10) in Figure 10-4 represent the variables that you want Excel to substitute for the 10.00% growth rate currently entered in cell C4 and used in the formula in cell C5. After substituting each of the new rates in this column into the formula, Excel puts the projected sales it computes into the associated blank cell to the right in the data table.

Creating a single-input data table

1. **Select all the cells in the data table, including the blank one in cell E3.**

   In this case, you select cell range E3:F10.

2. **Choose the Data⇨Table command on the pull-down menus to open the Table dialog box (see Figure 10-5).**

3. **In the Table dialog box, press Tab to advance to the Column Input Cell text box.**

   Because this one-input table contains variables only in the first column, you don't need to enter an address in the Row Input Cell text box.

4. **In the Column Input Cell text box, enter the address (in absolute values) of the cell whose value is to be substituted by the variable values in the first column of the data table.**

   Enter $C$4 in this example by clicking on the cell or typing the cell address.

5. **Click on OK or press Enter to have Excel fill in the second column of the data table, as shown in Figure 10-6.**

The nice thing about using the Data⇨Table command to test a series of assumptions is that you can see all the results together so that you can compare them. Not only that, but because Excel uses a special TABLE function to compute the projected sales figures (in the cell range F4:F10) of the data table, you can have the data table calculate new results based on a group of new assumptions simply by entering new growth rates in the first column. You don't even have to go through the rigmarole of selecting the cells in the data table, choosing the Data⇨Table command, and specifying the Column Input Cell again.

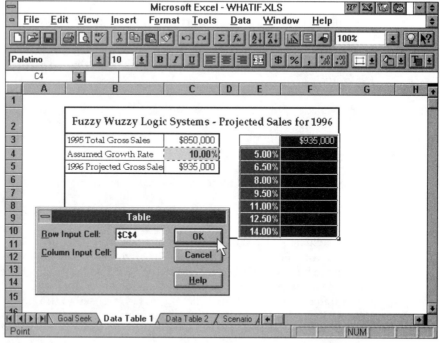

Figure 10-5:
Use the Table dialog box to create a one-input data table that shows the projected incomes for a series of different growth rates.

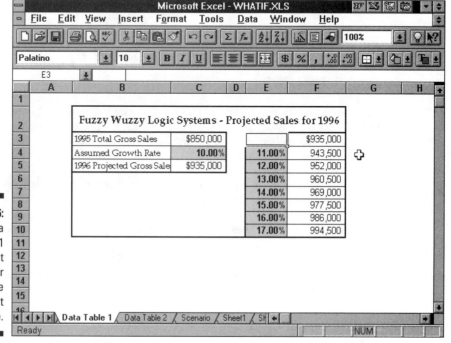

Figure 10-6:
The Data Table 1 worksheet after creating the one-input data table.

Figure 10-7 shows the Data Table 1 worksheet with the same one-input data table after changing the variable growth rates in the cell range E4:E10 from a spread of 11.00% to 17.00% to a spread of 5.00% to 14.00%. If you compare the table in this figure to the one in Figure 10-6, you can see that Excel has automatically recalculated the projected sales figures in the second column of Figure 10-7.

The downside of having Excel use the TABLE function to calculate the results in a data table is that you are effectively prevented from ever deleting a single TABLE formula from the data table. If you try to delete one of the formulas, you receive the Cannot change part of a table error message. To get rid of the formulas in a data table, you need to select all their cells before you press Delete or choose Clear Contents on the cell shortcut menu.

If you don't want Excel to automatically recalculate data tables in the worksheet, open the Options dialog box and select the Automatic Except Tables radio button in the Calculation tab. Selecting this option keeps the program from recalculating the figures in a data table until you press F9 or choose the Calc Now (F9) command or the Calc Sheet button in the Protection tab of the Options dialog box. Keep in mind, however, that when you choose the Automatic Except Tables radio button (as opposed to the Manual radio button), Excel doesn't display the Calculate indicator on the status bar to let you know that you've made changes to the variables or that your data table's values are out-of-date. To get this kind of message when the data table needs recalculating, you have to choose the Manual radio button and switch the whole blooming workbook to manual recalculation mode.

Tables that play with a couple of assumptions

Sometimes, you may want to see the results of changing more than just a single assumption in a particular formula. With the Data⇨Table command, you can play with up to two different variables. To see how this task is accomplished, take a look at the two-input data table set up in Figure 10-8. This table for calculating projected sales is just a bit more elaborate than the single-input table. The two-input table not only assumes that projected gross sales in 1996 will be increased a certain percentage over the gross sales in 1995 (the growth rate percentage in cell D4), but it also assumes that the expenses in 1996 will be a certain percentage of these 1995 sales, as well (the expenses percentage in cell D5). By creating a formula (in cell D6) that calculates the 1996 gross sales based on the growth percentage and then reducing that figure by an amount based on the expenses percentage, this table gives you the projected net sales for the next year.

Figure 10-7:
The Data
Table 1
worksheet
after
changing
the assumed
growth rates
to test for
new
projected
sales figures
in the one-
input data
table.

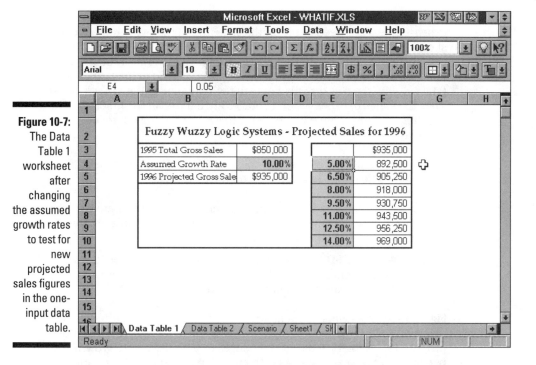

Figure 10-8:
Using the
Table dialog
box to
create a
two-input
data table in
the Data
Table 2
worksheet.

To have Excel create a data table based on changes to the growth rates and expense rates, you need to set up the structure of the two-input data table shown in Figure 10-8. In this table, the formula in cell D6 is brought forward to cell F3, the very first cell of the two-input data table. As in the single-input data table, the series of growth rate percentages are placed in the first column (starting with the row directly beneath the reference to the formula in cell F3). Then the series of expenses percentages are entered in the first row of the table (starting with the column immediately to the right of the reference to the formula).

After selecting all the cells in this table and opening the Table dialog box with the Data⇨Table command, you then do the following:

✔ Designate cell **$D$5** — the one with the expense rate where the series of the expense percentages in the first row of the data table are to be substituted — as the Row Input Cell.

✔ Designate cell **$D$4** — the one with the growth rate where the series of growth percentages in the first column of the data table are to be substituted — as the Column Input Cell.

Figure 10-9 shows what happens when you click on the OK button in the Table dialog box. Excel fills in all the blank cells of the table by calculating the projected sales for 1996 based on changes to both the rate of growth and the percentage of the expenses. As with one-input data tables, Excel computes these projected figures in this two-input data table with its TABLE function. And, as before, you can't modify or delete individual cells of this table. If you want to make a change to the cells, you must select all the cells that use the TABLE function (G4:J10) before doing so.

Creating a Real Scenario in Excel

When you really get into this data analysis stuff big time, you soon discover that playing around with only one or two variables with the Data⇨Table command is simply not adequate. When you reach this stage, you're ready for the Scenarios feature. This feature enables you to play around with any number of variables (referred to as *changing cells*) used in various formulas of a table and then save the results with a name, such as Best Case, Most Likely, and Worst Case.

After you've created a series of different scenarios for your table, you can then view the results of each one by selecting its scenario name. If you want to be able to compare each set of results in one take, you can have Excel generate a summary report that displays each scenario side by side, showing all the assumptions used in the changing cells as well as all the results calculated in the table.

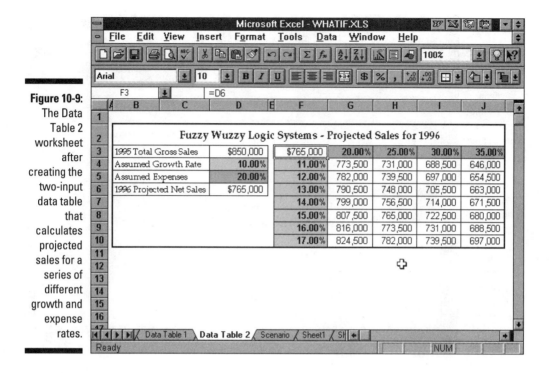

Figure 10-9:
The Data
Table 2
worksheet
after
creating the
two-input
data table
that
calculates
projected
sales for a
series of
different
growth and
expense
rates.

Scenario one, take one . . .

There are two ways to create scenarios in Excel: the short way and the long way. The short way (covered in the next section) uses the Scenarios drop-down list box in the Workgroup toolbar. This method is great when you are working with a what-if table and then suddenly decide that you want to preserve this table with its current values as a scenario. The long way uses the Scenario Manager dialog box and is a better method because you plan which scenarios you need to create, and you prepare to enter the values for each set of changing cells.

To see how the long way works, follow along with the steps for creating four plausible and not-so-plausible scenarios (Realistic, Pie in the Sky, Bad News, and Out of Business!) with the Scenario Manager for the version of the 1996 projected sales table shown in Figure 10-10. In this table, each of the four quarterly sales is based on three growth rates: a sales growth rate in cell H4, a cost of goods sold growth rate in cell H5, and an expenses growth rate in cell H7. Because these percentages are referred to by the appropriate formulas in their rows, you have only to change any or all of these three rates in the cells in column H to create a new scenario.

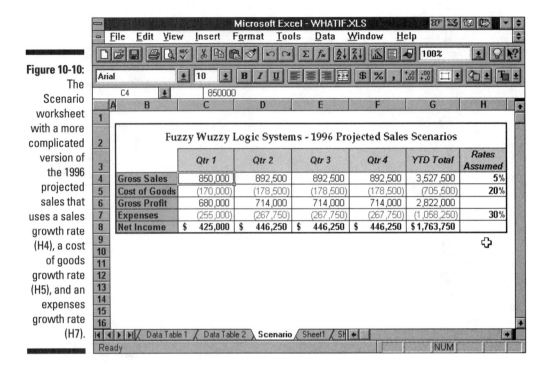

Figure 10-10:
The
Scenario
worksheet
with a more
complicated
version of
the 1996
projected
sales that
uses a sales
growth rate
(H4), a cost
of goods
growth rate
(H5), and an
expenses
growth rate
(H7).

Creating a scenario with the Scenario Manager

To create the most realistic scenario, I entered what I thought to be Fuzzy Wuzzy Logic Systems' best shot at growth in 1996 by putting **5%** in cell H4, **20%** in cell H5, and **30%** in cell H7. Then I followed these steps:

1. **Select cell H4, H5, and H7 by Ctrl+clicking on each of them.**

2. **Choose Tools⇨Scenarios to open the Scenario Manager dialog box.**

3. **Click on the Add button to open the Add Scenario dialog box, similar to the one shown in Figure 10-11.**

4. **Type in a name for the new scenario in the Scenario Name text box.**

   Be creative with names, such as Best Case, You got to be Kidding, and so on.

5. **Check over the cell references listed in the Changing Cells list box and modify them, if necessary.**

6. **Choose the Protection category you want.**

   By default, Excel protects a scenario from changes when you turn on protection for its worksheet. This protection means that you can't edit or delete the scenario in the Scenario Manager, nor can you make new entries in the scenario's changing cells in the worksheet. If you want Excel to hide the scenario as well, choose the Hide check box. If you don't wish to protect or hide the scenario, deselect the Prevent Changes check box and leave the Hide check box alone.

7. **Click on OK or press Enter to open the Scenario Values dialog box.**

8. **Check the values listed in each box for a different changing cell, making changes to them if necessary.**

9. **Click on OK or press Enter to return to the Scenario Manager dialog box.**

10. **To create another scenario, choose the Add button again, repeat Steps 4 – 9, and do not collect $200.**

11. **After you've had enough fun adding scenarios for one day, click on the Close button.**

After you've created your scenarios, be sure to save your workbook so that the scenarios are saved as part of the file.

Thereafter, when you want to take a look at the results in a table using a particular set of values, you simply open the Scenario Manager, choose the scenario you want in the Scenarios list box, and then click on OK or press Enter. Figure 10-12 shows the Scenario Manager with all four scenarios. I was just about to switch from the Realistic scenario to the Pie in the Sky scenario.

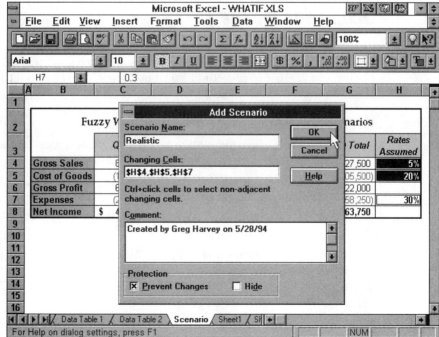

Figure 10-11:
The Add
Scenario
dialog box,
where you
name the
scenario
you're
creating.

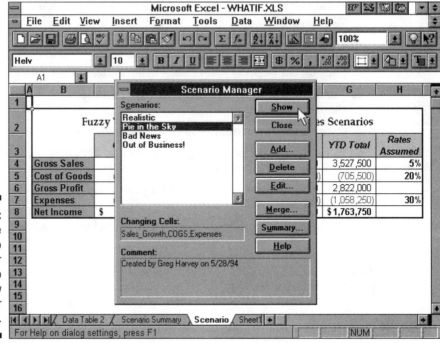

Figure 10-12:
Using the
Scenario
Manager
dialog box to
select a new
scenario for
the table.

Scenarios on the fly

As I promised at the start of this discussion on scenarios, you now get to learn about how to create a scenario on the fly (my so-called short way). Before you can use this handy-dandy method, you must have already entered the values you want saved in the changing cells.

Creating a scenario with the Workgroup toolbar

1. **Display the Workgroup toolbar by choosing Workgroup on the toolbar shortcut menu or by choosing the View⇨Toolbars command.**

2. **Select all the changing cells (by Ctrl+clicking on them, naturally) with the values you want saved in the new scenario.**

   In the example sales table, I selected cells H4, H5, and H7 after entering **55%**, **8%**, and **12%** in them, respectively.

3. **Click in the Scenarios text box in the Workgroup toolbar and type a name for the new scenario (see Figure 10-13).**

4. **Press the Enter key.**

That's all there is to the short method. Just keep in mind that you need to have all your changing cells up-to-snuff for the scenario you're creating before you select them and start typing in the new name in the Scenarios text box of the Workgroup toolbar.

Not only does the Workgroup toolbar provide the quickest way for adding a scenario, but it also provides the quickest way to select one. Simply click on the Scenarios drop-down list button and then select the name of the scenario in the drop-down list. Figure 10-14 shows my selection of the Pie in the Sky scenario right after creating the Too Good to be True! scenario.

Scenario summary reports

After you've added all the great (and not so great) scenarios for a particular table, you can then create a summary report that enables you to see the assumptions and results of each scenario side by side. When you create a scenario summary report for a table that has a number of scenarios, Excel generates the report containing all this information and puts it in a new worksheet called Scenario Summary. The Scenario Summary worksheet is inserted right in front of the worksheet containing the table with all the scenarios. You can move the Scenario Summary worksheet as you see fit or even delete it after printing or charting it. When generating a scenario summary, Excel takes whatever values are currently used in the changing cells of the table and contrasts them to those values specified by all the other scenarios created for that table.

To create a report, you need to open the Scenario Manager dialog box with the Tools⇨Scenarios command and then choose the Summary button to open up the Scenario Summary dialog box (see Figure 10-15). By default, Excel chooses the Scenario Summary option rather than the Scenario Pivot Table option (see Chapter 11). Before you click on OK to generate the summary, you need to select the range of cells in the table that contain the results upon which your changing cells depend so that its range address (in absolute values) is displayed in the Result Cells text box. In the case of the 1996 sales scenarios table, the result cells are those that show the net income figures in the cell range C8:G8.

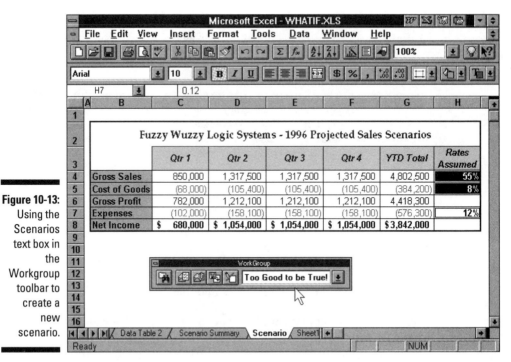

Figure 10-13:
Using the
Scenarios
text box in
the
Workgroup
toolbar to
create a
new
scenario.

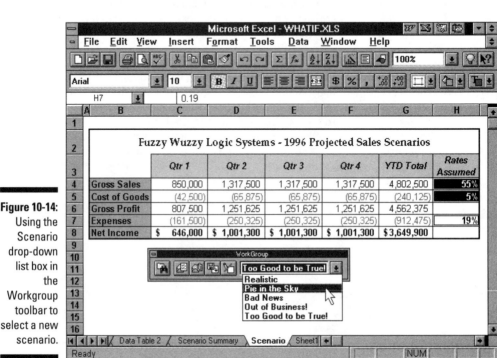

Figure 10-14:
Using the
Scenario
drop-down
list box in
the
Workgroup
toolbar to
select a new
scenario.

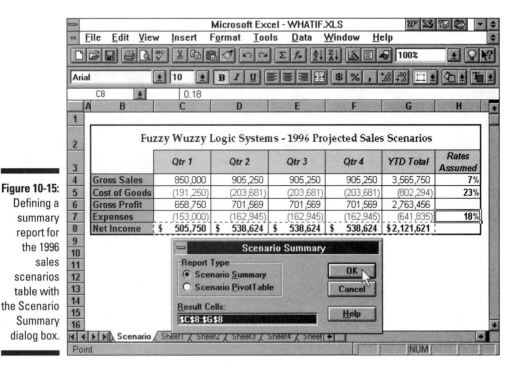

Figure 10-15:
Defining a
summary
report for
the 1996
sales
scenarios
table with
the Scenario
Summary
dialog box.

After you click on OK in the Scenario Summary dialog box, Excel goes to work
on generating a summary table that compares the changing values and results
of the current values to each scenario. This table is done in outline form (see
Chapter 8 for an explanation of this outline business) so that you can expand
and collapse levels as you need. Figure 10-16 shows the first part of the
summary report table on the new Scenario Summary worksheet that was
generated for the 1996 sales scenarios table. (I futzed with the column widths
so that you could see as much of the table as possible.) Note how the current
values (current at the moment this report was created) are contrasted to the
projected values for each set of scenarios and are presented in the order in
which they were originally created.

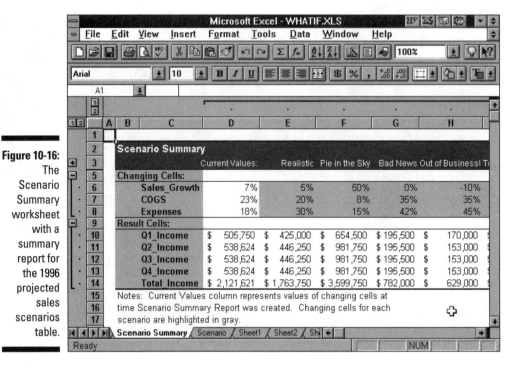

Figure 10-16:
The
Scenario
Summary
worksheet
with a
summary
report for
the 1996
projected
sales
scenarios
table.

Part IV
A Few of the More Advanced Features

The 5th Wave   **By Rich Tennant**

The computer virus crept silently from network to network, until it found its way into the cafeteria vending machines.

In this part . . .

*A*dvanced always has such a scary sound to it. In this section, you really don't get exposed so much to extra-difficult topics as to really *specialized* ones that are suitable for stu-dents who just can't get enough of the good things Excel has to offer. For example, Chapter 11 teaches you how to use the Pivot Table feature to cross-tabulate data in a list or database. Obviously, this a subject that you would pursue only when you really need to do that kind of analysis (or if you have become something of an Excel nerd — but we don't have to worry about that). Of more general interest, in this part you will also find information on how to edit macros that you record and create custom functions as well as a whole bunch of good information on using Excel as one of the programs that come bundled in Microsoft Office.

Chapter 11

Data Summaries, Thanks to Pivot Tables

*T*he subject of this chapter is pivot tables. The *pivot table* is another new Excel 5 feature for summarizing certain values in a list or database without having to actually create formulas to perform the calculations. Unlike the Automatic Subtotals feature, the other new Excel 5 summarizing feature (discussed in Chapter 6), pivot tables let you play around with the arrangement of the summarized data, even after you create the list. (The Automatic Subtotals feature only lets you hide and display different levels of totals in the list.) It's this ability to change the arrangement of the summarized data by rotating row and column headings that gives the pivot table its (strange) name.

Like automatic subtotals, pivot tables let you summarize data by using a variety of different summary functions (although totals created with the SUM function will probably remain your old standby). When setting up the original pivot table — with the wonderful PivotTable Wizard — you make several decisions: which summary functions to use, which columns (fields) the summary functions are applied to, and which columns (fields) these computations are tabulated with. You also can use pivot tables to cross-tabulate one set of data in your list or database with another. For example, you can use this feature to create a pivot table from an employee database that totals the salaries for each job category cross-tabulated (arranged) by department or job site.

"Where, oh where, has my little Crosstab Report Wizard gone?"

Pivot tables and the PivotTable Wizard in Excel 5 replace (thank heaven) crosstab tables and the Crosstab Report Wizard introduced in Excel 4.0. Although pivot tables, as presented by the PivotTable Wizard, are still considered by some to be too hard and cumbersome to use, believe you me, compared to using that skanky Cross Tab Report Wizard in 4.0, generating cross-tabulated data tables is a piece of cake with the PivotTable Wizard in Excel 5!

Pivot Tables, Courtesy of the PivotTable Wizard

Microsoft Windows programs these days are crawling with Wizards, so it should come as no surprise that pivot tables use yet another Excel Wizard, called the PivotTable Wizard. To use the PivotTable Wizard, you must first determine the following four points:

- ✔ Indicate the source of the data to be summarized. This source can be an Excel list or database; a database created with a bona fide database management program, such as Access, FoxPro, Paradox, or dBASE; a collection of different data tables (which must have both row and column headings) spread throughout a workbook; or data in another pivot table.

- ✔ Indicate the range of cells that contains the data you want summarized by the pivot table. This cell range must include the column headings (column and rows when using the Multiple Consolidation Range option).

- ✔ Arrange the columns (fields) in the list or database the way you want them to appear in the pivot table by dragging buttons with their field names onto different parts of a diagram of the report. As part of this process, you also decide which fields are to be summarized and which summary functions are to be used.

- ✔ Indicate where the pivot table is to be located in the worksheet: If you don't specify a starting cell location, Excel inserts the pivot table at the beginning of a new worksheet. Assign a name to the table: If you don't specify a name, Excel gives it a real original name like PivotTable1. And deselect any of the pivot table default options that you don't want used.

To see how easy it is to generate a simple pivot table from a list of data by using the PivotTable Wizard, follow along with the steps that summarize the sales data in the list shown in Figure 11-1. If this list looks familiar, it's because it was originally created in Chapter 6, where it was used to illustrate the advanced filtering and automatic subtotals features.

In case you haven't yet had the pleasure of reading Chapter 6, this list represents a sales database that tracks the daily sales in Simple Simon's world-famous Pastry Palace of four different pastry goodies (such as Queen's tarts and Muffet muffins) sold in four different locations (such as Muffet Street and Arachnid Rd.). For this particular example, I input bogus sales for these products for the first five days in January, 1995. In a *real* sales table like this, you would enter sales for all 31 days of the month, provided, that is, that the establishment runs seven days a week.

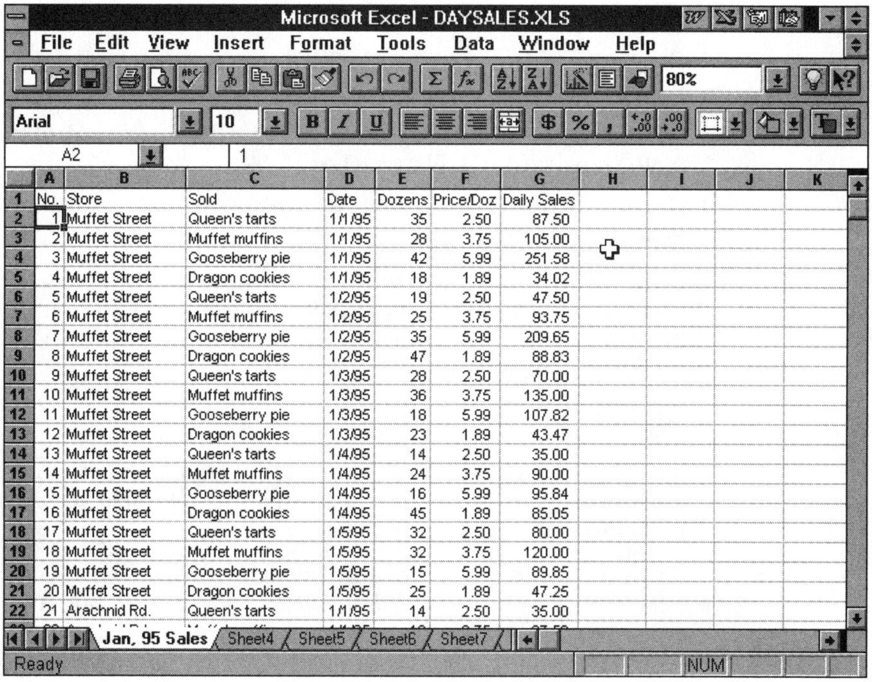

Figure 11-1:
The Jan, 95 Sales worksheet, with a list of sales for all stores during the first five days in January.

	A	B	C	D	E	F	G
1	No.	Store	Sold	Date	Dozens	Price/Doz	Daily Sales
2	1	Muffet Street	Queen's tarts	1/1/95	35	2.50	87.50
3	2	Muffet Street	Muffet muffins	1/1/95	28	3.75	105.00
4	3	Muffet Street	Gooseberry pie	1/1/95	42	5.99	251.58
5	4	Muffet Street	Dragon cookies	1/1/95	18	1.89	34.02
6	5	Muffet Street	Queen's tarts	1/2/95	19	2.50	47.50
7	6	Muffet Street	Muffet muffins	1/2/95	25	3.75	93.75
8	7	Muffet Street	Gooseberry pie	1/2/95	35	5.99	209.65
9	8	Muffet Street	Dragon cookies	1/2/95	47	1.89	88.83
10	9	Muffet Street	Queen's tarts	1/3/95	28	2.50	70.00
11	10	Muffet Street	Muffet muffins	1/3/95	36	3.75	135.00
12	11	Muffet Street	Gooseberry pie	1/3/95	18	5.99	107.82
13	12	Muffet Street	Dragon cookies	1/3/95	23	1.89	43.47
14	13	Muffet Street	Queen's tarts	1/4/95	14	2.50	35.00
15	14	Muffet Street	Muffet muffins	1/4/95	24	3.75	90.00
16	15	Muffet Street	Gooseberry pie	1/4/95	16	5.99	95.84
17	16	Muffet Street	Dragon cookies	1/4/95	45	1.89	85.05
18	17	Muffet Street	Queen's tarts	1/5/95	32	2.50	80.00
19	18	Muffet Street	Muffet muffins	1/5/95	32	3.75	120.00
20	19	Muffet Street	Gooseberry pie	1/5/95	15	5.99	89.85
21	20	Muffet Street	Dragon cookies	1/5/95	25	1.89	47.25
22	21	Arachnid Rd.	Queen's tarts	1/1/95	14	2.50	35.00

Microsoft Excel - DAYSALES.XLS

File   Edit   View   Insert   Format   Tools   Data   Window   Help

Arial   10

A2   1

Jan, 95 Sales / Sheet4 / Sheet5 / Sheet6 / Sheet7 /

Ready   NUM

Creating a pivot table

To create a pivot table that analyzes the sales data in Figure 11-1, follow these steps:

1. **Position the cell pointer in the first cell of the table data (cell A2 in this example).**

2. **Choose the Data⇨PivotTable command on the pull-down menus to display the PivotTable Wizard – Step 1 of 4 dialog box (shown in Figure 11-2).**

   By default, Excel chooses the Microsoft Excel List or Database radio button. If your data consists of multiple ranges, another pivot table, or an external database, choose the appropriate radio button.

3. **After you verify that all information is correct in the Step 1 dialog box, click on the Next button to open the PivotTable Wizard – Step 2 of 4 dialog box (shown in Figure 11-3).**

4. **Check the cell range shown in the Range text box and, if necessary, edit the cell range or select it again.**

5. **Click on the Next button to open the PivotTable Wizard – Step 3 of 4 dialog box (shown in Figure 11-4).**

6. **Drag the buttons for the fields whose data you want summarized to the appropriate areas on-screen.**

   In this example, I dragged the Daily Sales button (with the *s* cut off) to the DATA area of the report diagram. If you want to use some other summary function (such as AVERAGE or COUNT) rather than the SUM function, double-click on the button you dragged to the DATA area. Then select the function you want to use in the Summarize by list box in the PivotTable Field dialog box and click on the OK button.

   Drag the button of the field you want to appear in the columns of the pivot table to the COLUMN area. Drag the button of the field you want to appear in the rows of pivot table to the ROW area.

   If you want to separate the table data into "pages" so that you can display data for one item at a time, drag the appropriate field button to the PAGE area of the report diagram. In this example, I dragged the button of the Store field to the PAGE area so that I could flip through the daily sales for each store.

7. **Click on the Next button to open the PivotTable Wizard – Step 4 of 4 dialog box (shown in Figure 11-5).**

   If you want the pivot table to be generated in a new worksheet, leave the PivotTable Starting Cell text box empty. If you want the table to be located somewhere on the current sheet or on another existing sheet, indicate the address of the first cell of the range in this text box (be sure that there's no danger of overlaying and thereby wiping out existing data in the vicinity). If you want, enter a name of your own choosing for your pivot table in the Pivot Table Name text box and modify any of the PivotTable Options that need changing (you can usually live with these options selected).

8. **When you are satisfied with the choices you have made in the Step 4 dialog box, click on the Finish button.**

After you choose the Finish button, Excel generates the new pivot table, starting in the cell indicated in the PivotTable Starting Cell text box. If you left this text box blank (as I did in this example), Excel generates the pivot table at the beginning of a new worksheet, which is inserted right in front of the worksheet containing the list used to create the table. The program also automatically displays the Query and Pivot toolbar — a rather obscure toolbar that is so inconspicuous, it doesn't even show up on the toolbar shortcut menu — that you can use to edit the table (see Figure 11-6).

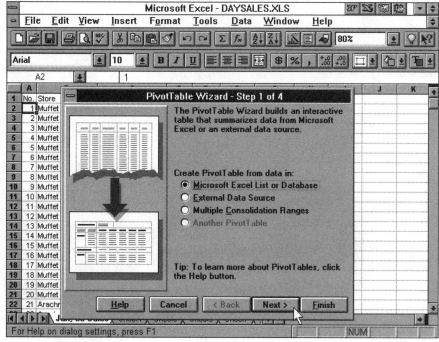

Figure 11-2:
Indicating the type of data to be used in the PivotTable Wizard – Step 1 of 4 dialog box.

Figure 11-3:
Indicating
the range of
data to be
used in the
PivotTable
Wizard –
Step 2 of 4
dialog box.

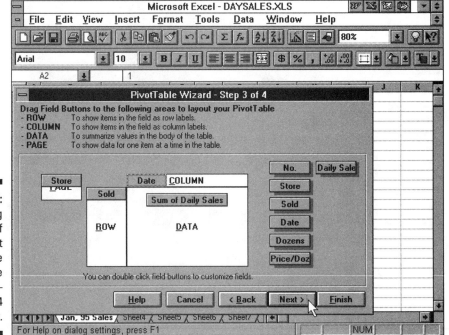

Figure 11-4:
Indicating
the layout of
the pivot
table in the
PivotTable
Wizard –
Step 3 of 4
dialog box.

Figure 11-5:
Indicating
the location
and name of
the pivot
table in the
PivotTable
Wizard –
Step 4 of 4
dialog box.

Figure 11-6 shows the completed pivot table created from the sales table according to the layout specified in the PivotTable Wizard – Step 3 of 4 dialog box. Note that the rows of the pivot table show the category of pastries sold, indicated by the shaded Sold label in cell A4. The columns of the table show the date of the sales, indicated by the shaded Date label in cell B3. The adjusted name of the field, Sum of Daily Sales, that I dragged to the DATA area in the Step 3 dialog box appears in this finished table as a label in cell A3, right above the Sold heading and immediately to the left of the Date heading.

Because the Store field was selected as the page item for this table, Excel set up a Page section above the data in the pivot table at the top of Sheet 1. Cell A1 contains the shaded Store label, and cell B1, sporting a shiny new drop-down list button, contains the name of the current store. The pivot table in Figure 11-6 is currently showing the sales figures by date and item sold for all three stores (indicated by (All) entered in cell B1). To see the sales by date and item sold for just one of the stores, simply click on the drop-down list button and select the store from the list.

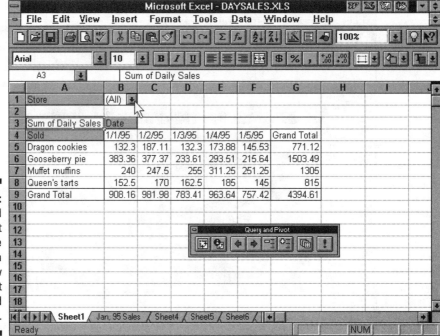

Figure 11-6:
The brand new pivot table created in a new worksheet called Sheet1.

Figures 11-7 and 11-8 demonstrate how easy it is to switch from the daily sales totals for all the stores to those made just in the Muffet Street location. In Figure 11-7, I clicked on the drop-down list box in cell B1 and then dragged down to the Muffet Street listing. Figure 11-8 shows the pivot table after I released the mouse.

Editing a Pivot Table

Pivot tables (despite their ugly name) are pretty neat creatures simply because they remain interactive even after you create them. In the example table in the preceding section, you saw how easy it is to display sales data for a particular store: You simply select the store name in the Store drop-down list box. Do you want to see the totals for all the stores? Bam! What could be easier! Just select (All) in this drop-down list.

Well, if you like making changes at the drop of a list (as I obviously do), you're really going to like editing pivot tables. Excel offers two methods for editing a pivot table after you've created it. You can either get back into the PivotTable Wizard and make your changes there, or you can use your good friend drag and drop to rearrange the field labels in the pivot table.

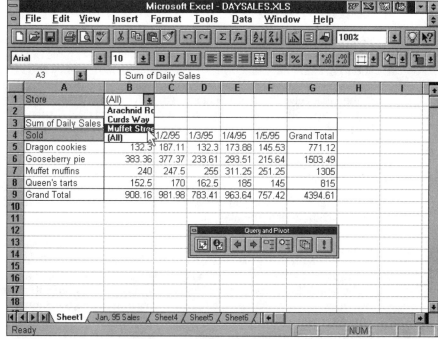

Figure 11-7:
Selecting
Muffet
Street as the
store whose
daily sales
totals are to
be displayed
in the pivot
table.

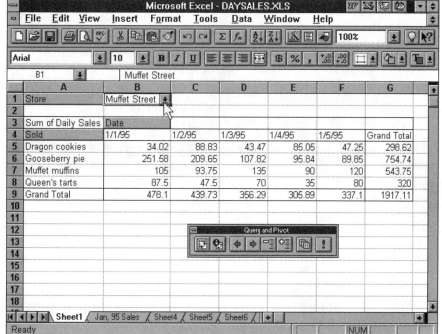

Figure 11-8:
The pivot
table after
displaying
the daily
sales for the
Muffet
Street store.

Editing, thanks to the PivotTable Wizard

You can use the PivotTable Wizard — by far the most ho-hum of the two ways to edit a pivot table — to rearrange the fields in a pivot table or to change or add to the summary functions used on its data. If the Query and Pivot table toolbar is on-screen, you can edit your pivot table by positioning the cell in one of the table cells and then clicking on the PivotTable Wizard tool, the very first tool on the toolbar (see Figure 11-6). If this toolbar is not displayed, bring up the PivotTable Wizard by choosing the Data➪PivotTable command.

Any way you do it, Excel redisplays the PivotTable Wizard – Step 3 of 4 dialog box, which shows the current layout of all the fields in your summary report. At this point, you can rearrange the fields by dragging them to new areas of the report diagram, or you can delete fields by dragging them to somewhere off their current area in the diagram.

If you want to change the summary function used by the field currently located in the DATA area, double-click on the field to open the PivotTable Field dialog box (similar to the one shown in Figure 11-9). There you can change the name of the field, which changes the label shown in the pivot table itself, in the Name text box. You also can change the summary function in the Summarize by list box. After you make your changes in this dialog box, click on OK to return to the PivotTable Wizard – Step 3 of 4 dialog box.

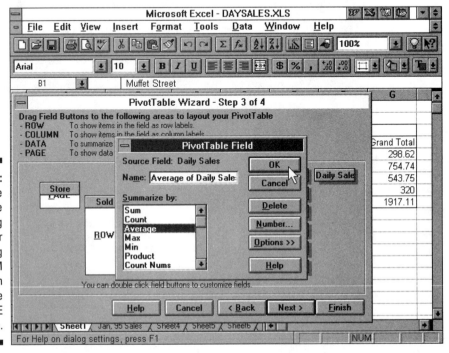

Figure 11-9: The PivotTable Field dialog box after replacing the SUM function with the AVERAGE function.

Pivot tables can display more than one summary function for a single field. If you want to define an additional summary function for a field in the DATA area, you need to drag another one of the field buttons to this area in the PivotTable Wizard dialog box. You can then double-click on this new summary button if you need to change its name or its function. When you add summary buttons for one field with different functions, the pivot table displays these calculations in the order in which their summary buttons appear in the DATA area. To rearrange one summary function ahead of another, you need to drag its summary button up and then drop it into position ahead of (slightly above) the summary button that is to follow it.

If you need to change only the name of a summary field or the function it uses, you can do this directly from the pivot table. Position the cell pointer on the cell with the summary field name and then click on the PivotTable Field tool on the Query and Pivot toolbar or choose the PivotTable Field command on the Data pull-down menu. This step opens the PivotTable Field dialog box, with the information on the current summary field, which you can then modify at will.

Figure 11-10 shows the sample pivot table after changing the summary function for the Daily Sales summary field from SUM to AVERAGE so that its label in cell A3 now reads Average of Daily Sales rather than Sum of Daily Sales.

Figures 11-11 and 11-12 show the process of making another modification to the pivot table. This time, I opened the PivotTable Wizard dialog box and switched the Date and Sold fields in the table by dragging the Date field from the COLUMN section to the ROW section and the Sold field from the ROW section to the COLUMN section (see Figure 11-11). Figure 11-12 shows the changes that Excel made to the pivot table after I clicked on the Finish button. As you can see, the dates now run down the rows of the table, and the items sold stretch across its columns.

Pivot tables can display more than one summary function for a single field. If you want to define an additional summary function for a field in the DATA area, you need to drag another one of the field buttons to this area in the PivotTable Wizard dialog box. You can then double-click on this new summary button if you need to change its name or its function. When you add summary buttons for one field with different functions, the pivot table displays these calculations in the order in which their summary buttons appear in the DATA area. To rearrange one summary function ahead of another, you need to drag its summary button up and then drop it into position ahead of (slightly above) the summary button that is to follow it.

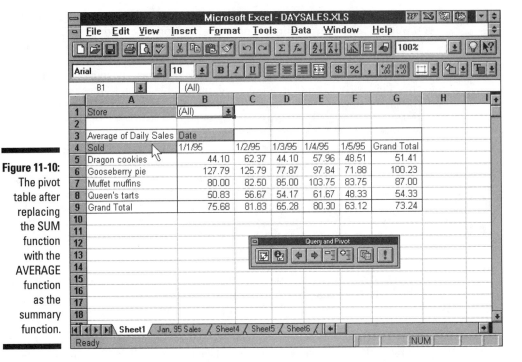

Figure 11-10:
The pivot table after replacing the SUM function with the AVERAGE function as the summary function.

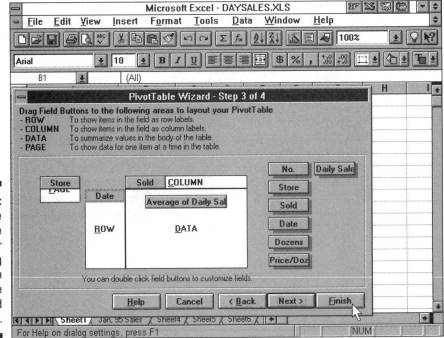

Figure 11-11:
The PivotTable Wizard after switching the position of the Date and Sold fields.

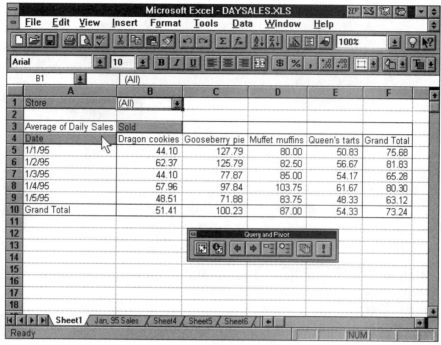

Figure 11-12:
The pivot
table, with
dates
running
down the
rows and
items sold
running
across the
columns.

Figure 11-13 shows the sample pivot table after I made yet another editing change with the PivotTable Wizard. This time, I added a second summary function, SUM, to the Daily Sales field and positioned it above the AVERAGE summary function so that the pivot table displays both the total and average sales. To make this change, I opened the PivotTable Wizard dialog box and added a Sum of Daily Sales summary field to the DATA area of the report diagram by dragging the Daily Sales field button to this area. Then I dragged this new summary button until it was on top of the Average of Daily Sales summary button and released the mouse button to position the totals on top of the averages in the pivot table.

In Figure 11-13, you can see the effect of adding this new summary function to the pivot table. Notice that the table contains two rows for each date: the first row shows the total sales, and the second row shows the average sales. Notice, also, that after making this change, this pivot table now contains a Data column (column B in the worksheet) that identifies the name of each summary field. Before I changed the names, this column contained the original summary field names: Sum of Daily Sales followed by Average of Daily Sales. However, these long labels looked really clunky in the table and were hard to read, so I shortened them to Total Sales and Average Sales.

	A	B	C	D	E	F	G
1	Store	(All)					
2							
3			Sold				
4	Date	Data	Dragon cookies	Gooseberry pie	Muffet muffins	Queen's tarts	Grand Total
5	1/1/95	Total Sales	$ 132.30	$ 383.36	$ 240.00	$ 152.50	$ 908.16
6		Average Sales	44.10	127.79	80.00	50.83	75.68
7	1/2/95	Total Sales	187.11	377.37	247.50	170.00	981.98
8		Average Sales	62.37	125.79	82.50	56.67	81.83
9	1/3/95	Total Sales	132.30	233.61	255.00	162.50	783.41
10		Average Sales	44.10	77.87	85.00	54.17	65.28
11	1/4/95	Total Sales	173.88	293.51	311.25	185.00	963.64
12		Average Sales	57.96	97.84	103.75	61.67	80.30
13	1/5/95	Total Sales	145.53	215.64	251.25	145.00	757.42
14		Average Sales	48.51	71.88	83.75	48.33	63.12
15	Total Total Sales		$ 771.12	$ 1,503.49	$ 1,305.00	$ 815.00	$ 4,394.61
16	Total Average Sales		$ 51.41	$ 100.23	$ 87.00	$ 54.33	$ 73.24
17							
18							
19							

Figure 11-13: The pivot table after adding a SUM function to the AVERAGE function in the Daily Sales field.

To change the field names, I selected cell B5 — the one containing the original Sum of Daily Sales label — clicked on the PivotTable Field tool in the Query and Pivot toolbar, and then edited the name in the PivotTable Field dialog box. Next, I selected cell B6 — the one containing the original Average of Daily Sales label — and repeated the procedure.

Musical summary functions

Any of the switching of the pivot table fields that I showed you in the preceding section using the PivotTable Wizard could (and probably, should) be done directly in the pivot table itself by using drag and drop. Actually, not until you drag a field label from one place in a pivot table to another and watch Excel change the orientation of the headings and update the data do you actually understand why Microsoft named these hummers *pivot tables*.

To rearrange the pivot table fields, you simply click on their field labels (the shaded ones) and drag them to their new locations. After you release the mouse button, Excel reconfigures the pivot table to include the information covered by that field label. Don't believe me? Well, then, take a look at Figures 11-14 through 11-17.

Figure 11-14 shows how I dragged the Date field label from the ROW area of the pivot table up to the PAGE area (I could just as well have dragged it to the COLUMN area). I could tell when it was safe to release the mouse button to drop the Date field into the PAGE area because a shaded I-beam appeared at the bottom of cells A2 and B2, and the mouse pointer icon took on the shape of three cascading header rows.

Figure 11-15 shows the pivot table after I finished dropping the Date field into the PAGE area and was in the process of dragging the Store field from the PAGE to the ROW area. I made this move to switch the Date field with the Store field so that I can page through the sales totals arranged by store location, day by day. I could tell when it was safe to drop the Store field into the ROW area because a shaded I-beam appeared at the left edge of rows 6 and 7, and the mouse pointer icon took on a table shape. (Please write me and tell me if you can figure out what this icon is really trying to show!)

Figure 11-16 shows how the pivot table looks after I made my last field drop. As you can see, this view represents the total and average sales for all (five) days in the list and is arranged in rows by store and in columns by items sold. Figure 11-17 shows the same pivot table after I selected 1/1/95 in the Date drop-down list to display just the totals and average sales for the first day in January, 1995.

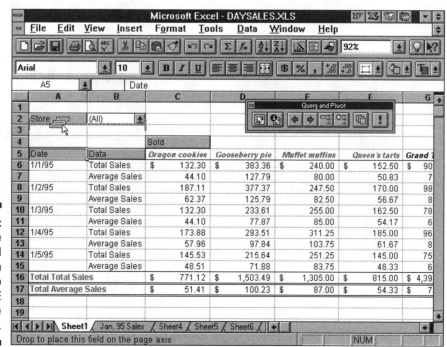

Figure 11-14: Dragging the Date field label from the ROW to the PAGE area of the pivot table.

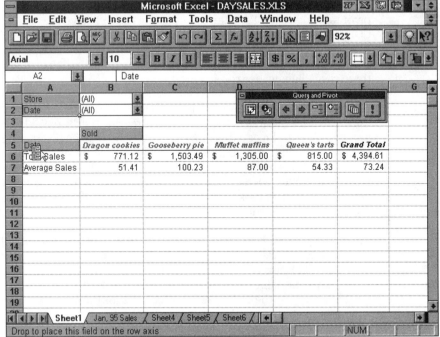

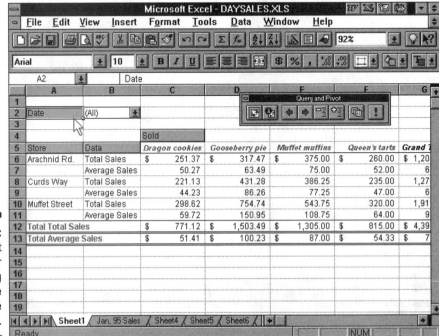

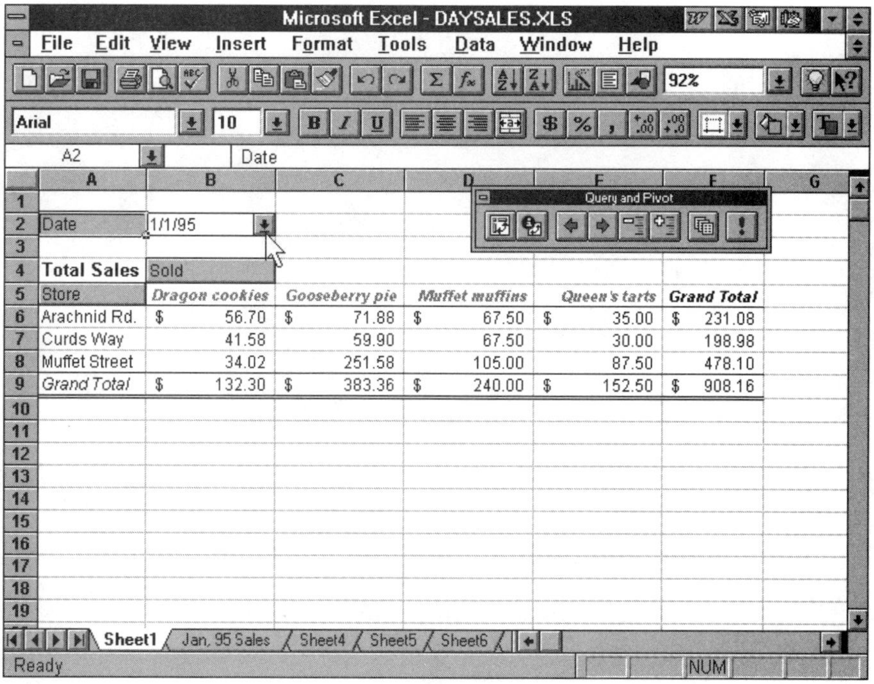

Figure 11-17:
The pivot
table after
selecting
1/1/95 in the
Date drop-
down list.

Prettying up the pivot table

Pivot tables are notorious (well, maybe they're too new to be notorious) for their lack of formatting. After creating a pivot table, Excel simply assigns the plain old General number format to the calculated values in the table. The best way (meaning both the easiest and the most efficient way) to format a pivot table is with the Autoformat feature. Then, if you later edit the pivot table by adding or removing a new summary function or summary field, you don't have to go through all the bother of formatting the changed parts of the table (which automatically revert back to that awful General format).

To format a pivot table with the Autoformat feature, position the cell pointer in any of the table's cells and then choose the Autoformat command on the Format pull-down menu. Select the formatting you want in the Table Format list box and then click on OK or press Enter. To get an idea of what a difference a table format can make, contrast the look of the numbers in the pivot table shown in Figure 11-12 (using the General format) with the look of the numbers in the table shown in Figure 11-13. For Figure 11-13, I selected the Accounting 1 table format that uses the number format with commas everywhere but the first and last rows of the table which use a mild form of the Currency format.

Chapter 12

More Macro Magic

. . . .

In This Chapter

▶ A quick review of recording macros

▶ A quick review of assigning shortcut keys to macros

▶ A quick review of assigning macros to buttons, graphics, and the Tools pull-down menu

▶ How to edit recorded macros

▶ How to create custom Excel functions with macros

. . . .

Macros in Excel 5 are complicated by the fact that the program is now in transition between two different and mutually exclusive coding systems: the so-called Excel 4.0 macro language (although it's been in use in some form in all earlier versions of Excel for Windows) and Visual Basic. Excel 5 still supports the Excel 4.0 macro language because such people as the local spread-sheet guru in your office, who've spent months developing super-sophisticated macros with this code, can still run their prize-winning macros after they upgrade to Excel 5.

Nevertheless, this dual support for the Excel 4.0 macro language and Visual Basic in Excel represents a reprieve, not a pardon. Microsoft is determined from here on out to push the use of Visual Basic as the macro language in all its major applications (it's already crept into Word for Windows 6.0). Because of Microsoft's Visual Basic fetish, you need to decide which language to use when you create your own macros in Excel. (I understand, however, that you, gentle reader, have absolutely no intention of actually, yuck, *learning to code in Visual Basic!!!*) When making this choice, keep in mind that version 5 undoubtedly re-presents the last version of Excel that will run macros in any language other than Visual Basic. So if you don't get on the bandwagon now and start creating macros in Visual Basic, you will either be stuck not being able to upgrade to the next version of Excel or face an even more daunting task of having to re-create all your macros in Visual Basic.

Microsoft doesn't include any type of automated translation features for converting macros recorded or written in the Excel 4.0 macro language to Visual Basic. Without this translation feature, you have to go through the tedious process of re-recording or manually rewriting every single one of your old macros to convert them from the Excel 4.0 macro language to Visual Basic.

Fortunately, because Excel 5 still runs macros coded in the old macro language, you can still use your old macros while you're in the process of re-creating them in Visual Basic. Just be sure that you assign a new name to the Visual Basic version of each macro so that you still can use the original macro in the meantime.

Seeing the coding written all over the wall, so to speak, this chapter introduces you to using Visual Basic in recording and editing simple macros and in writing your own custom functions. And, of course, if you find yourself so motivated from this meager introduction to Visual Basic that you actually want to learn how to do real *programming* in Visual Basic, you'll be all set to go.

Macro Recording Revisited

In *Excel For Dummies*, you learned how to create macros by using the macro recorder to record the steps you take to accomplish a particular task as you actually perform them. To use the macro recorder, choose Tools⇨Record Macro⇨Record New Macro, name the macro, and press Enter. Excel displays the Recording message on the status bar along with a tiny toolbar — which is named Stop Recording, although you can't see much more than *Sto* and part of a *p* in the toolbar's title bar — that has one measly little tool (called Stop Macro). You then do the things in Excel that you later want your macro to do for you. After you're finished, you click on the Stop Macro tool in the tiny Stop Recording toolbar, or you choose Tools⇨Record Macro⇨Stop Recording (for more detailed instructions on recording macros, please see Chapter 10 of *Excel For Dummies*).

As you may expect, Excel 5 automatically records the steps in a macro in the preferred Visual Basic language. In fact, if you want to record a macro in the old macro language, you have to go out of your way to open the Record New Macro dialog box and choose the MS Excel 4.0 Macro radio button, which is available only after you've expanded the dialog box by choosing its Options button.

How Can Ya Tell a Module Sheet from a Macro Sheet?

The code that Excel 5 writes when you record a new macro in Visual Basic is automatically stored in a special Module sheet, which is given a temporary name like Module1, Module2, and so on — just like the temporary names given to new chart sheets and worksheets in a workbook. The code that Excel writes when you record a macro in the Excel 4.0 macro language is stored in a Macro sheet, which is again given a temporary name like Macro1, Macro2, and so on.

Deciding where to record your macros

When you record a new macro, you can record it in any of three ways: as part of the current workbook, which causes Excel to insert its Module or Macro sheet at the end of the current workbook; as part of your Personal Macro Workbook, which causes Excel to insert its Module or Macro sheet at the end of the workbook named PERSONAL.XLS; or as part of a new workbook, which causes Excel to insert its Module or Macro sheet at the end of a brand new workbook. If you choose the Personal Macro Workbook option, the macro is available to you anytime you're using Excel. If you record the macro in the current workbook or in a new workbook, the macro runs only when you're working in that particular workbook. The PERSONAL.XLS workbook doesn't exist until you record your first macro by using the Personal Macro Workbook radio button *and* saving your changes in this workbook upon exiting Excel. When you exit, Excel saves this workbook in the C:\EXCEL\XLSTART directory (assuming that your Excel directory is called EXCEL and that you've installed Excel on the C drive).

As you can see from Figures 12-1 and 12-2, the most noticeable difference between a Module sheet and a Macro sheet is that a Module sheet doesn't use the column and row grid lines of a worksheet. To see all the text of the macro commands in a Macro sheet, you have to widen column A, as I have done in Figure 12-2. The lines of Visual Basic commands in the Module1 sheet, however, are normally all visible without requiring any fooling around other than vertical scrolling (notice, also, how nicely indented the Visual Basic commands are).

Beyond the obvious, if superficial, difference between the look of a Module and a Macro sheet, you will find other, more significant (if less obvious) differences in their coding, such as

- Each command in a Macro sheet is contained in its own cell in a single column; each command in the Visual Basic Module sheet is placed on its own line.

- The macro commands in the Macro sheet all begin with an equal sign, like Excel functions; Visual Basic commands in the Module sheet just start with the command words.

- The settings put into effect by the macro commands in the Macro sheet are located in the closed pair of parentheses, like arguments of a function; the settings put into effect by the Visual Basic commands in the Module sheet are located after an equal sign opposite the particular command or attribute.

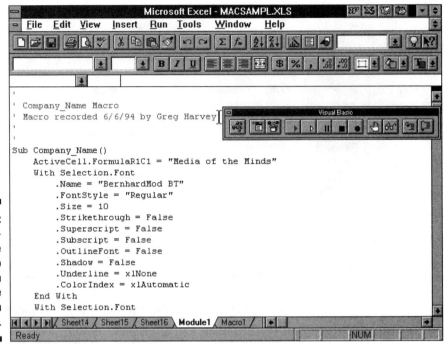

Figure 12-1:
The Company_Name macro recorded in a Module sheet in Visual Basic.

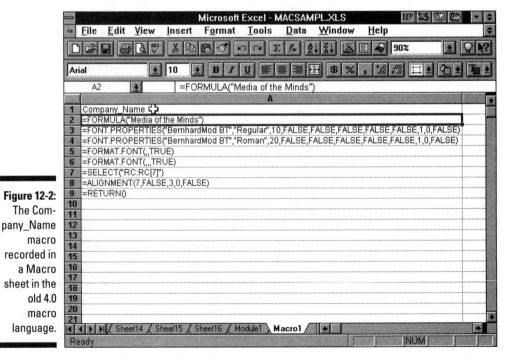

Figure 12-2:
The Company_Name macro recorded in a Macro sheet in the old 4.0 macro language.

When It's Playback Time

After you record a macro, you can play it back by choosing <u>T</u>ools⇨<u>M</u>acro, which opens the Macro dialog box. Excel lists the names of all the macros in the current workbook and in your Personal Macro Workbook (provided you've created one) in the <u>M</u>acro Name/Reference list box. Select the macro that you want and click on the <u>R</u>un button or press Enter.

Figure 12-3 shows the Macro dialog box after I recorded two macros (the ones in Figures 12-1 and 12-2) with the same name, one in the old macro language and one in the new Visual Basic language. The Visual Basic macro's name is automatically preceded with the Module1 sheet reference. The Excel 4.0 macro is automatically designated simply by its range name, without regard to its sheet location. The simple addition of the Module1 sheet reference to the Visual Basic macro's name is enough difference to let me get away with giving the macros the same name (usually a big no-no in Excel).

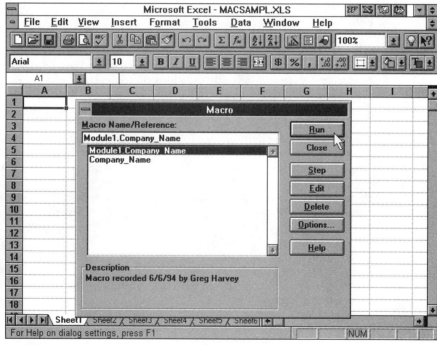

Figure 12-3:
The Macro dialog box, showing the macros recorded in the Macro1 and Module1 sheets of the MAC-SAMPL.XLS workbook.

The naming of macros points up another difference between the old style macros and the newfangled Visual Basic ones: Macros recorded in the old Excel 4.0 macro language are known by their bona fide range names. These names show up in the cell reference drop-down list on the formula bar, in the Go To dialog box, and just about everywhere else. Macros recorded in Visual Basic, on the other hand, are known by sheet and subroutine references. Yes, that's right. The *Company_Name* part of the Module1.Company_Name reference in the Macro dialog box refers to a subroutine name of the Visual Basic code — the `Sub Company_Name()` line at the top in Figure 12-1 — and not a cell or cell range of that name.

Assigning shortcut keys to macros and macros to menus

Although you can always play any of your macros from the Macro dialog box, going through the dialog box cuts down considerably on the convenience and efficiency of the macros. For most macros that you use frequently, you will either want to assign them shortcut keys or assign them to a menu.

When you first record a new macro, you can assign it shortcut keys and a place at the bottom of the Tools pull-down menu. To make these assignments, however, you need to select the Options button in the Record New Macro dialog box at the time you give the macro a name. To place the macro on the Tools menu, select the Menu Item on Tools Menu check box in the Assign to area. You then need to enter in the text box the name you want to appear on the Tools menu. Be sure to keep this name short so that it fits on the menu. To assign the macro its shortcut keys, select the Shortcut Key check box. Then select the Ctrl+ text box and type the letter you want to use to run the macro.

Remember that if you type a capital letter like uppercase *B*, you then assign the shortcut keys Ctrl+Shift+b to the macro. If you type a lowercase *b*, you assign the shortcut keys Ctrl+b.

If you didn't assign the macro to the Tools menu or to shortcut keys at the time you first recorded the macro, you can still do so after the fact. Choose Tools⇨Macro, select the macro in question, and then choose the Options button in the Macro dialog box. The Macro Options dialog box opens, similar to the one shown in Figure 12-4, where you can make these two assignments in the Assign to area. In the Help Information area, you can also decide on what Help text you want displayed on the status bar. Simply select the Status Bar Text option and type in the information you want to see on-screen. Figure 12-5 shows how this help text looks on the status bar after you open the Tools pull-down menu and select the Company Name macro at the very bottom of this menu.

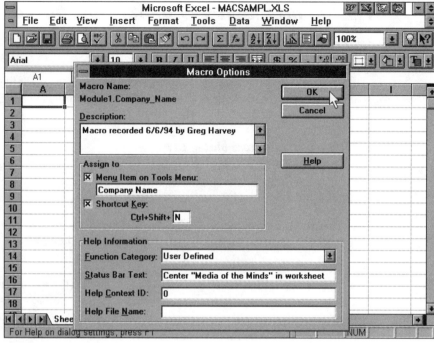

Figure 12-4:
Assigning
shortcut
keys to a
macro, the
macro to the
Tools menu,
and status
bar Help
text.

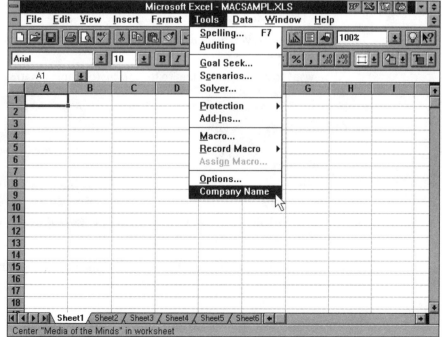

Figure 12-5:
Selecting
the
Company
Name
macro from
the Tools
menu now
displays the
Help text
on the
status bar.

Assigning macros to toolbar buttons or other amusing graphics

The Tools menu is not the only thing you can attach your macros to: You can also assign macros to custom buttons on toolbars and other graphic objects that you bring into a worksheet — a shaded text box, for example, that you've drawn with the Text Box tool on the Drawing toolbar.

Adding a macro custom button to a toolbar

To assign a macro to a toolbar, you need to create a new toolbar or select one of the existing toolbars and then, with the toolbar displayed, add a custom button for the macro, as follows:

1. **Choose View⇨Toolbars⇨Customize or choose Customize on the toolbar's shortcut menu to open the Customize dialog box.**

2. **Choose Custom in the Categories list box.**

    This option is all the way at the bottom of the list (the various toolbar categories are not in alphabetical order).

3. **Drag any one of the custom buttons, such as the bell or that stupid happy face, to the toolbar that you are editing.**

    Excel automatically opens the Assign Macro dialog box. Note that you can also create a new toolbar by dragging the custom button to any place in the workbook window other than an existing toolbar.

4. **Select the macro you want assigned to the custom button in the Macro Name/Reference list box.**

    If you want to record a new macro for the custom button rather than assign an existing macro to it, choose the Record button in the Assign Macro dialog box and then name and record the macro as usual.

5. **Click on OK or press Enter.**

    Excel closes the Assign Macro dialog box and returns you to the Customize dialog box.

    Repeat this procedure for any other macros that you want to assign to custom buttons on the toolbar you're editing or creating.

6. **When you're done, choose the Close button in the Customize dialog box.**

For more detail on creating and customizing toolbars in Excel, see Chapter 11 in *Excel For Dummies*.

Assigning a macro to a graphic object

To assign a macro to a graphic object that you have either imported into Excel or drawn in Excel, follow these steps:

1. **Select the graphic image in the worksheet by clicking on it (selection handles appear around its perimeter).**

2. **To open the Assign Macro dialog box, choose the Tools⇨Assign Macro command on the pull-down menus or the Assign Macro command on the graphic object's shortcut menu.**

3. **Choose the macro to be assigned to the graphic image in the Macro Name/Reference list box and then click on OK or press Enter.**

Just as you can record a macro when assigning it to a custom button, you can also record a new macro to be assigned to the selected graphic image by choosing the Record button in the Assign Macro dialog box. After choosing this button, you then name and record the macro as you would any other. (For more information on getting graphics into your charts and worksheets, see Chapter 7 *of Excel For Dummies.*)

Editing Recorded Macros

After you've created a macro, you don't always have to re-record it to change the way it behaves. In many cases, you will find it more expedient to change its behavior by simply editing its contents. In Excel 5, you can edit the workings of a macro by actually writing new Visual Basic code in the Module sheet (a really nerdy way of changing a macro that is far beyond the scope of any self-respecting . . . *For Dummies* book). Or you can record new code into the macro with your good friend the macro recorder (a much less demanding procedure which is more appropriate for nonprogrammers).

Before you can make any editing changes to a macro, however, you must activate the Module sheet that contains the macro to be edited. Simply choose Tools⇨Macro, select the macro to be edited in the Macro Name/Reference list box, and click on the Edit button. Taking these steps opens the Module sheet containing the macro and displays the Visual Basic toolbar (refer to Figure 12-1).

If you know which Module sheet in your workbook contains the macro you want to edit and where it's located in the workbook, you can also activate the macro by displaying and selecting the workbook's sheet tab.

If the macro you want to edit is stored in your Personal Macro Workbook (that PERSONAL.XLS file in the \XSTART directory), you *must* unhide this workbook before you can activate its Module sheet and edit its contents. To unhide the Personal Macro Workbook, choose Window⇨Unhide, select PERSONAL.XLS in the Unhide Workbook list box, and press Enter. This procedure unhides and activates the Personal Macro Workbook so that you can then select the appropriate Module sheet tab.

If you need to edit a macro recorded in the old Excel 4.0 macro language on a Macro sheet of your workbook, all you need to do is choose the macro's range name in the Go To dialog box (Ctrl+G or F5) and press Enter or drag to it in the cell reference drop-down list on the formula bar. When you select this range name, Excel positions the cell pointer on the first cell containing the macro name in the Macro sheet.

Recording new code into an existing macro

Before you use the macro recorder to add new tasks to an existing macro, you need to position the insertion point at the beginning of the line where the new macro commands are to be added. You can reposition the insertion point in the Visual Basic text either by clicking the I-beam cursor at the appropriate place or by using the arrow keys on your keyboard (editing Visual Basic commands in a Module sheet is a lot like editing lines of text in a word processing program).

Recording new macro commands

After you have the insertion point at the beginning of the proper line in the macro commands, you are ready to start recording the new macro commands, as follows:

1. **Check to make sure that the insertion point is really, *really* at a place in the Visual Basic commands where it makes sense to add the code for the new tasks you're about to record.**

   If not, reposition the insertion point at the beginning of the line of code where it does make sense.

2. **Choose Tools⇨Record Macro⇨Mark Position For Recording command.**

3. **Activate the worksheet (or chart sheet) where you want to record the new tasks that you're adding to the macro.**

4. **Choose Tools⇨Record Macro⇨Record At Mark command to start the macro recorder.**

5. **Perform all the tasks to be included in the macro by using the necessary pull-down menus, toolbars, shortcut menus, or whatever to get the job done.**

6. **Stop the macro recorder by clicking on the Stop Macro button on the Stop Recording toolbar (that shrimpy toolbar with only one tool) or by choosing Tools⇨Record Macro⇨Stop Recording.**

Changing settings in a macro command

Even when you don't know anything about programming in Visual Basic (and aim to keep it that way), you can still get the gist of some of the more obvious statements in a macro that change certain settings, such as number format or font attribute, by assigning new values. In the Company_Name macro shown in Figure 12-6, for example, you can tell that the section of Visual Basic commands between the line

```
With Selection.Font
```

and the line

```
End With
```

contains code to change various font attributes for the current cell selection.

Going a step farther, you probably can figure out that most of these attributes are being reset by making the attribute equal to a new entry or value, such as

```
.FontStyle = "Roman"
```

or

```
.Size = 20
```

Or an attribute is being reset by turning it on or off by setting it equal to True or False, such as

```
Selection.Font.Bold = True
```

to make the text in the current cell selection bold.

Now, it doesn't require a programming degree (at least, not the last time I checked) to get the bright idea that you can make your macro behave differently just by — carefully — editing these settings. For example, suppose that you want the final font size to be 30 points instead of 20. All you have to do is change

```
.Size = 20
```

to

```
.Size = 30
```

Figure 12-6:
The Module1 sheet, showing part of the Visual Basic commands in the Company_Name macro.

```
                Microsoft Excel - MACSAMPL.XLS
  File   Edit   View   Insert   Run   Tools   Window   Help

With Selection.Font
    .Name = "BernhardMod_BT"
    .FontStyle = "Roman"
    .Size = 20
    .Strikethrough = False
    .Superscript = False
    .Subscript = False
    .OutlineFont = False
    .Shadow = False
    .Underline = xlNone
    .ColorIndex = xlAutomatic
End With
Selection.Font.Bold = True
Selection.Font.Italic = True
ActiveCell.Range("A1:H1").Select
With Selection
    .HorizontalAlignment = xlCenterAcrossSelection
    .VerticalAlignment = xlBottom
    .WrapText = False
    .Orientation = xlHorizontal
```

Sheet13 / Sheet14 / Sheet15 / Sheet16 \ Module1 /

Ready   NUM

Likewise, you can have the macro apply single underlining to the cell selection by changing

```
.Underline = xlNone
```

to

```
.Underline = xlSingle
```

Many times, the alternate settings allowed in a particular Visual Basic code, such as the `.Underline` property, are anything but obvious (how's that for understatement?). When you encounter such a property in the macro code and would like to know what kinds of values it will accept, simply look it up in the on-line Visual Basic Reference. Press F1 to open the Visual Basic Reference window and then click on Programming Language Summary to open the Visual Basic Reference Index window. Click on the button with the appropriate letter of the alphabet (the U button if you're looking up the `.Underline` property). Then click on the appropriate index entry (Underline Property, in this example) to display Help information explaining the use and permissible values for that property in the Visual Basic Reference window. Remember, too, that you can obtain a printout of this Help information by choosing File⇨Print Topic.

Making a static macro interactive

One of the biggest problems with recording macros is that any text or values that you have the macro enter for you in a worksheet or chart sheet can never vary thereafter. If you create a macro that enters the heading *Bubba Bob's Barbecue Pit* in the current cell of your worksheet, this is the only heading you'll ever get out of that macro. However, you can get around this inflexibility by using the InputBox function. When you run the macro, this Visual Basic function causes Excel to display an input dialog box, where you can enter whatever title makes sense for the new worksheet. The macro then puts that text into the current cell and formats this text, if that's what you've trained your macro to do next.

To see how easy it is to use the InputBox function to add interactivity to an otherwise staid macro, follow along with the steps for converting the Company_Name macro that currently inputs the text *Media of the Minds* to one that actually prompts you for the name you want entered.

Using the InputBox function to make a macro interactive

Before you can add the line of code to the macro with the InputBox function, you need to find the place in the Visual Basic commands where the line should go. To enter the *Media of the Minds* text into the active cell, the Company_Name macro uses the following Visual Basic command:

```
ActiveCell.FormulaR1C1 = "Media of the Minds"
```

To add interactivity to the macro, you need to insert the InputBox function on a line right above this `ActiveCell.FormulaR1C1` statement, as follows:

1. **Position the insertion point at the beginning of the**
   `ActiveCell.FormulaR1C1` **statement and press Enter to insert a new line.**

2. **Press the ↑ key to position the insertion point at the beginning of this new line.**

3. **Type the following and press Enter to start a new line:**

   InputMsg = "Enter the title for this worksheet in the text box below:"

   Be sure that you put quotation marks at both the beginning and the end of your message text. This statement sets up a temporary holder called InputMsg (which is a made-up name describing the type of information it will contain) with the text that will appear as the prompt in the input dialog box.

4. On the next line type the following and press Enter:

Titlebar = "Worksheet Title"

Again, be sure to enclose the name for the dialog box title bar in quotation marks. This statement sets up another temporary holder called Titlebar with the text that will appear as the title bar for the input dialog box (making this the Worksheet Title dialog box).

5. On the next line, type the following and press Enter:

StockText = "Media of the Minds"

This statement sets up a temporary holder called StockText with the default worksheet title that will appear as the text box of the Worksheet Title dialog box.

6. On the next line, type the following:

WorksheetTitle = InputBox(InputMsg, Titlebar, StockText)

This statement sets up a temporary holder called WorksheetTitle with whatever text is returned by the InputBox function. The InputBox function uses three arguments (although only the first one is mandatory): *prompt*, which contains the text that prompts the user for input; *title*, which supplies the text for the dialog box title bar; and *default*, which supplies the text of the default entry. In this case, the InputMsg holder supplies the prompt argument; the Titlebar holder supplies the title argument; and the StockText holder supplies the default argument of the InputBox function.

7. In the `ActiveCell.FormulaR1C1 = "Media of the Minds"` **statement, select** `Media of the Minds` **and replace it by typing the following as a single word with NO quotation marks:**

WorksheetTitle

The edited statement should now read as follows:

```
ActiveCell.FormulaR1C1 = WorksheetTitle
```

This statement enters whatever is in the Worksheet Title temporary holder (which, in turn, contains the text entered into the Worksheet Title dialog box created with the InputBox function) into the current cell.

Figure 12-7 shows the Module1 sheet with the Company_Name macro after adding the statements that make it interactive. Figure 12-8 shows the Worksheet Title dialog box that appears when you now run the interactive version of the Company_Name macro.

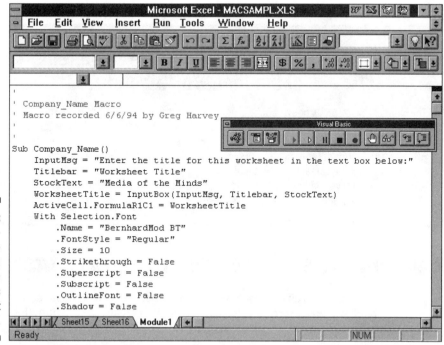

Figure 12-7:
The Company_Name macro, with the commands to make it interactive.

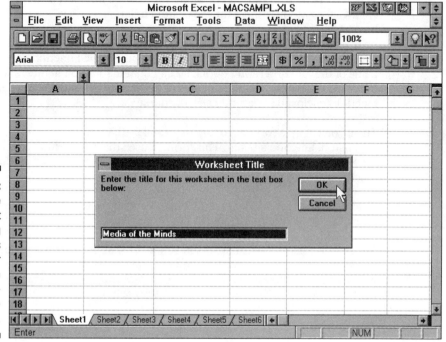

Figure 12-8:
The Worksheet Title dialog box displays whenever you now run the Company_Name macro.

Why not simply type in the arguments of the InputBox function?

The biggest reason for using *variables* (programmer jargon for temporary holders, such as InputMsg, Titlebar, and StockText) to supply the prompt, title, and default arguments of the InputBox function — rather than just typing them — is their length. If you typed in all three pieces of text within the parentheses of the InputBox function, you would end up with one of the longest (and hardest to read) lines of code in history. When you use variables to do the job, as in the example, you end up with lines of code that fit on one screen, making the lines of code easier to read and also making it possible to print them on a normal piece of paper.

Custom Excel Functions through Macros

Being as good as my word, your experience with Visual Basic coding in this book will go no farther than learning how to create custom functions (also referred to as user-defined functions).

To create a user-defined function, you must do four little things. First, you must select or create a Module sheet where the custom function is to be defined. To create a new Module sheet for the custom function, choose Insert⇨Macro⇨Module.

Next, you enter the following in order: the Visual Basic Function command, the name of the function (don't duplicate any built-in function names, such as SUM or AVERAGE, please), and the names of the arguments allowed in your custom function (enclosed in parentheses, of course).

Then, you set up a formula, or set of formulas, that tells Excel how to calculate the custom function's result. This formula uses the argument names listed in the Function command with whatever arithmetic operators and/or built-in functions are required to get the calculation made.

Finally, you indicate that you're finished defining the custom function by entering the End Function command on the last line.

To see how this procedure works in action, look at this scenario. Suppose that you want to create a custom function that calculates the sales commissions for your salespeople based on the number of sales they make in a month as well as the total amount of their monthly sales (they sell big ticket items, such as RVs).

Your custom Commission function will then have two arguments — TotalSales and ItemsSold — so that the first line of code in your Module sheet will be

```
Function Commission(TotalSales,ItemsSold)
```

In determining how the commissions are actually calculated, suppose that you base the commission percentage on the number of sales made during the month. For 5 sales or less in a month, you pay a commission rate of 4.5 percent of the salesperson's total monthly sales; for sales of 6 or more, you pay a commission rate of 5 percent.

To define the formula section of the Commission custom function, you need to set up an IF construction. This IF construction is similar to the IF function you enter into a worksheet cell except that you use different lines in the macro code for the construction in the custom function. An ELSE command separates the command that is performed if the expression is True from the command that is performed if the expression is False. The macro code is terminated by an END IF command. To set the custom function so that your salespeople get 4.5 percent of total sales for 5 or less items sold and 5 percent of total sales for more than 5 items sold, you enter the following lines of code underneath the line with the Function command:

```
If ItemsSold <= 5 Then
    Commission = TotalSales * 0.045
Else
    Commission = TotalSales * 0.05
End If
```

The indents are made with the Tab key to keep it easy to differentiate the parts of the IF construction. The first formula, Commission = TotalSales * 0.045, is used when the IF expression ItemsSold <= 5 is True. Otherwise, the second formula underneath the Else command, Commission = TotalSales * 0.05, is used. After the IF construction, all you need to add is an End Function statement to tell Excel that you're done. Figure 12-9 shows you the finished custom Commission function.

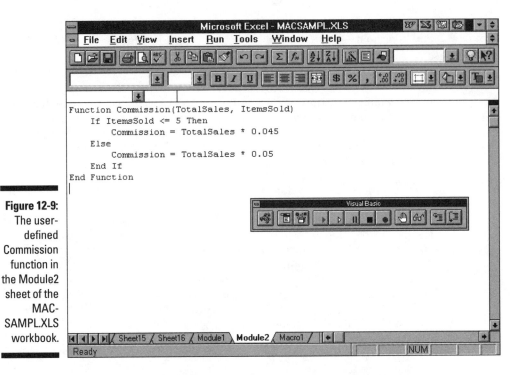

```
Microsoft Excel - MACSAMPL.XLS
File   Edit   View   Insert   Run   Tools   Window   Help

Function Commission(TotalSales, ItemsSold)
    If ItemsSold <= 5 Then
        Commission = TotalSales * 0.045
    Else
        Commission = TotalSales * 0.05
    End If
End Function
```

Figure 12-9:
The user-
defined
Commission
function in
the Module2
sheet of the
MAC-
SAMPL.XLS
workbook.

Assigning a custom function to a function category

All the custom functions that you define in Excel are added to the User Defined
category in the Function Wizard – Step 1 of 2 dialog box. You can assign your
custom function to one of the other function categories in the Function Wizard,
however.

Assigning custom functions to another function category

1. **Select the Module sheet in your workbook that contains the custom
   function for which you want to assign a new category.**

2. **Choose View⇨Object Browser on the pull-down menus or press F2.**

3. **In the Object Browser dialog box, choose the name of the custom
   function in the Methods/Properties list box.**

4. **Choose the Options button to open the Macro Options dialog box.**

5. In the **F**unction Category drop-down list box, choose the category you want the custom function to be in.

For example, to assign the custom Commission function to the Financial category in the Function Wizard, choose Financial in this drop-down list.

6. **Click on OK or press Enter to close the Macro Options dialog and return to the Object Browser dialog box.**

7. **Click on the S**how button or press Enter.

Entering custom functions with the Function Wizard

The great thing about custom functions is that they can be inserted into your worksheets with your old friend the Function Wizard. Figures 12-10 through 12-13 illustrate how easy it is to enter the custom Commission function in a worksheet with the Function Wizard (after moving the Commission function from the User Defined category to the Financial category, as described in the preceding section).

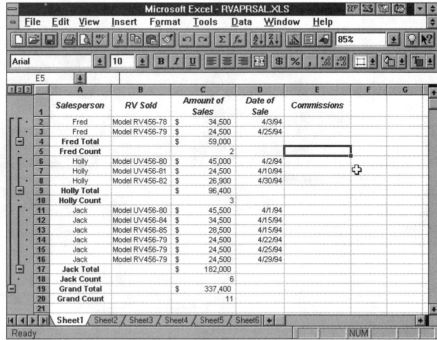

Figure 12-10:
The April sales table with subtotals that show monthly sales totals and number of sales.

	Salesperson	RV Sold	Amount of Sales	Date of Sale	Commissions		
1							
2	Fred	Model RV456-78	$ 34,500	4/3/94			
3	Fred	Model RV456-79	$ 24,500	4/25/94			
4	Fred Total		$ 59,000				
5	Fred Count		2				
6	Holly	Model UV456-80	$ 45,000	4/2/94			
7	Holly	Model UV456-81	$ 24,500	4/10/94			
8	Holly	Model RV456-82	$ 26,900	4/30/94			
9	Holly Total		$ 96,400				
10	Holly Count		3				
11	Jack	Model UV456-80	$ 45,500	4/1/94			
12	Jack	Model UV456-84	$ 34,500	4/15/94			
13	Jack	Model RV456-85	$ 28,500	4/15/94			
14	Jack	Model RV456-79	$ 24,500	4/22/94			
15	Jack	Model RV456-79	$ 24,500	4/25/94			
16	Jack	Model RV456-79	$ 24,500	4/29/94			
17	Jack Total		$ 182,000				
18	Jack Count		6				
19	Grand Total		$ 337,400				
20	Grand Count		11				
21							

Figure 12-10 shows a worksheet that contains a table with the April, 1994, RV sales for three salespeople: Fred, Holly, and Jack. As you can see, the Automatic Subtotals feature (covered in Chapter 6) has been used to compute both the monthly total sales (with the SUM function) and the number of sales (with the COUNT function) for each of these three salespeople.

To calculate the April monthly commissions for each salesperson in this table, you select the cell where you want the first commission to be calculated (Fred's commission in cell E5). Click on the Function Wizard tool on the Standard toolbar and then select Financial in the Function Category list box and Commission (preceded with the sheet name) in the Function Name list box (as shown in Figure 12-11).

The arguments of the custom functions that you create show up in the Function Wizard – Step 2 of 2 dialog box. For example, to fill in the TotalSales argument for the Commission function that calculates Fred's April commission (as shown in Figure 12-12), click on cell C4 (containing the sum of Fred's sales) in the worksheet while the insertion point is in the TotalSales text box in the Step 2 dialog box. Then press Tab to advance the insertion point to the ItemsSold text box. While the insertion point is in this text box, you click on cell C5 (containing the count of Fred's sales).

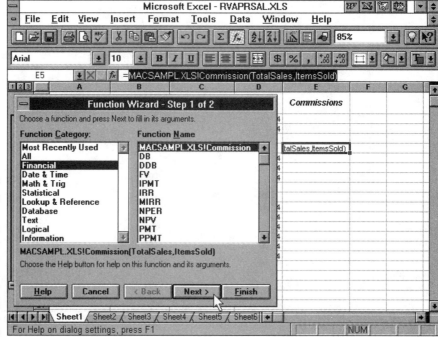

Figure 12-11:
Selecting
the custom
Commission
function in
the Function
Wizard –
Step 1 of 2
dialog box.

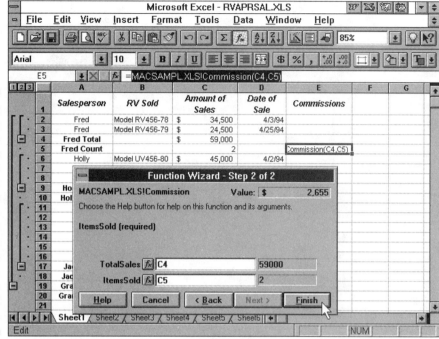

Figure 12-12:
Selecting
the
TotalSales
and
ItemsSold
arguments
for the
custom
Commission
function in
the Function
Wizard Step
– 2 of 2
dialog box.

When you click on the Finish button in the Function Wizard – Step 2 of 2 dialog box, Excel calculates Fred's commission by using the 4.5 percent commission rate because his two sales made in April are well below the 6 sales necessary to bump him up to the 5 percent commission rate used by the custom Commission function. Figure 12-13 shows the completed April sales table after calculating the monthly commissions for Fred, Holly, and Jack. In using the Commission function, both Fred and Holly fall into the 4.5 percent commission rate. Only Jack, the April RV sales king, gets paid the higher 5 percent commission rate for his 6 sales during this month.

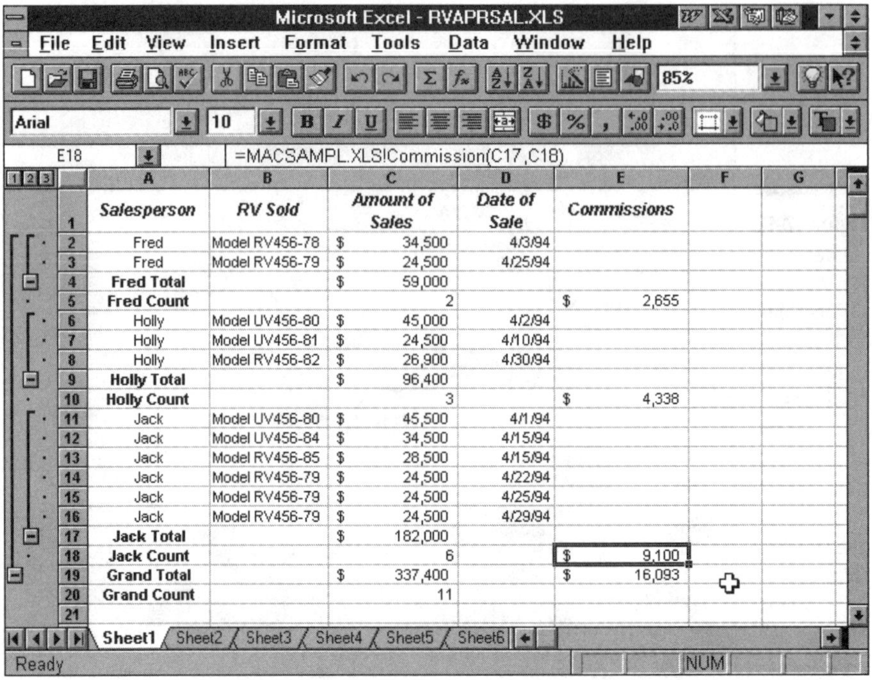

Figure 12-13:
The
completed
April sales
table with
the monthly
commissions
for all three
salespeople,
calculated
with the
custom
Commission
function.

Microsoft Excel - RVAPRSAL.XLS

File   Edit   View   Insert   Format   Tools   Data   Window   Help

Arial   10   **B** *I* U

E18   =MACSAMPL.XLS!Commission(C17,C18)

	A	B	C	D	E	F	G
1	Salesperson	RV Sold	Amount of Sales	Date of Sale	Commissions		
2	Fred	Model RV456-78	$ 34,500	4/3/94			
3	Fred	Model RV456-79	$ 24,500	4/25/94			
4	**Fred Total**		$ 59,000				
5	**Fred Count**		2		$ 2,655		
6	Holly	Model UV456-80	$ 45,000	4/2/94			
7	Holly	Model UV456-81	$ 24,500	4/10/94			
8	Holly	Model RV456-82	$ 26,900	4/30/94			
9	**Holly Total**		$ 96,400				
10	**Holly Count**		3		$ 4,338		
11	Jack	Model UV456-80	$ 45,500	4/1/94			
12	Jack	Model UV456-84	$ 34,500	4/15/94			
13	Jack	Model UV456-85	$ 28,500	4/15/94			
14	Jack	Model RV456-79	$ 24,500	4/22/94			
15	Jack	Model RV456-79	$ 24,500	4/25/94			
16	Jack	Model RV456-79	$ 24,500	4/29/94			
17	**Jack Total**		$ 182,000				
18	**Jack Count**		6		$ 9,100		
19	**Grand Total**		$ 337,400		$ 16,093		
20	**Grand Count**		11				
21							

Sheet1 / Sheet2 / Sheet3 / Sheet4 / Sheet5 / Sheet6

Ready   NUM

Chapter 13

Using Excel as Part of Microsoft Office

A growing number of Excel 5 users are getting Excel as part of a package (or suite) of Microsoft Windows application programs, known collectively as Microsoft Office. If you are one of these Excel users (that is, Bill Gates owns you lock, stock, and barrel), this chapter gives you some basic information for surviving your first attempts at exchanging information between Excel and one of the other Office programs. Keep in mind that all of this information is given from the perspective of an Excel user (this is, after all, an Excel book) and is in no way meant to teach you how the heck to use the other programs you scored when you got your copy of Excel as part of Microsoft Office.

Food for thought: it may look good on your resume to be able to say (with some verisimilitude) that you know how to take the data you create in Excel and place it in a Word document or PowerPoint presentation, and you know how to take data that's been entered into an Access database and bring it into Excel, where you can actually do something with it.

Microsoft Office: How Suite It Is!

First of all, you need to be clear on just what the heck someone means when he or she says, "I use Microsoft Office." There are, after all, a couple of flavors of Office that you can purchase. The most common (translated: *cheaper*) version is just plain old Microsoft Office made up of the following applications:

- ✔ Excel 5, the spreadsheet/charting/database program, which you know how to use (more or less)

- ✔ Word 6, the word processing/report writing/mail merge program, which you may also use regularly or somewhat regularly in getting your work done

- ✔ PowerPoint 4, the outlining/slide show/business presentation program, which you will probably never have any use for until you join "management" or unless you work in the marketing department of your company

- ✔ Mail 3, the electronic mail/message utility, which you can use to pass messages and copies of your workbooks back and forth to coworkers, provided that your computer is hooked up to some kind of local area network (LAN)

- ✔ Microsoft Office 4, the terminate-and-stay resident (TSR) utility that coordinates your movements between different Office programs

In addition to the fabulous programs you get when you purchase plain old Microsoft Office, when you buy the more advanced (translated: *expensive*) version of Office, called Microsoft Office Pro (for professional), you also get this lovely application:

- ✔ Access 2, the sophisticated (translated: *complicated*) relational database management program, which you would probably use only if your work involved converting mass quantities of work-related data into meaningful information that even a human could love

Keep in mind that even though you got a great deal on Microsoft Office or Microsoft Office Pro, you don't have to install each and every one of its programs (you may not have that much hard disk space available). To preserve much needed free space on your hard disk, you can install only those programs that you know you may someday need (say, Excel and Word, or Excel and PowerPoint). Unfortunately, Microsoft Office doesn't have an installation program that enables you to install some or all of the programs in one operation. Instead, you have to go through the installation drill — nearly identical to the one you went through when installing Excel — for each and every Office program you want to install. You do know somebody you can bribe to do this part for you, don't you?

To and Fro in a Flash

Microsoft Office itself is not really much of a program. It's biggest claim to fame is that it creates an Office toolbar. You can see this toolbar to the right on Excel's title bar, and you can use the toolbar to open or jump to and from any of the Office programs you have installed. When this toolbar is displayed, you have access to its buttons from anywhere within Windows (talk about persistent advertising).

To go to another Office program via the toolbar, you simply click on its program button. If the program is already running, clicking on its button causes the active document to be displayed on-screen. If the program is not yet running, clicking on its button starts the program with a new empty document.

If you need to customize the Office toolbar or uninstall one of the Office programs (other than your beloved Excel, of course), you can use the pull-down menu attached to the Microsoft Office button. By clicking on this button, you display a menu of commands that you can use to go to a new Office program (or the Windows Program Manager or File Manager), customize the Office toolbar, or change the setup or uninstall one of the Office crew.

If you choose the Customize command on this menu, you are presented with the Customize dialog box with three tabs: Toolbar, Menu, and View. From the Toolbar tab, you can add or remove buttons or move the buttons to a new position on the Office toolbar. You move a button by selecting its program description in the list box and then clicking on the up- or down-arrow button until its description appears in the correct order. You can also add buttons that take you all sorts of places in Windows, such as to the Program Manager, the File Manager, the Control Panel, or the Print Manger. There's even a button to take you out of Windows to the dreaded DOS prompt!?!

From the Menu tab, you add or remove menu commands that are displayed when you click on the Microsoft Office button, or you move the commands to new positions (by using the up- and down-arrow buttons). From the View tab, you can modify the size of the buttons on the Office toolbar, get rid of its display, or just suppress the display of tooltips, which identify the name of each of the buttons when you position the mouse pointer on it. If you want the Office toolbar to appear in a free-standing dialog box that you can move about and resize at will (instead of staying dry-docked on the program window's title bar), choose the Regular Buttons or Large Buttons radio button in the Toolbar Button Size area of the View tab.

Early to Embed and Late to Link

Before you rush off and start wildly throwing Excel worksheets into Word documents and Excel charts into PowerPoint presentations, you need to realize that Microsoft offers you a choice in the way you exchange data between your various Office programs. Namely, you can either embed the worksheet or chart in the other program, or you can set up a link between the Excel-generated object in the other program and Excel itself.

- ✔ *Embedding* means that the Excel object (be it a worksheet or a chart) actually becomes part of the Word document or PowerPoint presentation. For any changes you then need to make to the worksheet or chart, you must make within the Word document or PowerPoint presentation. This presupposes, however, that you have Excel on the same computer as Word or PowerPoint and that your computer has enough memory to run them both.

- ✔ *Linking* means that the Excel object (worksheet or chart) is only referred to in the Word document or PowerPoint presentation. Any changes you make to the worksheet or chart must be made in Excel itself and then updated in the Word document or PowerPoint presentation to which it is linked.

Use the embedding method when the Excel object (worksheet or chart) is not apt to change very often and when the document or file you're adding it to is not so large that the additional Excel data makes it too big to back up on a diskette. Use the linking method when the Excel object (worksheet or chart) changes fairly often, when you always need the latest and greatest version of the object to appear in your Word document or PowerPoint presentation, or when you don't want to make the Word or PowerPoint document any bigger by adding the Excel data to it.

Be aware that when you link an Excel worksheet or chart to another Office document and you want to show that document or print it on another computer, you must copy both the Excel workbook with the linked worksheet/chart and the Word or PowerPoint file to that computer. Also be aware that when you embed an Excel worksheet or chart in another Office document and then want to edit it on another computer, that computer must have both Excel and the other Microsoft Office program (Word or PowerPoint) installed on it.

Use the embedding or linking techniques only when you have a pretty good suspicion that the Excel stuff is far from final and that you want to be able to update the Excel data either manually (with embedding) or automatically (with linking). If your Excel stuff will remain unchanged, just use the old standby method of copying the Excel data to the Clipboard with Edit⇨Copy (Ctrl+C) and then switching to the Word or PowerPoint document and pasting it in place there with the Edit⇨Paste (Ctrl+V) command.

Excel 5 and Word 6

Of all the Office programs (besides our beloved Excel), Word is the one you are most apt to use. You will probably find yourself using Word to type up any memos, letters, and reports that you need in the course of your daily work (even if you really don't understand how the program works). From time to time, you may need to bring in some worksheet data or charts that you've created in your Excel workbooks into a Word document that you're creating. When those occasions arise, check out the information in the next section.

For the benefit of those of you who get stuck doing mass mailings (you know, that form letter stuff) in Word, I've also included a section called "Mail Merge using Excel data" that tells you how to use the records you've created in an Excel database or list in generating form letters, mailing labels, and envelopes in Word.

Although Word has a Table feature that supports calculations through a kind of mini-spreadsheet operation, you will probably be more productive if you create the data (formulas, formatting, and all) in an Excel workbook and then bring that data into your Word document by following the steps outlined in the next section. Likewise, although you can keep, create, and manage the data records you use in mail merge operations within Word, you will probably find it more expedient to create and maintain them in Excel — seeing as how you are already familiar with how to create, sort, and filter database records in Excel — and then select them as described in the mail merge section.

Getting Excel data into a Word document

As with all the other Office programs, you have two choices when bringing Excel data (worksheet cell data or charts) into a Word document: You can embed the data in the Word document, or you can link the data you bring into Word to its original Excel worksheet. Embed when you want to be able to edit right within Word. Link when you want to be able to edit in Excel and have the changes automatically updated when you open the Word document.

Happily embedded after

The easiest way to embed a table of worksheet data or a chart is to use the good old drag-and-drop method: Simply drag the selected cells or chart be-tween the Excel and Word program windows rather than to a new place in a worksheet. The only trick to drag and drop between programs is the sizing and maneuvering of the Excel and Word program windows themselves. Figures 13-1 and 13-2 illustrate the procedure for dragging a table of worksheet data (with first quarter sales for the Miss Muffet St. store) from its workbook to a memo started in Word.

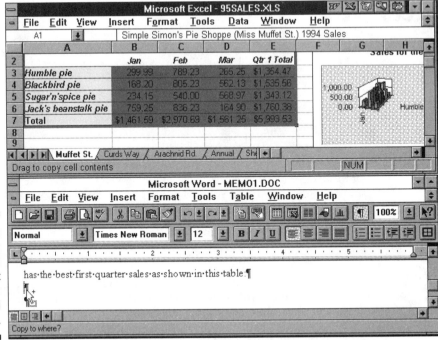

Figure 13-1:
Dragging
the Excel
worksheet
data into a
Word
document.

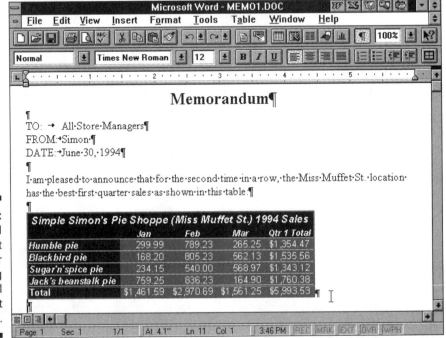

Figure 13-2:
The Word
document
after
embedding
Excel
worksheet
data.

Before I could drag the selected worksheet data, I had to size and position the Excel program window. In Figure 13-1, you can see that the Excel window is positioned above the Word window and sized to about half the full screen size. After futzing with these two program windows, I had only to select the worksheet data in the Excel worksheet and then hold down the Ctrl key (to copy) as I dragged the outline down to the Word window.

As I passed over the border between the Excel and Word program windows, the mouse pointer changed shape to the international "oh-no-you-don't" symbol. When I reached the safe havens of the Word document area, however, the pointer changes again, this time to the shape of an arrowhead sticking up from a box with a plus sign (how's that for a description?). To indicate where in the Word document to embed the selected data, I simply positioned the arrowhead-sticking-up-from-a-box with-a-plus-sign pointer at the place in the document where the Excel stuff is to appear. Then I released the mouse button. Figure 13-2 shows you the embedded worksheet table that appears after I released the mouse button.

Editing embedded stuff

The great thing about embedding Excel stuff (as opposed to linking, which I'll get to in a minute) is that you can edit the data right from within Word. Figure 13-3 shows the table after I centered it with the Center button on Word's Formatting toolbar. Notice what happens when I double-clicked on the embedded table (or chose the Edit Spreadsheet command on the table's shortcut menu). A frame with columns and rows, scroll bars, and sheet tabs miraculously appears around the table. Notice, also, that the pull-down menus and toolbars in the Word window have changed to Excel's pull-down menus and Excel's Standard and Formatting toolbars (it's like being at home when you're still on the road). At this point, you can edit any of the table's contents by using the Excel commands that you already know.

The links that bind

Of course, as nice as embedding is, there are times when linking the Excel data to the Word document is just fine (in fact, even easier to do). Figures 13-4 through 13-6 illustrate the linking process. In Figure 13-4, I selected a chart that I created in the worksheet by single-clicking on it, not double-clicking on it as I would do to edit the chart in the worksheet. I was about to select the Copy command on its shortcut menu (Edit➪Copy or Ctrl+C) to send a copy of it to the Clipboard.

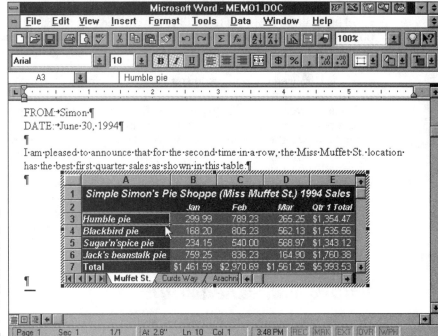

Figure 13-3:
Editing the
embedded
Excel
worksheet
data within
Word.

After copying the chart (or selected data) to the Clipboard, I then switched over to Word and my memo to all store managers. After positioning the insertion point at the beginning of the paragraph where the chart needs to be, I selected the Paste Special command on the Edit pull-down menu (in Word). Figure 13-5 shows the Paste Special dialog box that appears. In this dialog box, the crucial thing is to select the Paste Link radio button before choosing OK. (It doesn't make a whole lot of difference whether you paste the chart as an Excel 5 chart object or a picture.) Figure 13-6 shows the Word memo after I clicked on OK and pasted the Excel chart into place.

Editing linked junk

Editing data linked to Excel (as a chart or cells) is not quite as delightful as editing embedded worksheet data. For one thing, you first have to go back to Excel and make your changes there — although you can easily open Excel and its workbook just by double-clicking on the linked chart. For another thing, after making changes to the data in Excel, you may find that you have lost the formatting that you originally gave to the data (especially charts) when you return to Word.

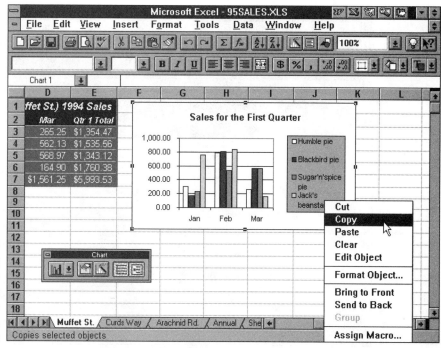

Figure 13-4:
Copying an
Excel chart
to the
Clipboard.

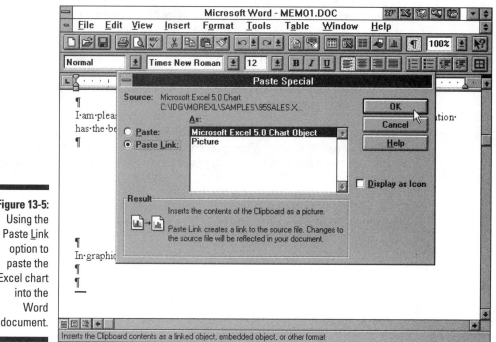

Figure 13-5:
Using the
Paste Link
option to
paste the
Excel chart
into the
Word
document.

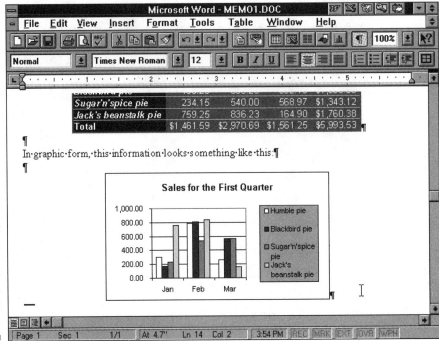

Figure 13-6:
The Word
memo after
pasting the
linked Excel
chart.

Figures 13-7 and 13-8 illustrate the problem of lost formatting. In Figure 13-7, I returned to Excel and edited the chart title. After I returned to Word (as shown in Figure 13-8), I found that the chart title was automatically updated but that Word had removed the border around the chart. And, unfortunately, the only way to restore this original formatting to the chart once it's lost is to repeat the whole procedure for cutting and pasting the chart from Excel into Word (negating the whole reason for using linking in the first place).

To avoid the problem of losing formatting when you update data via linking, use embedding instead of linking. When you embed something in another Microsoft program, nine times out of ten, you will never have trouble with the formatting. If, on the tenth time, you do have trouble, you can just double-click on the thing and fix it with the program's menus and toolbars. Continue to use linking, however, when your main concern is keeping the data (values and text) current without much regard for formatting (which you may want to control with the program where the data is pasted, anyway).

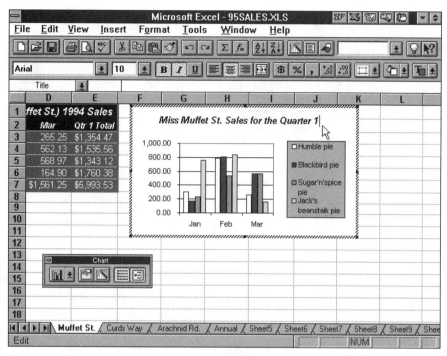

Figure 13-7:
Editing the
chart's title
in Excel.

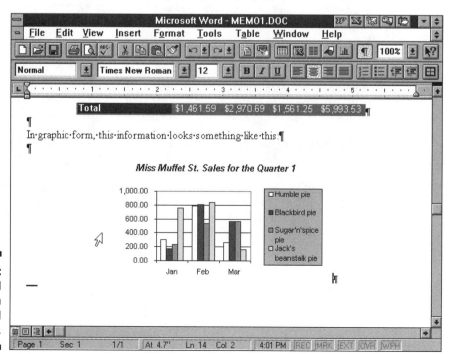

Figure 13-8:
The Word
memo with
the edited
Excel chart.

Mail Merge using Excel data

In some offices, you may find that mass mailings — you know, the "personal-ized" form letters, envelopes, and mailing labels all generated by the computer — make up a big part of your job. Although it's well beyond the scope of this book to teach you how to use the Mail Merge feature in Word, suffice it to say that Word makes it really easy to create the forms for the letters, envelopes, and mailing labels. What you may not find so easy to do is to generate and maintain the data — you know, the names and addresses of the folks you want to send "personalized" form letters to — in Word.

Because you already know a fair amount about creating, sorting, and filtering data within Excel, you may want to maintain the data records used in Mail Merge within Excel, too. (It's really not that hard to create the records in Word, but it *is* another thing to learn!)

Figures 13-9 and 13-10 illustrate how easy it is (and I *do* mean easy) to use the records you've created, sorted, and filtered in Excel in a Mail Merge in Word. In Figure 13-9, you see the Mail Merge Helper (Word prefers Helpers to Wizards), which I opened by selecting the Tools⇨Mail Merge command. I selected Form Letters as the type of Main Document to create (you can choose Mailing Labels or Envelopes, as well), and I selected the current document window as the place to create the form letter with the Create drop-down list button. Then I selected the Get Data drop-down list button under Data Source and dragged down to the Open Data Source command.

When you select Open Data Source, Word opens a dialog box that looks (and acts) a lot like the Open dialog box in Excel. The big thing to remember when using this dialog box is that it is set to find Word documents (those that use the .doc extension). To help you find the Excel workbook file that contains the data records as you browse the directories on your disk, you need to remember to change the List Files of Type setting to MS Excel Worksheets (*.xls).

After selecting the Excel file to use in the Open Data Source dialog box, you need to indicate which range in the workbook to use. In most cases, you want to choose Database in the list box in the Microsoft Excel dialog box that shows all the ranges in the Excel file. You can choose the Entire Spreadsheet selection when the workbook contains only the database you want to use or the range name given to a particular database if the workbook contains more than one database on different sheets.

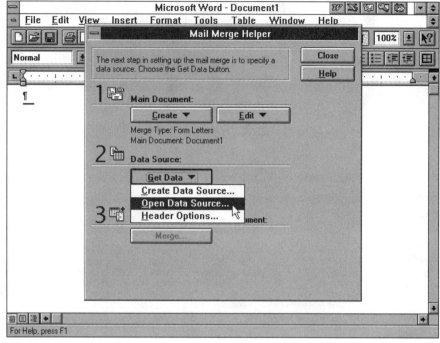

Figure 13-9:
Using the
Mail Merge
Helper to
select an
Excel
database as
the data
source.

After choosing the Excel file and the range that contains the data records, Word adds the Merge toolbar below its Formatting toolbar at the top of the window (see Figure 13-10). You can then use this toolbar's Insert Merge Field drop-down list button to select the name of the field in the Excel database that you want merged when the actual form letters are generated. In Figure 13-10, I used this button to insert the First Name, Last Name, City, State, and ZIP fields from the sample Clients database.

I finished composing my form letter by typing in the canned text and inserting field codes at all the places where information from a particular field in the Excel Clients database is to appear — this is the stuff that fools the person receiving the letter into believing that I really wrote this letter to him! I then previewed the merge with a few records by selecting the record number in the Go to Record text box (the one containing the number 7 in Figure 13-10) and then clicking on the View Merged Data button on the Merge toolbar (the one to the right of the Insert Word Field button).

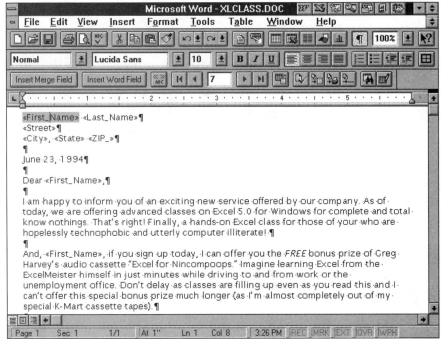

Figure 13-10:
The form
letter with
merge fields
for merging
with the
Excel Clients
database.

If you find errors in the data while previewing the merge, you can use the Edit
Data Source button on the Merge toolbar to go to the Excel worksheet containing the data records where the changes were made. After completing the record
editing, switch back to Word (via the Microsoft Word button on the Office
toolbar) and click on the Mail Merge Helper button (the one after the two arrow
buttons pointing right) on the Merge toolbar to perform the merge operation.

When you specify an Excel database as the data source for doing a merge, Word
automatically starts Excel and opens the workbook with the database each time
you open the merge document. Be aware that this procedure requires more
overall computer memory to accomplish and slows down the time it takes to
open the merge document in Word.

Excel 5 and PowerPoint 4

You may start dabbling with PowerPoint just because it's so much fun to use!
Be aware that this program is very Wizard-driven. It seems like there are
Wizards to help you in creating every type of presentation. Even though I'm a
complete dummy when it comes to using PowerPoint, I was able to create a

slide-show presentation (or at least the beginnings of one) to help explain how easy it is to exchange data between the programs in Microsoft Office. To create the basic presentation, I used the Pick a Look Wizard, which walked me through selecting a basic template for the presentation and got me going in no time at all.

Figures 13-11 through 13-14 show the result. As you can see in Figure 13-11, I chose a slide template that used a map of the world as the background (appropriate enough, considering the worldwide influence of Microsoft products in personal computing). In this first slide, I merely replaced the placeholder headings with text of my own.

Figure 13-12 shows the second slide in my presentation. For this slide, I embedded the Excel column chart underneath my heading. To do this, I switched to Excel (which was running in the background) and then opened the workbook with the worksheet containing the chart. After sizing and positioning the Excel program window in the upper half of the screen, I selected the chart in Excel, held down Ctrl, and dragged the chart to the second PowerPoint slide, partially visible in the lower half of the screen. When I released the mouse button, a copy of the chart appeared at the insertion point's position in the PowerPoint slide, where I was then able to size and position it as you see it in Figure 13-12.

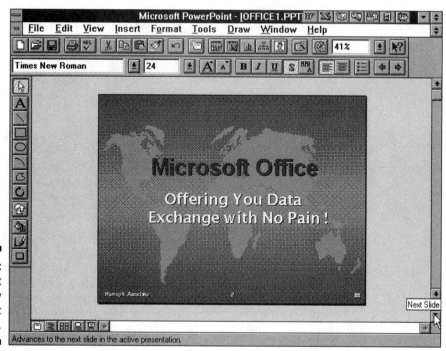

Figure 13-11:
The first slide in my PowerPoint presentation.

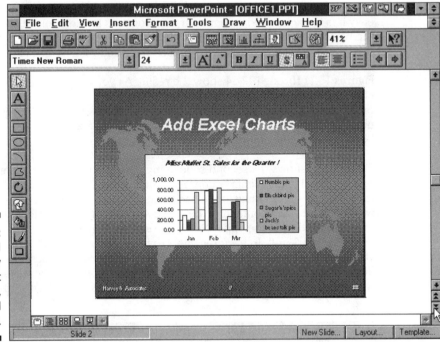

Figure 13-12:
The second slide in my PowerPoint presentation, with a linked Excel chart.

Figure 13-13 shows the third slide in my PowerPoint presentation. For this slide, I embedded a table of Excel worksheet data (formatted with the Colorful 1 table autoformat) underneath my heading and first bullet point. To do this, I once again used drag and drop with the Ctrl key to copy the selected worksheet data from the Excel program window on the top to the PowerPoint window on the bottom.

Once embedded, the chart or worksheet data in the PowerPoint slides can be edited from within PowerPoint. All you have to do is double-click on the chart or table (or choose the Edit Chart Object or Edit Spreadsheet Object command on the chart's or table's shortcut menu).

Figure 13-14 shows the third slide after I double-clicked on the table of Excel worksheet data. As you saw earlier in Word, double-clicking places a frame with column and row information, scroll bars, and sheet tabs around the table. Double-clicking also inserts the Excel pull-down menus and toolbars into PowerPoint, which enables you to make any changes to the contents or formatting of the data in the table with the familiar Excel commands. And as soon as you deselect the worksheet data table by clicking somewhere else in the slide, the menus and toolbars revert back to those used by PowerPoint, and the table of data appears as before, except for the changes made with Excel.

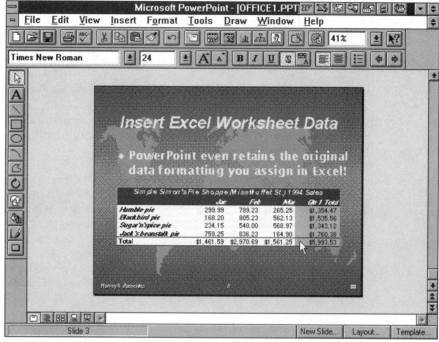

Figure 13-13:
The third slide in my PowerPoint presentation, with embedded Excel data.

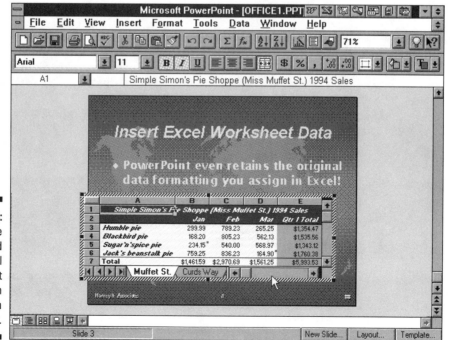

Figure 13-14:
Editing the embedded Excel worksheet data from within PowerPoint.

Excel 5 and Access 2

Access is probably the program in the Office Pro collection that you will be least tempted to start using — not because Access is not a very useful program (because it really is) — but because the program is pretty deep (translation: *nerdy*) and requires a basic understanding of how relational database management systems (a real mouthful) work to be used successfully. Even though you personally may not have any use for Access, somebody in the office may start using the program to create databases that store all sorts of important information that you may need to use.

If this situation comes to pass, you'll be happy to know that you can bring the information stored in an Access database into an Excel worksheet where you can work with it just as though it were an Excel database. To be able to link up with Access and copy records from its database files, you must first have the MS Query add-in program installed in Excel. You can easily tell whether this add-in program is installed by simply starting Excel and then choosing the Data menu. If the Get External Data command appears at the very bottom of the Data menu, then MS Query is installed. If not, you need to follow these steps to install the program:

1. **Choose Tools⇨Add-Ins.**

2. **Select the MS Query Add-In check box.**

3. **Choose OK or press Enter.**

If the MS Query Add-In check box doesn't appear in the Add-Ins Available list box of the Add-Ins dialog box, the data access parts of Excel weren't installed when Excel was originally installed on your computer. (This problem occurs when you do a typical installation instead of the custom Excel installation.)

Installing the data access part of Excel on your computer

1. **Go the Windows File Manager.**

2. **Choose File⇨Run.**

3. **Put the Excel Disk 1 – Setup disk in your floppy drive (A or B).**

4. **If you put the disk in drive A, type** a:setup.

   If you put the disk in drive B, type **b:setup**. If you don't know which drive you put the disk in, please get a hold of a copy of *DOS For Dummies* right away!

5. **Click on the Add/Remove button when the installation program is loaded.**

6. **Choose the Data Access check box and then select the Continue button or press Enter.**

7. **Switch Excel disks in your floppy disk drive as prompted by the installation to do so (have all your Excel disks ready just in case).**

As part of this installation of the data access parts of Excel, the MS Query add-in is automatically installed in Excel. So the next time you start Excel, the Get External Data command will appear on the Data pull-down menu.

After the MS Query add-in is successfully installed, the procedure for getting Access data into an Excel worksheet is pretty straightforward.

Inserting Access data into an Excel worksheet

1. **Open the workbook and select the worksheet where you want the Access data.**

2. **Position the cell pointer in the first cell to contain the Access data and then choose Data⇨Get External Data.**

3. **Select the name of the database to use in the Data Sources dialog box and then choose the Use button.**

4. **Select the database tables that contain the data you want to use within the database and then choose the Add button. When you're finished selecting the database tables you want to use, choose the Close button.**

   In the Query window that appears (similar to the one shown in Figure 13-15), you will see list boxes for each of the database tables you selected in Step 4.

5. **Drag the name of each field you want to use from the tables list boxes to the query table area in the bottom half of the Query window.**

   If you want to add the field to the last column of the query table, you can just double-click on the name. If you add a field to the wrong column in the query table, move the field by clicking on its field name to select the field and then dragging its icon to the correct column of the query table. If you add a field by mistake, you can get rid of it by clicking on the field name and then pressing the Delete key.

6. **When you have added the fields you want to the Query window, choose File⇨Return Data to Microsoft Excel or click on the Return Data button on the MS Query toolbar.**

   You are returned to Excel, where you will see the Get External Data dialog box (shown in Figure 13-16).

7. To have the Access data copied into the current worksheet, starting with the active cell, click on the OK button in the Get External Data dialog box or press Enter.

After you click on OK, the data in the selected fields of the specified Access database tables is copied into your worksheet. Unless you deselect the Include Field Names check box in the Get External Data dialog box, the Access data will start with a row of field names (as shown in Figure 13-17), followed by rows of data.

If, after clicking on OK in the Get External Data dialog box, you find yourself still staring at a blank worksheet, you need to open the Options dialog box (Tools⇨Options), select the General tab, and make sure that the Ignore Other Applications check box is *not* selected. If it is, remove the X from its check box, close the Options dialog box, and try the whole data query procedure all over again. This time, after you click on the OK button in the Get External Data dialog box, you should see your worksheet fill up with Access data!

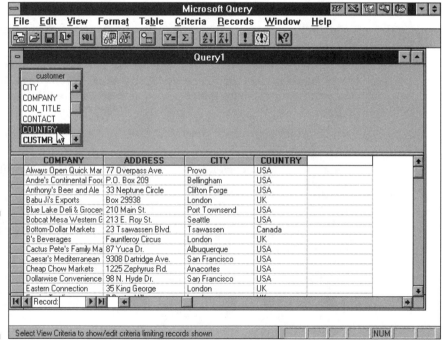

Figure 13-15:
Selecting the fields to copy from the Access database table.

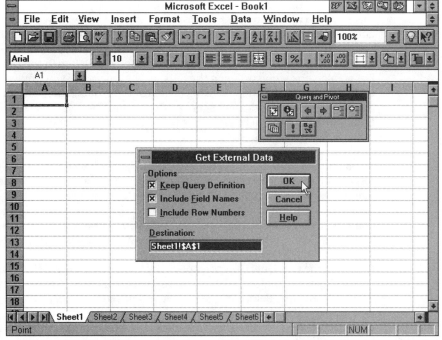

Figure 13-16:
Specifying
where to
copy the
records
from the
Access
database to
the Excel
worksheet.

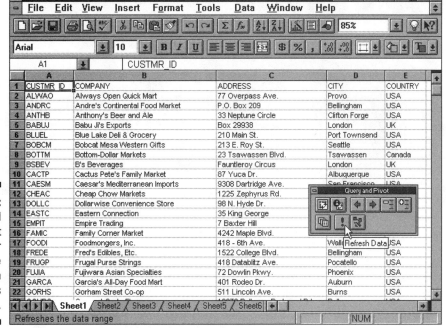

Figure 13-17:
The Excel
worksheet
after
copying the
records from
the Access
database.

After you get the data from the Access database into your Excel worksheet in this manner (which, for your information, is technically known as *performing a data query*), the Microsoft Query program retains a link between the data copied to the worksheet and the original data in the Access database — as long as you don't deselect the Keep Query Definition check box in the Get External Data dialog box when bringing the data in. Now, if you're working on a network and somebody else is busy making changes to the database, you can update the data in your Excel worksheet simply by choosing Data⇨Refresh (or the Refresh Data button on the Query and Pivot toolbar, if you happen to have this little guy open).

If you find that you didn't get all the Access data you needed (let's say you forgot a critical field), you can choose Data⇨Get External Data (or the Get External Data button, which is added to the Query and Pivot toolbar only after you make your first query with the Microsoft Query program). Choosing this command selects all the data brought into your worksheet from Access and opens the Get External Data dialog box again, this time with an Edit Query button.

Choosing the Edit Query button opens the Query window in Microsoft Query, which shows the tables and fields you specified in the first query. You can then add fields, remove fields, or rearrange the fields in the query table as you see fit (see Step 5 in the preceding Tootorial for details). When you're ready to get the data, choose File⇨Return Data to Microsoft Excel or click on the Return Data button on the MS Query toolbar. Then click on OK or press Enter in the Get External Data dialog box in Excel. Microsoft Query replaces the selected data in your worksheet with the Access data from your edited query.

The 5th Wave   By Rich Tennant

Part V
Tips and Tricks Galore

The 5th Wave   By Rich Tennant

"IT'S A SOFTWARE PROGRAM THAT MORE FULLY RE-FLECTS AN ACTUAL OFFICE ENVIRONMENT. IT MULTI-TASKS WITH OTHER USERS, INTEGRATES SHARED DATA, AND THEN USES THAT INFORMATION TO NETWORK VICIOUS RUMORS THROUGH AN INTER-OFFICE LINK-UP."

In this part . . .

I've obviously saved the best for last. The last section is composed of three little chapters that are chock-full of tips, shortcuts, and ways to get yourself out of trouble. The best thing about this part is that you don't have to do very much reading (certainly not of long, boring paragraphs) to get to the info you want to use.

Chapter 14

A Potpourri of Tips

I don't know anyone who couldn't use a few hints and inside pointers on Excel to help him or her work better. And if you're looking for hints, you've come to the right place. In this chapter, I've collected helpful tips on doing all sorts of things in Excel — from entering, editing, formatting, and printing data all the way to working with charts and graphic objects.

While we're on the subject of tips, don't forget about the TipWizard tool on the Formatting toolbar. When the lightbulb icon turns yellow (gray-shaded, if you only have a monochrome monitor), Excel has a new tip for you, based on the actions that you've recently taken in the program. To display the tip or tips, click on the TipWizard tool. After you finish reading the tip(s) displayed above the formula bar, click on the TipWizard tool again to remove its display.

Tips on Data Entry

Data entry is one of those Excel activities where you simply can't get too many tips. The problem, of course, is that the predominant types of data entry vary enormously from workbook to workbook, making it very difficult for one group of data entry pointers to apply to all the data entry situations you'll find yourself in.

When creating a new workbook, these hints can come in pretty handy:

- When creating a new workbook whose worksheets use a standard design common to workbooks you've previously created, convert one of the existing workbooks into a template (Chapter 7) and then create the new worksheet from that template.

- To have a template appear in the New dialog box when you choose File⇨New or press Ctrl+N, save the .xlt file in the \XLSTART directory (usually located under the C:\EXCEL directory on your hard disk).

- To create a generic template which changes Excel's default fonts and formatting to those of your own preferences in all new workbooks that you open, create a template file called BOOK.XLT in the \XLSTART directory.

When doing boring, regular data entry, keep these pointers in mind:

- To restrict your data entry to a particular range or nonadjacent selection in a worksheet, select *all* the cells and then begin your data entry.

- To make a single entry in multiple cells at one time, select the range or nonadjacent cell selection, type the entry, and then press Ctrl+Enter to put the entry in all the highlighted cells.

- To copy a formula up or down a column or across a row, select its cell and then drag the fill handle (the black cross that appears when you position the mouse pointer on the tiny square in the lower right-hand corner of the cell) in the appropriate direction until you have selected all the cells you want to copy the formula to.

- Use the AutoFill feature to fill in a series of dates — days of the week, months, and years — by entering the first date in the first cell and then using the fill handle to enter the rest of the series in the column or row.

- Hold down the Ctrl key as you drag the fill handle to copy an entry (such as a date) into a cell range that would normally be filled with a series. Note that when the active cell contains a single number (such as *1*) and you hold the Ctrl key as you drag the fill handle, Excel creates a series of numbers (*1, 2, 3, 4,* and so on).

- Create a custom AutoFill list (see Chapter 2 of *Excel For Dummies* for details) for any series of entries that you routinely have to enter in your worksheets that are not normally created by Excel when you drag the fill handle.

Tips on Editing Data

In Excel workbooks, as in life, dear reader, change seems to be the only constant you can count on. To help get you through the ups and downs of making modifications (both major and minor) in your worksheets, remember these tempting tips:

- To quickly move a single range of cells to a new place in the worksheet, use the drag-and-drop method: Select the range, position the cell pointer on one of the edges of the highlighted range, and after the pointer assumes the arrowhead shape, drag the outline of the range to its new position.

- To copy a range of cells with drag and drop, hold down the Ctrl key as you position the cell pointer on one of the edges of the highlighted range. After the pointer assumes the arrowhead shape with a plus sign, drag the outline of the range to the place where you want the copy.

- To move or copy a range of cells from one worksheet to another in a workbook, use the Cut or Copy command on the cells' shortcut menu. Select the range, click on it with the secondary mouse button, and then select Cut or Copy on the shortcut menu. Then click on the sheet tab of the appropriate worksheet, position the cell pointer, and press Enter.

- To perform group editing on a bunch of worksheets in the same workbook, select all their sheet tabs (by holding down the Ctrl key as you click on each tab) and then start making your editing changes. To break the editing link between the selected worksheets and go back to one-at-a-time worksheet editing, just click on the sheet tab of that worksheet.

- To really speed up scrolling through a worksheet, hold down the Shift key as you drag the scroll box in the vertical or horizontal scroll bar. Be sure to watch the cell reference area at the beginning of the formula to get an idea of what column or row you're at as you move this box.

- To select only the blank cells in a cell range (for data entry or formatting), select the entire range of cells that contains these blanks and then press Ctrl+G or F5 to open the Go To dialog box. Then choose the Special button to open the Go To Special dialog box, where you choose the Blanks radio button and then click on OK.

- To convert a single formula into its current calculated value in a worksheet, select its cell, press F2 (Edit), press F9 (Calculate), and, finally, press Enter. To convert a range of formulas into their current calculated values, select the range, choose Edit⇨Copy (Ctrl+C) and then Edit⇨Paste Special. In the Paste Special dialog box, choose the Values radio button and press Enter.

Tips on Formatting Data

The biggest tip I can give you on formatting the data in your worksheet is to select all the cells that require a certain format and then open the Format Cells dialog box (Ctrl+1), with its many tabs (Number, Alignment, Font, Border, Patterns, and Protection). From this dialog box, you can choose any and all the formatting options you need. In addition to this general (and very valuable) pointer, there are a few more specific formatting tips that you will want to keep in mind:

- ✔ Whenever possible, use the AutoFormat feature to format an entire table of data. To use this feature, you have to select only one of the cells in the table before you choose Format⇨AutoFormat. Then you select the format you want to use in the Table Format list and press Enter.

- ✔ Use the Format Painter tool on the Formatting toolbar to copy the formatting from one cell to other ranges in a worksheet. Simply double-click on this tool to "paint" multiple ranges. The Format Painter tool remains selected until you click on it again. This enables you to paint as many cell ranges as you need anywhere in the workbook.

Tips on Printing Data

Printing tips are worth their weight in gold. Not only can they save you valuable time, but they also can save you from wasting tons of paper! The following advice should come in handy when printing reports in Excel — not to mention saving a bunch of trees:

- ✔ To have Excel default to printing a particular range (such as one with a particularly important table of data) in a worksheet each time you open its workbook and print, choose File⇨Page Setup and choose the Sheet tab in the Page Setup dialog box. Then designate the range's address in the Print Area text box by typing the range address, selecting the range, or pasting in its range name.

- ✔ Always preview the pages on-screen for a report that you've never printed before. Choose the File⇨Print Preview command, the Print Preview tool on the Formatting toolbar, or the Print Preview button in the Print or Page Setup dialog box before you actually go ahead and print the data.

- ✔ To select more than one worksheet for printing in a workbook, select the sheet tabs for all the worksheets (by holding down the Ctrl key as you click on each one). Then choose File⇨Print or click on the Print tool on the Standard toolbar.

✔ To print your report without the worksheet grid lines, choose File➪Page Setup and then choose the Sheet tab in the Page Setup dialog box. Deselect the Gridlines check box and choose the Print or Print Preview button.

✔ To print column headings at the top of each page of a report, choose File➪Page Setup and then choose the Sheet tab in the Page Setup dialog box. Designate the row or range of rows with the headings in the Rows to Repeat text box before you choose the Print or Print Preview button.

✔ To print row headings on the left side of each page of a report, choose File➪Page Setup and then choose the Sheet tab in the Page Setup dialog box. Designate the column or range of columns with the headings in the Columns to Repeat text box before you choose the Print or Print Preview button.

✔ If the tables of information you need to print are wider than they are tall, save paper by switching the orientation of the printing from Portrait mode to Landscape mode. To make this change, choose File➪Page Setup and then choose the Page tab in the Page Setup dialog box. Select the Landscape radio button before you choose the Print or Print Preview button.

✔ To print all the data on your worksheet on one page, choose File➪Page Setup and then choose the Page tab in the Page Setup dialog box. Select the Fit to radio button. Make sure that both the page(s) wide and the page(s) tall text boxes associated with this radio button contain a *1* before you choose the Print or Print Preview button.

✔ To remove all the page breaks from a worksheet after printing or print previewing it, choose all the cells (Ctrl+Shift+spacebar) and then choose Insert➪Remove Page Break.

Tips on Charting and Working with Graphics

If you have reason to work with charts and other types of graphics in your work, you already know how time-consuming and downright frustrating futzing with the little angels can sometimes be. To help cut down on time lost and eliminate undue stress and high blood pressure, I offer you the following charting tips and tips for working with graphic objects.

When creating and editing a chart, keep these pointers in mind:

✔ To select a chart that is embedded in a worksheet, double-click on the chart. To select a chart that is on its own chart sheet, select the tab of the chart sheet.

✔ To chart the chart type without losing the custom formatting that you've applied to the chart, select the chart and then choose the Chart Type command on the Format menu.

✔ To open a dialog box for formatting a part of a chart (like the y-axis or the legend), double-click on the object after selecting the chart.

✔ To create a column chart on its own chart sheet for the data you've selected in your worksheet, highlight all the cells and then press F11.

✔ To add data to an embedded chart, select the cells with the data to be added and then position the pointer on a side of the cell selection. When the pointer changes to an arrowhead, drag the outline of the cell selection to the embedded chart and release the mouse button.

✔ To copy a chart created in its own chart sheet to a worksheet where it becomes an embedded chart, select the chart and then choose Edit⇨Copy (Ctrl+C). Next select the sheet tab and cell where the upper left-hand corner of the chart is to appear and choose Edit⇨Paste (Ctrl+V).

✔ You may discover that a chart copied from a chart sheet to a worksheet takes up far too many cells of the worksheet where it's embedded. The easiest way to resize the newly embedded chart is to select a smaller percentage (such as 50 percent or 25 percent) in the Zoom Control drop-down list box on the Formatting toolbar. Then drag the lower right-hand corner of the embedded chart up and to the left. After resizing the chart in the zoomed-out worksheet, you can return to the normal view by choosing 100 percent in the Zoom Control drop-down list box.

When working with other graphic objects (such as text boxes, arrows, ovals, imported pictures, and so on), keep these tips in mind:

✔ To select a single graphic object in a worksheet, click on the graphic. To select multiple graphic objects, hold down the Ctrl key as you click on each one. To select all the graphic objects in a worksheet, select one and then press Ctrl+A (Select All).

✔ If you need to move a group of graphic objects (such as an embedded chart, arrows, and a text box) as a single unit in a worksheet, group them together by selecting each object and then choosing Format⇨Placement⇨Group or by choosing the Group Objects tool on the Drawing toolbar.

✔ If you're having trouble selecting a graphic because each time you click on it, Excel selects another object that overlaps it in some way, choose the Format⇨Placement⇨Send to Back command or the Send to Back tool on the Drawing toolbar to send the unwanted graphic to the background. Then try selecting the graphic you really want. (You can also use the Send to Back feature with graphics that partially overlap each other to change which overlaid part is hidden and which is displayed.)

✔ If you want to create a text box whose text is linked to a particular cell in the worksheet, select the Text Box tool on the Formatting or Drawing toolbar and then draw the box. Next press F2 or click on the formula bar to activate Edit mode. Type = and then select or type in the address of the cell that contains the text you want to use and press Enter. After linking the contents of the text box to a particular cell, Excel changes the text displayed in the text box as soon as you edit or replace the text in that cell.

✔ If you need to edit a graphic (such as a text box or other shape) that has a macro assigned to it, hold down the Ctrl key as you click on the object to select it. By holding down the Ctrl key as you click, you prevent Excel from running the macro assigned to the object.

✔ To change the way a graphic that sits on top of cells is sized and moved when you resize or move the columns or rows containing these cells, select the graphic and then choose Format⇨Object (Ctrl+1). Select the Properties tab and then choose between the Move and Size with Cells, Move But Don't Size with Cells, or Don't Move or Size with Cells radio buttons.

✔ To remove from the printed report a particular graphic object that sits on top of the print area, choose Format⇨Object (Ctrl+1). Select the Properties tab and then deselect the Print Object check box.

✔ To make a copy of the graphic you've selected, hold down Ctrl as you drag it to a new position. To constrain the movement of the graphic you've selected to its current vertical or horizontal plane, hold down Shift as you drag it to a new position. To align the graphic you've selected on the invisible grid used in the worksheet, hold down Alt as you drag it to a new position.

✔ To draw a square with the Rectangle or Filled Rectangle tool on the Drawing toolbar, hold down Shift as you drag the crosshair pointer.

✔ To draw a circle with the Ellipse or the Filled Ellipse tool on the Drawing toolbar, hold down Shift as you drag the crosshair pointer.

✔ To constrain an arrow drawn with the Arrow tool on the Drawing toolbar to a 45 degree angle in any direction around an imaginary circle, hold down Shift as you drag the crosshair pointer.

✔ To maintain the original proportions of a graphic as you resize it, hold down the Shift key as you drag its corner with the double-headed arrow pointer.

Chapter 15

Shortcuts for Every Occasion

● ●

In This Chapter

▶ Selection shortcuts

▶ Data entry shortcuts

▶ Editing shortcuts

▶ Formatting shortcuts

▶ Window and workbook shortcuts

● ●

*A*s the pace continues to get faster and faster in today's modern, hurry-up-and-wait offices, you need all the shortcuts you can get your hot little hands on. Well, between the shortcut keys, shortcut menus, and toolbars in Excel 5, you should have all the shortcuts you can possibly deal with when working in this program. The biggest problem you'll have with all these short-cuts is just remembering that they exist and what they do. Of course, that's where this nifty little chapter comes into play.

Shortcuts for Selecting Cells

No doubt about it, you probably spend more time than you care to admit with selecting worksheet cells to do one darn thing or another. When selecting a cell range that forms a table that is so many columns wide and so many rows long, you'll want to keep these cell selection shortcuts in mind:

✔ When all the cells of the table are visible on-screen, click on the first cell in the upper left-hand corner of the table, hold down the Shift key, and then click on the last cell in the lower right-hand corner.

✔ When the table is too wide and too long to fit on-screen, click on the first cell in the upper left-hand corner, hold down the Shift key, and double-click somewhere on the right side of the first cell to select the entire first row. Next, double-click somewhere on the bottom side of one of the cells in the selected first row to select vertically down to the last row.

Excel also includes some powerful shortcut keystrokes for extending a cell selection in a particular direction. You can use the following shortcuts without the Shift key if you first press F8 to put Excel into Extend mode:

- ✔ Press Ctrl+Shift+→ or End+Shift, → to extend the selection to the right all the way to the last occupied cell in that row.
- ✔ Press Ctrl+Shift+← or End+Shift, ← to extend the selection to the left all the way to the first occupied cell in that row.
- ✔ Press Ctrl+Shift+↑ or End+Shift, ↑ to extend the selection up all the way to the first occupied cell in that column.
- ✔ Press Ctrl+Shift+↓ or End+Shift, ↓ to extend the selection down all the way to the last occupied cell in that column.
- ✔ Press Ctrl+Shift+Home to extend the selection to the very first cell of the worksheet.
- ✔ Press Ctrl+Shift+End or End+Shift, Home to extend the selection to the last active cell in your worksheet.
- ✔ Press Shift+Page Down to extend the selection down one screenful.
- ✔ Press Shift+Page Up to extend the selection up one screenful.
- ✔ Press Alt+Shift+Page Down to extend the selection right one screenful.
- ✔ Press Alt+Shift+Page Up to extend the selection left one screenful.

For selecting larger areas of the worksheet, keep these mouse and keystroke shortcuts in mind:

- ✔ To select an entire column, click on the column letter or press Ctrl+spacebar.
- ✔ To select an entire row, click on the row number or press Shift+spacebar.
- ✔ To select the entire worksheet, click on the Select All button at the intersection of the row of column letters and column of row numbers or press Ctrl+A.

While the preceding shortcuts are great for selecting individual cell ranges in a worksheet, don't forget that you can select dissimilar, disassociated cell ranges (better known as a *nonadjacent selection*) at one time by holding down the Ctrl key as you drag through each new range to be selected.

Simply press F8 to put Excel in Extend mode to select the first range with the keyboard. Then press Shift+F8 to switch to Add mode and move the cell pointer to the first cell of the second range. Press F8 to put Excel back into Extend mode so that you can select the second range with the keyboard.

Selecting graphic objects

While cells of a worksheet are the most likely candidates for being selected, they are by no means the only items in town. A worksheet can contain many graphic objects, such as text boxes, arrows, embedded charts, pictures of your boss, and who knows what else. To select a graphic object in the worksheet, you simply click on it (which causes its selection handles to be displayed around its perimeter).

If you're working in a worksheet that contains lots of graphics, you can select all the graphics in a flash by clicking on one of the graphic objects and then pressing Ctrl+Shift+spacebar to select all the other objects in the worksheet.

You may sometimes want to hide the display of graphic objects or, at a minimum, display only placeholders for them in a worksheet to speed up scrolling (especially if you're forced to run Excel 5 on one of those slow 386 machines). Simply press Ctrl+6 (that's 6, not F6 — and I mean the 6 on the top row of the keyboard, not the one on the numeric keypad) to cycle through replacing all the graphic objects in the worksheet with placeholders, hiding them all, and redisplaying them.

Selecting parts of a chart

A chart that has been embedded in worksheet is the one selectable graphic object that is itself composed of a whole bunch of selectable objects. Before you can select objects in an embedded chart, you must select the chart itself by double-clicking on it (single-clicking selects the chart as a graphic object to be manipulated in the worksheet). Dealing with a chart that is in its own chart sheet is another story, however, because then you can single-click anywhere on the chart after selecting its chart sheet.

After a chart is selected, you can then select particular chart items by clicking on them or by using the following keystrokes:

- ✔ Press ↓ to select the next group of items in the chart.
- ✔ Press ↑ to select the preceding group of items in the chart.
- ✔ Press → to select the next chart item within the group.
- ✔ Press ← to select the preceding chart item within a group.

Selecting cells with special attributes

As you may remember, if you open the Go To dialog box (by pressing F5 or Ctrl+G) and then choose the Special button to open the Go To Special dialog box, you can select only the cells in the worksheet with some special characteristic — such as the cells with notes or graphics, or only the visible cells in a selected range (which is very helpful when you need to chart just the cells with quarterly totals in a collapsed outline).

Instead of going to all the trouble to open up the Go To Special dialog box, you can use the following shortcut keys:

- Press Ctrl+Shift+/ (Ctrl+?) to select all the cells with notes.
- Press Ctrl+Shift+8 (Ctrl+*) to select a rectangular range of cells surrounding the active cell.
- Press Ctrl+Shift+spacebar to select all the graphic objects in the worksheet.
- Press Alt+; (semicolon) to select only the visible cells in the highlighted range.

Shortcuts for Entering Data in Cells

Data entry in a worksheet can be a real drag on the old wrists. To help get the job done without a good case of carpal tunnel syndrome, keep these data entry shortcuts foremost in your mind:

- Press Ctrl+Enter to make the same entry in all the cells that are currently selected.
- Press Ctrl+R so that the entry in the first (active) cell of the range is copied to the right to all the cells in the same row of the current cell selection.
- Press Ctrl+D so that the entry in the first (active) cell of the range is copied down to all the other cells in the same column of the current cell selection.
- Press Ctrl+' (single quotation mark) to copy the formula from the cell above into the current cell.
- Press Ctrl+Shift+" (double quotation mark) to copy the value (as opposed to the formula) from the cell above into the current cell.
- Press Ctrl+; (semicolon) to enter the current date in a cell.
- Press Ctrl+Shift+: (colon) to enter the current time in a cell.

✔ Press Alt+= (equal sign) to insert **=SUM()** in the current cell, waiting for you to select the cells to be summed.

✔ Press Shift+F3 to open the Function Wizard — Step 1 of 2 dialog box.

✔ Press Ctrl+A to open the Function Wizard – Step 2 of 2 dialog box (where you specify the function's arguments) after typing the name of an Excel function in the current cell (such as **=sum** or **=vlookup**).

✔ Press Ctrl+Shift+A to insert the names of a function's arguments after typing the function name in the current cell (such as typing **=sum** to get =sum(number1,number2,...) displayed in the cell).

✔ Press F3 to paste a range name in the formula you're building.

✔ Press Ctrl+F3 to define a range name in the Define Names dialog box.

✔ Press Ctrl+Shift+F3 to define a range name in the Create Names dialog box from existing worksheet labels.

✔ Press Shift+F2 to open the Cell Note dialog box to add a note to the current cell.

Shortcuts for Editing Cells

No sooner do you get the data entry done for a worksheet than it's time to edit the darned thing! Don't despair. By using the editing shortcuts covered in this section, you'll be on the golf course in no time at all. When editing the contents of a particular cell, the following shortcuts should be uppermost in your mind:

✔ Press Backspace to clear the current contents of the cell and to put Excel into Enter mode so that you can make a brand new entry.

✔ Press F2 or double-click on a cell to put Excel in Edit mode so that you can modify its contents (either on the formula bar or in the cell itself).

✔ Press Home to move the insertion point to the beginning of the cell entry that you're editing.

✔ Press End to move the insertion point to the end of the cell entry that you're editing.

✔ Press Backspace to delete the character to the left of the insertion point or press Delete to delete the character to the right of the insertion point in the cell that you're editing.

✔ Press Ctrl+Shift+Delete to delete from the insertion point to the end of the cell entry that you're editing.

✔ Press Alt+Enter to insert a new line into the cell entry that you're editing.

✔ Press Ctrl+Alt+Tab to insert a tab into the cell entry that you're editing.

✔ Press F4 to convert the cell reference at the insertion point in the cell you're editing from relative to absolute, from absolute to mixed, or from mixed back to relative.

When doing other kinds of editing in your worksheet, these shortcuts can come in handy:

✔ Press Ctrl+O (as in *open*) or Ctrl+F12, or click on the Open button on the Formatting toolbar to open a workbook for editing.

✔ Press Ctrl+N (as in *new*) or click on the New button on the Formatting toolbar to open a new workbook for editing.

✔ Press Ctrl+S (as in *save*) or Shift+F12, or click on the Save button on the Formatting toolbar to save your editing changes in the workbook you're editing.

✔ Press F12 to open the Save As dialog box, where you can rename a workbook and/or save the workbook in another file format.

✔ Press Ctrl+Z or click on the Undo button on the Standard toolbar to undo your very last action in Excel.

✔ Press F4 or Alt+Enter, or click on the Repeat button on the Standard toolbar to repeat your very last action in Excel.

✔ Press Delete to clear all the entries in the current cell selection.

✔ Press Ctrl+X or click on the Cut button on the Formatting toolbar to cut the current cell selection and place it in the Clipboard.

✔ Press Ctrl+C or click on the Copy button on the Formatting toolbar to copy the current cell selection to the Clipboard.

✔ Press Ctrl+V or click on the Paste button on the Formatting toolbar to paste the contents of the Clipboard into the worksheet.

✔ Press Ctrl+Shift++ (plus sign on the top row) or Ctrl++ (plus sign on the numeric keypad) to display the Insert Cell dialog box.

✔ Press Ctrl+− (minus key on the top row or on the numeric keypad) to display the Delete Cell dialog box.

✔ Press F9 or Ctrl+= (equal sign) to calculate all the worksheets in all the workbooks you have open.

✔ Press Shift+F9 to calculate only the active worksheet of the current workbook.

✔ Press Ctrl+P (as in *print*) or Ctrl+Shift+F12 to print the workbook or a part thereof with the options in the Print dialog box. Click on the Print button on the Formatting toolbar to print the entire worksheet using the current print settings.

✔ Press Shift+F11 to insert a new worksheet in the current workbook.

✔ Press F11 to insert a new chart sheet in the current workbook.

✔ Press F7 or click on the Spelling button on the Formatting toolbar to spell check the current worksheet or the current selection in that worksheet.

Shortcuts for Formatting Cells

With the advent of one-stop-shopping dialog boxes — such as the Format Cells dialog box (Ctrl+1) — that use tabs to enable you to get at all the different types of formatting you may want to apply to the current cell selection, you don't need to rely on the following formatting shortcuts keys nearly as much as in the past:

✔ Press Ctrl+Shift+$ or click on the Currency Style button on the Standard toolbar to assign the currency number format to the current cell selection, as in $12,250.00.

✔ Press Ctrl+Shift+% or click on the Percent Style button on the Standard toolbar to assign the percentage number format to the current cell selection, as in 12%.

✔ Press Ctrl+Shift+! or click on the Comma Style button on the Standard toolbar to assign the comma number format to the current cell selection, as in 12,250.00.

✔ Click on the Increase Decimal button on the Standard toolbar to add a decimal place to the number style in the current cell selection.

✔ Click on the Decrease Decimal button on the Standard toolbar to remove a decimal place from the number style in the current cell selection.

✔ Press Ctrl+Shift+# to assign the date number format with the day, month, and year to the current cell selection, as in 31-Oct-94.

✔ Press Ctrl+Shift+~ to assign the general number format to the current cell selection.

✔ Press Ctrl+Shift+& to apply a single line border to the current cell selection.

✔ Press Ctrl+Shift+_ (underscore) to remove all borders from the current cell selection.

✔ Press Ctrl+B (as in *bold*) or click on the Bold button on the Standard toolbar to apply or remove bold in the current cell selection.

✔ Press Ctrl+I (as in *italics*) or click on the Italic button on the Standard toolbar to apply or remove italics in the current cell selection.

✔ Press Ctrl+U (as in *underline*) or click on the Underline button on the Standard toolbar to apply or remove underlining in the current cell selection.

✔ Press Ctrl+5 (on the top row of the keyboard) to apply or remove strikethrough in the current cell selection.

✔ Click on the Font drop-down list button on the Standard toolbar and drag to the desired font to apply a new font to the current cell selection.

✔ Click on the Size drop-down list button on the Standard toolbar and drag to the desired font size to apply a new font size to the current cell selection.

✔ Click on the Left button on the Standard toolbar to left-align the entries in the current cell selection.

✔ Click on the Center button on the Standard toolbar to center the entries in the current cell selection.

✔ Click on the Right button on the Standard toolbar to right-align the entries in the current cell selection.

✔ Click on the Center Across Columns button on the Standard toolbar to center the entry in the active cell across all the columns in the current cell selection.

✔ Click on the Border button on the Standard toolbar and then drag its palette off to display the Border tear-off palette, from which you can assign different borders to the current cell selection.

✔ Click on the Color button on the Standard toolbar and then drag its palette off to display the Color tear-off palette, from which you can assign different colors to cells in the current cell selection.

✔ Click on the Font Color button on the Standard toolbar and then drag its palette off to display the Font Color tear-off palette, from which you can assign different colors to entries in the cells in the current cell selection.

✔ Click on the Format Painter button on the Formatting toolbar and then drag through a range of cells to assign the formatting in the active cell to all the cells in the range you select.

✔ Press Alt+' (apostrophe or single quotation mark) to display the Style dialog box, where you can apply or define a new formatting style to the current cell selection.

Shortcuts for Changing What Is Displayed

In Excel 5, as you've probably noticed, there's always a lot on-screen. Fortunately, the program has included a few very useful shortcut keys for changing what's hidden or displayed:

- ✔ Press Ctrl+7 (not F7, just *7* on the top row of the keyboard) to switch between hiding and displaying the Formatting toolbar.

- ✔ Press Ctrl+9 (not F9, just *9* on the top row of the keyboard) to hide the rows you have selected in the worksheet.

- ✔ Press Ctrl+Shift+(to display the rows you have hidden in the worksheet.

- ✔ Press Ctrl+0 (zero on the top row of the keyboard) to hide the columns you have selected in the worksheet.

- ✔ Press Ctrl+Shift+) to display the columns you have hidden in the worksheet.

- ✔ Press Ctrl+8 (not F8, just *8* on the top row of the keyboard) to hide and redisplay outline symbols on-screen for an outlined table of data.

- ✔ Press Ctrl+` (the accent next to the 1 key on the top row) to switch between displaying the values and the formulas in the cells of the worksheet.

Shortcuts for Fooling Around with Windows

Admit it: Windows and Windows programs like Excel wouldn't be so bad if it weren't for all those darned windows you have to fool with! Think of it: First, you gotta keep track of Windows itself, within which you run Excel. Then, within Excel, you have to keep track of all the different document windows with the different workbooks you have open. Finally, within each document window, you have to keep track of all the different worksheets that are inside of the particular workbook that's active.

And, if that's not enough, Windows is just full of all those obscure little buttons that do different window-sizing tricks, such as shrink a window down to an itty-bitty icon or puff it up so that it takes over the entire screen. Whoa! It's enough to make you go out and buy a Macintosh!

Although they're not much help, the following shortcut keys may make your task of dealing with these windows a little easier (they certainly couldn't hurt):

✔ Press Ctrl+Esc to display the Task List dialog box, which shows what programs are running in Windows and enables you to choose any one of your choice.

✔ Press Alt+Esc to switch to the next program that is running.

✔ Press Alt+Shift+Esc to switch to the Windows program that is running.

✔ Press Alt+Tab to switch to the next Windows program that is running.

✔ Press Alt+Shift+Tab to switch to the preceding Windows program that is running.

In addition to these program-switching shortcuts, there a few generic windows shortcuts that you can use when dealing with Excel workbooks and the various sheets within each workbook:

✔ Press Ctrl+F9 to minimize a document window to a book icon in Excel.

✔ Press Ctrl+F10 to maximize a document window to full size.

✔ Press Ctrl+F5 to restore a document window to its regular size.

✔ Press Ctrl+F6 or Ctrl+Tab to activate the next document window that you have open.

✔ Press Ctrl+Shift+F6 or Ctrl+Shift+Tab to activate the preceding document window that you have open.

✔ Press Ctrl+F4 to close the active document window and remove its workbook from the computer's memory.

✔ Press Ctrl+PageDown to activate the next worksheet of the workbook in the active document window.

✔ Press Ctrl+PageUp to activate the preceding worksheet of the workbook in the active document window.

Chapter 16

What to Do When Things Go Wrong

. . . .

In This Chapter

▶ What to do when you zap something you shouldn't have

▶ What to do when error values show up in your formula

▶ What to do when you can't find something in a workbook

▶ What to do when you can't find the workbook you need

. . . .

I hate to end things in this book on a sour note by mentioning the bad times you may encounter when using Excel, but, as you all know, mistakes are inevitable (at least, every once in awhile). The best solution to encountering these problems is to be prepared and to know how to get out of them in the fastest way possible. In this chapter, I point out some of the more salient hints for keeping yourself sane when any of the following problems occur:

✔ You zap something in the worksheet that you really, really shouldn't have.

✔ You enter a perfectly fine-looking formula in a cell, and Excel returns one of those horrid-looking error values. Or even worse, you open up a workbook to find that it's now full of those horrid-looking error values.

✔ You need to open a workbook, but you can't remember where in blazes you saved it or, even worse, what the blasted thing is called.

Data Recovery 101

It's nothing to be ashamed of. It happens to the best of us (at the worst times, I might add). At one time or another, you're going to get rid of something that you didn't mean to (although you won't realize it until the instant after you deleted the stuff!). When that day dawns, you need to go through the following procedure the very moment you realize that you did something really stupid:

1. **Say a string of bad words: $#!@#%^&*!!!**

2. **Press Ctrl+Z or click on the Undo button on the Formatting toolbar or, if you're really desperate, choose Undo on the Edit pull-down menu.**

3. **Sigh a big sigh of relief!**

Remember that you apply this little three-step Undo procedure whenever you make a boo-boo, not just when you foolishly eradicate the whole left side of a worksheet. The Undo operation works when you insert a new column or row that you don't really need, when you add number formatting to the wrong cells, when you sort a list of data without checking and changing the Sort by column, when you insert a new worksheet that you don't really need in the workbook, or when you do any of a million other actions that seem really stupid and unnecessary the moment you do them.

Unfortunately for us all, there are some things that Undo just can't put back the way they ought to be. Moreover, even with actions that Undo can set right, you need to perform your little Undo procedure before you do anything else (foolish) in the workbook. The worst possible thing you can do when you realize that you've just done something crazy to your worksheet is to panic and immediately try a bunch of new things in Excel in an attempt to set things right. Most of the time, all the extra things you do to correct the problem make it impossible to use Undo to set things right and often make things worse (you can tell I'm speaking with the voice of experience here!).

In this worst-case scenario, you may find that you have no choice but to abandon the workbook you've messed up and fall back to the last-saved version of the file. Simply choose File⇨Close and then click on the No button when asked if you want to save the changes to the file. Of course, this cure can be as bad as the disease if you haven't been exactly regular in the saving of your changes (in which case, you lose more data by going back to the last-saved version than by sticking with the mess you made of the current version).

To avoid a lot of problems that can crop up when you find it difficult to get in the habit of saving changes on a regular basis, simply enable Excel's AutoSave feature and then forget about going through the saving routine except when you're ready to close the workbook or exit Excel altogether.

Before you can use the AutoSave command, you may have to add the command to the Tools menu. If you open the Tools menu and don't see AutoSave, first choose Tools⇨Add-Ins to open the Add-Ins dialog box. Then choose the AutoSave check box in the Add-Ins Available list box and click on OK or press Enter. At the time you select the AutoSave option in the Add-Ins dialog box,

Excel automatically activates the AutoSave feature and sets the interval for saving the active workbook to every ten minutes. But you can adjust this amount of time and other options, as well.

Changing AutoSave settings

To set a different AutoSave time interval, to deactivate AutoSave, or to change any of its other settings, follow these steps:

1. **Choose Tools➪AutoSave to open the AutoSave dialog box.**

2. **To change the time interval between saves, replace or edit the value in the Automatic Save Every *blank* Minutes text box.**

3. **To have Excel save changes in all workbooks you have open, not just the active one, choose the Save All Open Workbooks radio button in the Save Options area.**

4. **To have Excel save your changes without bothering to prompt you each time (which can become a real pain), choose the Prompt Before Saving check box to deselect it.**

5. **When you've finished changing the AutoSave options, choose OK or press Enter.**

Error Value Village

As you are undoubtedly painfully aware, Excel displays an error value in a cell when, for whatever reason, the program cannot properly calculate the formula that you've entered there. There are currently seven error values to choose from:

- #DIV/0! appears when a formula is trying to divide by zero or when a cell contains zero or is empty. The best bet for getting rid of this error value is to go to the cell that is being used as the divisor in the formula and enter a nonzero value there.

- #N/A appears when a formula contains a special #N/A value or a reference to a cell that contains such a value (used by some spreadsheet jockeys to indicate that a required value is not currently available). The only way to enter an #N/A value in a worksheet is with the NA( ) function. The best way to find and eliminate the #N/A value is to use the Edit➪Find command, switch to Values in the Look in text box, and enter **#n/a** as the search text in the Find What text box.

✔ #NAME? appears when a formula refers to a range name that Excel does not recognize as legitimate. This error can happen when you misspell the range name. (The best way to correct this problem is to paste the correct name in the formula with the Insert⇨Name⇨Paste command.) You can also get this error message when you forget to enclose formula text in quotation marks or forget a colon between cell references in a range so that Excel thinks you're referring to a named range rather than some text or a particular cell range.

✔ #NULL! appears when a formula refers to an intersection between two areas of a worksheet that do not intersect. Because you probably don't even know what this error means in English, chances are good that this error value has popped up because you inserted a space between a series of function arguments when you should have entered a comma (,).

✔ #NUM! appears when a formula has some kind of number woe. In most cases, the error occurs because the formula uses a function with an argument that contains unacceptable values of some sort or the formula is trying to calculate a number that is either too large or too tiny for Excel to deal with.

✔ #REF! appears when a formula refers to an invalid cell reference. This error occurs most often after you delete a part of a worksheet that contains cells that are referred to in the formula or you replace them by pasting in new values. Here's a perfect occasion for using your old friend, the Undo feature.

✔ #VALUE! appears when a formula contains the wrong type of argument or is trying to perform an operation that is not possible with the type of data you've entered or referred to. The most common cause of this type of error value is a mathematical formula of some kind that refers to cells that contain text rather than values, such as the formula =B2+B3, where B2 contains *Ted* and B3 contains *Bill*.

Knowing the probable cause for a particular error value can go a long way towards finding out how to get rid of the error. Just remember that these little joys have the really bad habit of spreading throughout a worksheet to any and all cells containing formulas that refer to them. This means that in some situations, you may have to track down the formulas that are actually the cause of the error values before you can eliminate them.

Consult Chapter 9 for loads of information about finding and eliminating the source of error values in a worksheet and avoiding them altogether with error trapping.

In the Data Lost and Found

The last type of error that you are bound to encounter is definitely one of omission: this error occurs when you can't find something in a worksheet or, even worse (and more common), you can't find the entire workbook you need to work on.

For those times when you've temporarily mislaid some very important data in a worksheet, I can offer two very different methods for locating the missing information:

✔ To locate the data by sight, use the Zoom Control button on the Formatting toolbar to zoom out on the worksheet by choosing a percentage, such as 25% or 50% (at the most). After you think you've located the target area, click on one of its (tiny) cells and then zoom in on the area by choosing 100% in the Zoom Control drop-down list.

✔ To locate the data by words, use the Edit⇨Find command and use the Find feature to locate some key text or value that's contained in the region you need to locate. When searching for text, you don't have to worry about what option appears in the Look in text box. However, when searching for a value that is used in the formula as opposed to a value returned by a formula, you need to be sure that Values appears in the Look in text box rather than Formulas, before you begin the search.

For more information on using the Edit⇨Find command in Excel, see Chapter 3.

Finding misplaced information in a workbook can be a piece of cake compared to finding a misplaced workbook file. For this kind of problem, you're probably going to have to resort to the use of the File⇨Find File command and search for files that either meet a particular filename pattern or contain certain keywords (used in the workbook's summary information). The greatest benefit in using this nifty utility is that you can use the Preview window in the Find File dialog box to determine which of the listed files returned by a Find File search is really the one you want to open.

For more complete information on using the Find File feature, consult Chapter 4.

Of course, you can save yourself a lot of hassle and wasted time in searching with the Find File feature by not losing the workbook in the first place. And the best antidote for misplacing workbooks is to set the directory where Excel automatically saves your workbooks so that you don't have to look anywhere else for the workbooks you create.

Setting the default directory

To set the default directory that Excel automatically reverts to whenever you choose File⇨Save (Ctrl+S) or File⇨Open (Ctrl+O), take the following steps:

1. **Choose Tools⇨Options.**

2. **Choose the General tab in the Options dialog box.**

3. **Select the Default File Location text box and enter the path of the directory that you want to set up as the place where Excel automatically saves your files.**

   For example, to set the directory I created beneath the Excel directory that bears my first name, I would enter **c:\excel\greg** in this text box.

4. **Choose OK or press Enter.**

After you set up a new default directory in this manner, Excel automatically suggests this directory any time you save a new file or go to open up an existing file. In this way, you don't even have to worry twice about yucky stuff like drives and directory paths when all you want to do is get your work done!

When you don't have anything entered in the Default File Location text box in the General tab of the Options dialog box, Excel always defaults to the directory that contains the Excel program files. This is the last place you want to save your workbook files because they get mixed in with about a billion other unrelated program files. Should you ever have to remove the Excel program (prior to reinstalling it or upgrading it), you then would have a devil of a time moving your files so that they don't get zapped.

Also, when setting a new default directory, be extra careful *not* to enter the directory pathname in the Alternate Startup File Location text box. (Remember, you want to enter the pathname in the Default File Location text box.) If you enter the pathname in the wrong text box, Excel will try to open up any and *all* files located in the directory that you specify in the Alternate Startup File Location text box *each* time you start the program. If you have lots of workbooks in the directory you specify there, I guarantee you'll be sorry the next time you start Excel!

Glossary

● ●

absolute cell reference

A cell reference that Excel cannot automatically adjust. If you're about to copy a formula and you want to prevent Excel from adjusting one or more of the cell references (the program has a tendency to change the column and row reference in copies), make the cell references absolute. Absolute cell references are indicated by a dollar sign (yes, a $) in front of the column letter and the row number — $K$11, for example. You can convert a relative reference to an absolute reference with the F4 key. See also **relative cell reference**.

active

The program window, workbook window, worksheet window, or dialog box currently in use. The color of the title bar of an active window or dialog box is different from the color of nonactive window title bars. When several document windows are displayed, you can activate an inactive window by clicking on it.

arguments

Not what you have with your spouse, but rather the values you give to a worksheet function to compute. Arguments are enclosed in parentheses and separated from one another by commas. See also **function**.

borders

The different types of lines Excel can draw around the edges of each cell or the outside edge of a bunch of cells. Excel offers a wide variety of different line styles and colors for this purpose.

cell

The basic building block of plant and animal life and also of the Excel worksheet. The *worksheet cell* is a block formed by the intersections of column and row grid lines displayed in the sheet. Cells are where all worksheet data is stored. Each cell is identified by the letter of its column and the number of its row, the so-called *cell reference*.

cell pointer

A heavy outline that indicates which cell in the worksheet is currently selected. You must move the cell pointer to a particular cell before you can enter or edit information in that cell.

cell range

A bunch of cells that are all right next to each other. To select a range of cells with the mouse, you simply point at the beginning of the range, click the mouse button, and drag through the cells.

cell reference

Identifies the location of a cell in the worksheet. Normally, the cell reference consists of the column letter followed by the row number. For example, B3 indicates the cell in the second column and third row of the worksheet. When you place the cell pointer in a cell, Excel displays its cell reference at the beginning of the formula bar. See also *relative cell reference* and *absolute cell reference.*

chart

Also known as a *graph.* This is a graphic representation of a set of values stored in a worksheet. You can create a chart right in a worksheet, where it is saved and printed along with the worksheet data. You can also display a chart in its own chart window, where you can edit its contents or print it independently of the worksheet data. (Such a chart is called, appropriately enough, a *chart sheet.*)

check box

Turns an option on or off in a dialog box. If the check box contains an *X* (sorry, not a check mark) the option is turned on. If the check box is blank, the option is turned off. The nice thing about check boxes is that you can select more than one of the multiple options presented as a group. See also *radio button.*

click

The simplest mouse technique. You press and immediately release the mouse button. See also *double-click.*

Clipboard

The Windows equivalent of a hand-held Clipboard to which you attach papers and information you need to work with. The Windows Clipboard is a special area of memory, a holding place where text and graphics can be stored to await further action. You can paste the contents of the Clipboard into any open Excel document (or any document in other Windows programs). The contents of the Clipboard are automatically replaced as soon as you place new information there (whether in Excel or some other program).

command button

A dialog box button that initiates an action. The default command button is indicated by a dotted rectangle and a darker border. A button with an ellipsis (. . .) opens another dialog box or window. Frequently, after you choose options in the dialog box, you click on the OK or Cancel command button.

control menu

A standard pull-down menu attached to all Windows program and workbook windows. It contains commands that open, close, maximize, minimize, or restore a window or dialog box. You can display a control menu by clicking on the control menu box — the one with a minus sign in the upper left-hand corner of the program or document window.

database

A tool for organizing, managing, and retrieving large amounts of information. A database is created right on a worksheet. The first row of the database contains column headings called *field names,* which identify each item of information you are tracking (like First Name, Last Name, City, and the like). Below the field names you enter the information you want to store for each field (column) of each record. See also **field** and **record.**

default

Don't be alarmed, I'm not talking blame here. A *default* is a setting, value, or response that Excel automatically provides unless you choose something else. Some defaults can be changed and rearranged.

dialog box

A box containing various options that appears when you select Excel commands followed by an ellipsis (. . .). The options in a dialog box are presented in groups of buttons and boxes (oh boy!). Many dialog boxes in Excel 5 contain different tabs (see **tab**) that you click on to bring up a different set of options. A dialog box can also display warnings and messages. Each dialog box contains a title bar and a control menu but has no menu bar. You can move a dialog box around the active document window by dragging its title bar.

docking

Has nothing at all to do with the space shuttle. Docking in Excel refers to dragging one of the toolbars to a stationary position along the perimeter of the Excel window with the mouse. See also **toolbar.**

document

A file where you store the information you generate in Excel. In Excel, a workbook is equivalent to a document (or file). To save the information in an Excel for Windows

document, you must name the document in accordance with the horrid DOS naming conventions. To retrieve a document so that you can do more work on it or print it, you must remember the name you gave it. See also **file** and **workbook.**

double-click

To click the mouse button twice in rapid succession. Double-clicking opens such things as a program or a document. You can double-click to close things, too.

drag and drop

A really direct way to move stuff around in a worksheet. Select the cell or range (bunch) of cells you want to move, position the mouse pointer on one of its edges, and then press and hold down the primary mouse button. The pointer assumes the shape of an arrowhead pointing up towards the left. Hold down the mouse button as you move the mouse and drag the outline of the selection to the new location. When you get where you're going, let it all go.

drop-down list box

A text box that displays the currently selected option accompanied by an arrow button. When you click on the associated arrow button, a list box with other options that you can choose from drops down (or sometimes pops up) from the text box. To select a new option from this list and close the drop-down list box, click on the option.

error value

A value Excel displays in a cell when it cannot calculate the formula for that cell. Error values start with # and end with ! and they have various capitalized informative words in the middle. An example is #DIV/0!, which appears when you try to divide by zero. Error values look like they have been censored.

field

A column in an Excel database that tracks just one type of item, such as a city, state, ZIP code, and so on. See also **database** and **record.**

file

Any workbook document saved to a computer disk. See also **document** and **workbook.**

font

Shapes for characters — typeface. Fonts have a point size, weight, and style, such as Helvetica Modern 20-point Bold Italic. You can pick and choose fonts used to display information in an Excel worksheet and change their settings at any time.

footer

Information you specify to be printed in the bottom margin of each page of a printed report. See also **header.**

formula

Ready for some math anxiety? A sequence of values, cell references, names, functions, or operators that is contained in a cell and produces a new value from existing values. In other words, a mathematical expression. Formulas in Excel always begin with an equal sign (=).

formula bar

Sounds like a high-energy treat. Well, it is, sort of. Located at the top of the Excel window under the menu bar, the formula bar displays the contents of the current cell (in the case of formulas, this means you see the formula rather than the calculated result, which shows up in the cell itself). You can also use the formula bar for entering or editing values and formulas in a cell or chart. When activated, the formula bar displays an Enter box, Cancel box, and Function Wizard button between the current cell reference on the left and the place where the cell contents appear on the right. Click on the Enter box or press Enter to complete an entry or edit. Click on the Cancel box or press Esc to leave the contents of the formula bar unchanged.

function

(Let's see, I know what *dysfunction* is . . . .) A function simplifies and shortens lengthy calculations. Functions have built-in formulas that use a series of values called *arguments* to perform the specified operations and return the results. The easiest way to enter a function in a cell is with the Function Wizard, which walks you through the entry of the function's arguments. The Function Wizard tool is the one with the *fx* on it, appearing on both the Standard toolbar and the formula bar.

graphic object

Any of the various shapes or graphic images you can bring into any of the sheets in your workbook document (including charts). All graphic objects remain in a separate layer on top of the cells in the sheet so that they can be selected, moved, resized, and formatted independently of the other information stored in the sheet.

header

Information you specify to be printed in the top margin of each page of a printed report. See also **footer.**

I-beam cursor

The I-beam shape, which looks like the end of a girder or a capital *I*, is what the mouse pointer assumes when you position it somewhere on the screen where you can enter or edit text. Click the I-beam cursor in the formula bar or a text box in a dialog box, for example, to place the insertion point where you want to add or delete text. When you double-click on a cell or press F2, Excel positions the insertion point (see next glossary entry) at the end of the entry in that cell — you can then click the I-beam cursor in the cell entry to reposition the insertion point for editing.

insertion point

The blinking vertical bar that indicates your current location in the text. The insertion point shows where the next character you type will appear or where the next one you delete will disappear. When you double-click on a cell or press F2, Excel positions the insertion point at the end of the entry in that cell: You can then move the insertion point through the characters as required to edit the cell entry.

list box

A boxed area in a dialog box that displays a list of choices you can choose from. When a list is too long for all the choices to be displayed, the list box has a scroll bar you can use to bring new options into view.

Most list boxes are already open and have the list on display. Those that you must open by clicking on an arrow button are called *drop-down list boxes.*

macro

A sequence of frequently performed, repetitive tasks and calculations that you record. From then on, at the touch of a couple keystrokes, you can have Excel play back the steps in the macro much faster than is humanly possible.

marquee

The moving lights around the movie stars' names, right? Well, a marquee exists in Excel in a slightly toned-down version. It's the moving dotted line around a selection that shows what information is selected when you move or copy data with the Cut, Copy, and Paste commands on the Edit menu. Looks sort of like marching ants.

maximize button

A little teeny box at the right of a window's title bar containing an upward-pointing triangle. When you click on the maximize button, the document or program window that has been at a medium size expands to full size and fills the screen. See also **minimize button** and **restore button.**

menu

A vertical list of commands that can be applied to the active window or application. Also known as a *pull-down menu* because the menu opens down from the menu bar when you select the menu name. When an option is currently unavailable on a pull-down menu, the option is dimmed or *disabled.* See also **shortcut menus.**

menu bar

The row at the top of a program window that contains the names of the menu items available for the active document window.

message box

Also known as an *alert box.* This is a type of dialog box that appears when Excel gives you information, a warning, or an error message, or when it asks for confirmation before carrying out a command.

minimize button

A minuscule box containing a downward-pointing triangle, located next to the maximize button at the right-hand end of a window's title bar. When you click on a minimize button, the document window or application shrinks to an icon at the bottom of the screen. See also **maximize button** and **restore button.**

mode indicators

The information on the right side of the status bar (the row at the bottom of the screen) that tells you what keyboard modes are currently active. Some examples are ADD, NUM, and CAPS.

mouse pointer

Indicates your position on-screen as you move the mouse on the desk. It assumes various forms to indicate a change in the action when you use different features: the arrowhead when you point, select, or drag; the I-beam when you place the insertion

point in text; the double-headed arrow when you drag to adjust row height or column width; and the hourglass when you need to wait.

nonadjacent selection

Also called a *discontinuous selection* (is that any better?). A nonadjacent selection is one composed of various cells and cell ranges that don't all touch each other. To accomplish this feat, click on the first cell or click and drag through the first range. Then hold down Ctrl as you click on or drag through the remaining cells or ranges you want to select.

notes (text and sound)

Comments that you attach to a particular worksheet cell to remind yourself of something important (or trivial) about the cell's contents. Text notes can be displayed in a separate dialog box or printed with the worksheet. If your computer is wired for sound, you can record sound notes to be played back directly through your computer's speaker for all the world to hear.

pane

A part of a divided worksheet window. You can display different parts of the same worksheet together on one window in different panes. Horizontal and vertical split bars are involved with creating and sizing.

paste

Yum, yum — remember kindergarten? Alas, in the computer age *paste* means to transfer the cut or copied contents of the Clipboard into a document, either into the cell with the cell pointer or into a line of text at the location of the insertion point.

pointing

Babies do it, politicians do it, and so can you. *Pointing* also means selecting a cell or cell range as you enter a formula in the formula bar to automatically record cell references.

primary mouse button

Politically correct name for the mouse button that used to be known as the left mouse button (on the two-button mouse commonly used with IBM compatibles). This is the button that you use to click on pull-down menus, cells, charts, or whatever. If you're right-handed and you keep the mouse on the right side of your keyboard, the primary mouse button continues to be the left button. However, if you are left-handed, have switched the mouse button functions, and keep the mouse on the left side of the keyboard, the right mouse button becomes the primary mouse button. In both cases, we are talking about the inmost button that is closest to the keyboard. Calling this button the primary button (rather than the inmost button) calls attention to the fact that in Excel you use the secondary mouse button to open shortcut menus. See also **secondary mouse button** and **shortcut menus**.

program icon

Not the idol for our new cult, but a graphical representation of an application, such as Excel, that appears in the Microsoft Office window in the Windows Program Manager. To start a program from the Microsoft Office window, you either double-click on the program icon or click on it and then press Enter.

radio button

A radio button in a dialog box works like an old-fashioned push-button radio when it's selected (shown by a dot in the middle). Radio buttons are used for dialog box items that contain mutually exclusive options. This means that you can select only one of the options at a time (only one can have the dot in the middle). See also **check box.**

range

Also called a *cell range.* A range is a bunch of neighboring cells that form some type of solid block when selected with the mouse or the keyboard.

record

A single row in a database that defines one entity (such as an employee, a client, or a sales transaction). See also **database** and **field**.

relative cell reference

The normal cell reference (such as A2) that is automatically adjusted when you copy formulas that refer to the cell. Row references are adjusted when you copy up or down, column references when you copy left or right. See also **absolute cell reference** and **cell reference.**

restore button

The double-triangle button at the right edge of the title bar. Mouse users can click on the restore button to shrink a window or return a window to the size and location it had before it was sized. See also **maximize button** and **minimize button.**

scroll bar

The vertical or horizontal bar in the active document window and in some list boxes. Use a scroll bar to move rapidly through a document or list by clicking on the scroll arrows or dragging the slider box.

secondary mouse button

Politically correct name for what used to be known as the right mouse button. This is the button that you use to click on various screen objects in Excel to display their shortcut menus. If you're right-handed and you keep the mouse on the right side of your keyboard, the secondary mouse button continues to be the right button. If, however, you are left-handed, have switched the mouse button functions, and keep the mouse on the left side of the keyboard, the left mouse button becomes the secondary mouse button. In both cases, we are talking about the outermost button that is furthest from the keyboard. Calling this button the secondary button (rather than the outermost button) calls attention to the fact that in Excel you use the primary mouse button much more often than the secondary mouse button. See also **primary mouse button** and **shortcut menus**.

selection

The chosen element, such as a cell, cell range, nonadjacent selection, file, directory, dialog box option, graphic object, or text. To make a selection, highlight it by clicking (and possibly dragging) the mouse or pressing keystroke shortcuts. You normally select an element before choosing the actions you want to apply to that element.

sheet tabs

The tabs that appear at the bottom of each workbook window in Excel 5. To select a new sheet (worksheet, chart, and so on) in your workbook, you click on its sheet tab. To display new sheet tabs, you use the tab scrolling buttons. Excel indicates which sheet is the active one by displaying the sheet name in bold on its tab. To rename a sheet tab (which is normally given a boring name, such as Sheet1, Sheet2, and so on), double-click on the tab and enter the new name in the Rename Sheet dialog box; then select OK or press Enter. See also *tab*.

shortcut menus

Nutritious meals for the whole family in 30 minutes or less. No, not really — *these* menus are attached to certain things on the screen, namely the toolbar, worksheet cell, or parts of a chart open in a chart window. They contain a quick list of command options related to the object they're attached to. You must use the mouse to open a shortcut menu and choose its commands. In Windows, you click on the object with the *secondary mouse button*.

size box

The little square box in the lower right-hand corner of the document window with the scrolling arrows pointing to it. Use the size box to manually size any open document window by dragging it until the window is the size and shape you want.

spreadsheet

A type of computer program that enables you to develop and perform all sorts of calculations between the text and values stored in a document. Most spreadsheet programs like Excel also include charting and database capabilities. *Spreadsheet* is also commonly used as an alternative term for *worksheet* — so see also **worksheet.**

status bar

The bar at the bottom of the Excel window. The status bar displays messages, such as Ready, or a short description of the menu option you have chosen and indicates any active modes, such as CAPS or NUM when you press Caps Lock or Num Lock.

style

If you've got it, flaunt it. Also known to some of us as a group of formatting instructions, all combined, that you can apply to the cells in a worksheet. Use styles to save time and keep things consistent. Styles can deal with the number format, font, alignment, border, patterns, and protection of the cells.

tab

You find tabs in two places in Excel 5: in some larger dialog boxes, such as the Format Cells or Options dialog boxes, and attached to the bottom of each worksheet in a workbook. In the case of dialog box tabs, you simply click on a tab to display its set of options on the top of all the others in the dialog box. In the case of sheet tabs, you click on a tab to display its sheet on top of all the others in the workbook. See also **dialog box** and **sheet tabs**.

text box

The area in a dialog box where you type a new selection or edit the current one.

title bar

The top bar of a program window, workbook window, or dialog box that contains its title. You can move an active window or dialog box around the screen by dragging its title bar.

toolbar

A series of related tools (buttons with icons) that you simply click on to perform common tasks like opening, saving, or printing a document. Excel comes with several built-in toolbars you can use as-is or customize. You can create toolbars of your own design, using predefined tools or blank tools that you assign macros to. Toolbars can be displayed in their own little dialog boxes that float around the active document window. They can also dock along the perimeter of the screen. See also **docking.**

window

A framed area on-screen that contains the program (called a *program window*) or the workbook (called a *workbook window*) you're working with. The Excel program window typically contains a title bar, control menu, menu bar, Standard toolbar, open document windows (with the active one on top), and status bar. The program and workbook windows can be resized and moved around the screen as needed.

workbook

The Excel file which contains multiple related sheets such as worksheets, charts, and macro sheets. When you start a new workbook, Excel automatically puts 16 blank worksheets in it (named Sheet1 through Sheet16) and gives the workbook a temporary name (such as Book1, Book2, and so on). You can then add or remove worksheets as needed as well as add chart and or module/macro sheets as needed. When you save the workbook, you can then give the workbook a permanent filename. See also *chart*, *document*, *file*, and *worksheet*.

worksheet

Also called a *spreadsheet.* This is the primary document for recording, analyzing, and calculating data. The Excel worksheet is organized in a series of 256 columns and 16,384 rows, making for a heck of a lot of cells. Each new workbook you open contains 16 blank worksheets. See also *workbook*.

Index

• *P* •

Notes

Notes

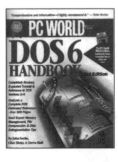

Order Form

Order Center: (800) 762-2974 (8 a.m.-5 p.m., PST, weekdays) or (415) 312-0650

For Fastest Service: Photocopy This Order Form and FAX it to: (415) 358-1260

Quantity	ISBN	Title	Price	Total

Shipping & Handling Charges

Subtotal	U.S.	Canada & International	International Air Mail
Up to $20.00	Add $3.00	Add $4.00	Add $10.00
$20.01-40.00	$4.00	$5.00	$20.00
$40.01-60.00	$5.00	$6.00	$25.00
$60.01-80.00	$6.00	$8.00	$35.00
Over $80.00	$7.00	$10.00	$50.00

In U.S. and Canada, shipping is UPS ground or equivalent.
For Rush shipping call (800) 762-2974.

Subtotal _____

CA residents add applicable sales tax _____

IN and MA residents add 5% sales tax _____

IL residents add 6.25% sales tax _____

RI residents add 7% sales tax _____

Shipping _____

Total _____

Ship to:

Name _____

Company _____

Address _____

City/State/Zip _____

Daytime Phone _____

Payment: ❏ Check to IDG Books (US Funds Only) ❏ Visa ❏ Mastercard ❏ American Express

Card# _____ Exp._____ Signature_____

Please send this order form to: IDG Books, 155 Bovet Road, Suite 310, San Mateo, CA 94402.

Allow up to 3 weeks for delivery. Thank you!

IDG BOOKS WORLDWIDE REGISTRATION CARD

RETURN THIS REGISTRATION CARD FOR FREE CATALOG

Title of this book: **MORE EXCEL 5 FOR WINDOWS FOR DUMMIES**

My overall rating of this book: ❏ Very good [1]   ❏ Good [2]   ❏ Satisfactory [3]   ❏ Fair [4]   ❏ Poor [5]

How I first heard about this book:

❏ Found in bookstore; name: [6] _____   ❏ Book review: [7]

❏ Advertisement: [8] _____   ❏ Catalog: [9]

❏ Word of mouth; heard about book from friend, co-worker, etc.: [10]   ❏ Other: [11]

What I liked most about this book:

_____

_____

What I would change, add, delete, etc., in future editions of this book:

_____

_____

Other comments:

_____

Number of computer books I purchase in a year: ❏ 1 [12]   ❏ 2-5 [13]   ❏ 6-10 [14]   ❏ More than 10 [15]

I would characterize my computer skills as: ❏ Beginner [16] ❏ Intermediate [17] ❏ Advanced [18] ❏ Professional [19]

I use ❏ DOS [20] ❏ Windows [21] ❏ OS/2 [22] ❏ Unix [23] ❏ Macintosh [24] ❏ Other: [25] _____
                                                         (please specify)

I would be interested in new books on the following subjects:
(please check all that apply, and use the spaces provided to identify specific software)

❏ Word processing: [26] _____   ❏ Spreadsheets: [27]

❏ Data bases: [28] _____   ❏ Desktop publishing: [29]

❏ File Utilities: [30] _____   ❏ Money management: [31]

❏ Networking: [32] _____   ❏ Programming languages: [33]

❏ Other: [34]

I use a PC at (please check all that apply): ❏ home [35] ❏ work [36] ❏ school [37] ❏ other: [38] _____

The disks I prefer to use are ❏ 5.25 [39] ❏ 3.5 [40] ❏ other: [41] _____

I have a CD ROM: ❏ yes [42]   ❏ no [43]

I plan to buy or upgrade computer hardware this year: ❏ yes [44]   ❏ no [45]

I plan to buy or upgrade computer software this year: ❏ yes [46]   ❏ no [47]

Name: _____   Business title: [48] _____   Type of Business: [49]

Address (❏ home [50] ❏ work [51] /Company name: _____)

Street/Suite# _____

City [52] /State [53] /Zipcode [54]: _____   Country [55]

❏ **I liked this book!** You may quote me by name in future
IDG Books Worldwide promotional materials.

My daytime phone number is _____

IDG BOOKS

THE WORLD OF
COMPUTER
KNOWLEDGE